Feminism and Psychotherapy

☎ 01603 773114
email: tis@ccn.ac.uk

7 DAY LOAN ITEM

CITY
COLLEGE
NORWICH

D1439910

Perspectives on Psychotherapy

editor: Colin Feltham
Sheffield Hallam University

Each book in this challenging and incisive series takes a particular perspective on psychotherapy to place it in its intellectual and cultural context. Disciplines which will be brought to bear in this series will include sociology, anthropology, philosophy, psychology, science and feminism.

Books in the series:

Philosophy and Psychotherapy
Edward Erwin

Psychotherapy and Society
David Pilgrim

Feminism and Psychotherapy
edited by
I. Bruna Seu and M. Colleen Heenan

Therapy Across Culture
Inga-Britt Krause

Feminism and Psychotherapy

*Reflections on Contemporary
Theories and Practices*

EDITED BY
I. BRUNA SEU AND
M. COLLEEN HEENAN

SAGE Publications
London • Thousand Oaks • New Delhi

First published 1998

SAGE Publications Ltd
6 Bonhill Street
London EC2A 4PU

SAGE Publications Inc
2455 Teller Road
Thousand Oaks, California 91320

SAGE Publications India Pvt Ltd
32, M-Block Market
Greater Kailash – I
New Delhi 110 048

British Library Cataloguing in Publication data

A catalogue record for this book is available
from the British Library

ISBN 0 7619 5190 3
ISBN 0 7619 5191 1 (pbk)

Library of Congress catalog card number 97–062310

Typeset by Mayhew Typesetting, Rhayader, Powys
Printed in Great Britain by Biddles Ltd, Guildford, Surrey

Contents

Notes on Contributors

Tessa Adams, PhD, is responsible for the MA in Psychoanalytic Studies and the Postgraduate Diploma in Counselling at Goldsmiths College, University of London. She originally qualified as a fine artist before training as a psychoanalytic psychotherapist and is UKCP registered. Her PhD, entitled *Creative Experience and the Authenticity of Psychoanalytic Discourse* (1993), focuses on the dynamics of creative process with the emphasis on critique. She has published articles combining art theory and psychoanalysis with reference to each practice. She is co-editor of a forthcoming publication, *The Feminine Case: Jung, Women's Language and the Creative Discourse* (Rebus Press).

Aileen Alleyne is a black psychotherapist (UKCP Reg.) and clinical supervisor in private practice with a background in mental health and nursing. She lectures on topics of 'Difference and Diversity' in counselling and psychotherapy practice and also works as a part-time clinician at Nafsiyat Inter-Cultural Therapy Centre. Her particular interests include furthering understanding of internalized racism and black identity development, and re-working concepts of attachment in black/white relations. She is the author of a chapter in *Race and Groupwork* (Whiting and Birch, 1997) which examines race dynamics in training groups.

Jocelyn Chaplin is a feminist psychotherapist in private practice living in Shepherds Bush, London. She is the co-founder with John Rowan of the Serpent Institute, a centre for training psychotherapists and counsellors within a framework of goddess spirituality. Her publications include *Feminist Counselling in Action* (Sage 1988). She has lectured widely and run workshops for 20 years on such topics as 'Images of Women', 'Social Anthropology' and 'Psychology and Mythology' and in such diverse places as the Women's Therapy Centre and the Festival of Mind, Body, Spirit. Jocelyn is also a painter, a writer and a mother.

M. Colleen Heenan was a founder member of the Leeds Women's Counselling and Therapy Service. At present she is a UKCP-registered psychotherapist in private practice and a university lecturer. Colleen recently completed her PhD thesis – a post-structural deconstruction of feminist psychotherapeutic theory and practice, with particular reference to the object relations approach to women's eating problems. She is the author of several book chapters and journal articles on this subject.

Elsa Jones works independently as a systemic psychotherapist and consultant, and conducts workshops and other training events with many systemic training organizations throughout Britain and abroad. She has been one of the pioneers of feminist critiques of the systemic model, and has written two books and numerous papers.

Melanie Katzman, PhD, is a senior lecturer at the Institute of Psychiatry and a clinical psychologist for the Eating Disorders Unit of the Bethlem and Maudsley NHS Trust. She is also assistant professor at Cornell Medical Centre in New York City. Melanie is the co-author/co-editor of four books on eating disorders: *Treating Bulimia: A Psycho-Educational Approach; You Can't Have Your Cake and Eat It Too: A Self Guided Program; Feminist Perspectives on Eating Disorders*; and the upcoming volume *Recent Advances in the Integration of Neurobiology and Treatment in Eating Disorders*. In addition, Melanie is the co-chair of the International Task Force for the Academy of Eating Disorders, and is on the editorial board of *Eating Disorders: Journal of Treatment and Prevention* and the scientific advisory board, American Anorexia and Bulimic Association.

Diane Kravetz is professor of social work at the University of Wisconsin-Madison. Her work focuses on feminist issues in social work, women's mental health, and feminist service agencies. She is completing a book on the beliefs and experiences of feminist activists involved in the early development of feminist agencies.

Jeanne Marecek is professor of psychology and women's studies at Swarthmore College. She is the co-author (with Rachel Hare-Mustin) of *Making a Difference: Psychology and the Construction of Gender* (Yale, 1990). Trained as a clinical psychologist, Jeanne's interests include feminist theory and postmodern thought and qualitative research in psychology.

Joy Schaverien, PhD, is a member of the Society of Analytical Psychology in London. She is in private practice as a Jungian analyst in Leicestershire. Formerly an art therapist in the NHS and senior lecturer in art therapy, she now lectures widely in Britain and abroad on gender and the links between art and psychoanalysis. Among her many publications she is the author of *The Revealing Image: Analytical Art Psychotherapy in Theory and Practice* (Routledge, 1991) and *Desire and the Female Therapist: Engendered Gazes in Psychotherapy and Art Therapy* (Routledge, 1995) and co-editor (with Katherine Killick) of *Art, Psychotherapy and Psychosis* (Routledge, 1997).

Robin Sesan, PhD, is Director of the Brandywine Center, LLC in Wilmington, Delaware, USA, a group practice specializing in therapy for women. She received her doctorate from Michigan State University and has been a practising clinician for 15 years. Robin focuses her clinical work on eating disorders, recovery from trauma and women's reproductive health. She provides education and training to a wide range of professionals, lectures at the University of Delaware, is the author of numerous journal articles and book chapters on the treatment of eating disorders and is on the editorial board of *Eating Disorders: Journal of Treatment and Prevention*.

I. Bruna Seu is a psychoanalytic psychotherapist in private practice and a lecturer in human sciences at Brunel University. With a background in philosophy, her work focuses on the mutual interrogation of feminist, post-structuralist and psychoanalytic theories. She has conducted a discourse analytic research on women's accounts of shame and is editing a book on *The Ego and the Self; Agency and Psychic Structures*.

Vanessa Swan recently moved to Vancouver, Canada, to take up a narrative therapy position at Yaletown Family Therapy. She works as a therapist and teaches narrative therapy. Her undergraduate background was in social work, and since then she has trained as a family therapist both at the Tavistock Clinic in London and at the Dulwich Centre in Adelaide, Australia. She was a member of the teaching faculty at the Dulwich Centre for four years. Her main interests are in feminist therapy; she worked at Dale St Women's Health Centre in Adelaide, Australia for five years and will return there in 1999 as the director. She has published several journal articles in this area.

Pamela Trevithick is a part-time lecturer in social work at the University of Bristol and a project leader for Barnardo's at 114 Child and Family Support Centre. She was a founder member of Womankind, a women and mental health project, where she worked for 10 years as a groupworker and counsellor. Her main interests lie in exploring how psychoanalytic theory and practice, particularly the work of Winnicott, can be adapted to meet the needs of people from more deprived and disadvantaged sections of the population. She is currently writing a book commissioned by Gower on communication skills for social workers.

Moira Walker originally trained and practised in social work and later as a psychotherapist, and now works mainly at Leicester University as a lecturer in counselling and psychotherapy. She also remains in practice and supervises, mainly in the area of abuse. She has written *Women in Therapy and Counselling*, and *Surviving Secrets: the Experience of Abuse for the Child, the Adult and the Helper*, as well as various chapters and articles. She has also co-edited two series, *Counselling in Context*, and *In Search of a Therapist*, all published by the Open University Press.

Acknowledgements

Colleen would like to thank her co-editor, Bruna Seu, for her invitation to work with her in compiling this book. The clarity of her theoretical and therapeutic insights, her ongoing support and the delights of her friendship have made the experience of editing a pleasure – even the awful bits! Thanks must go to Gabriela Rieberer as well, for putting up with me throughout.

Bruna would like to thank her dear friend and co-editor Colleen Heenan for her integrity, unflinching critical stance and stamina in editing this book. Thanks also to Sally Rose, Estelle King and Ros Gill for their continuous support and trust in this project.

We would also like to thank all the contributors for their hard work and for their faith in the value of this project and in us; it is because of their flexibility and courage in questioning themselves that this book has been possible. Foremost, our deep gratitude goes to all our patients/clients.

Introduction

M. Colleen Heenan and I. Bruna Seu

> What makes practice feminist is not who the clients are but how the
> therapist *thinks* about what she does, her epistemologies and underlying
> theoretical models rather than her specific techniques, the kinds of
> problems she addresses, or the demographic makeup of the client popu-
> lation. Feminist therapy requires a continuous and conscious awareness
> by the therapist that the apparently private transaction between therapist
> and client occurs within a social and political framework that can inform,
> transform, or distort the meanings given to individual experience in ways
> that must be uncovered in the process of the feminist therapeutic
> relationship. (Brown, 1994: 22)

This book discusses the theory and practice of contemporary feminist
therapies. As the editors, we invited the contributors to take a critically
reflexive stance in relation to both their therapeutic frameworks and their
feminist beliefs. This has engaged us as a group in acknowledging the
valuable contribution of feminist psychotherapy *models*, whilst simultaneously positioning feminist therapy as problematic. As such, although
the book is united by the contributors' belief in both the social oppression
of women and the usefulness of psychotherapy in understanding and
resolving some of the manifestations of these inequalities, the individual
chapters represent diverse viewpoints and practices which do not
necessarily concur with those of their fellow authors, or the editors. The
idea of a single, unitary feminist therapy, as well as the belief that one
model of therapy or one feminist stance can be privileged above others, is
refuted. However, a common theme which runs throughout is the ways in
which each woman is committed to struggling with the inherent tensions
between her political commitments to social change, and her therapeutic
commitments to women.

Given the number of texts already in existence, on the subject of
feminism and psychotherapy, the reader may well wonder why there is a
need for any additions. For instance, Eichenbaum and Orbach's (1982)
Outside In, Inside Out, Dutton-Douglas and Walker's (1988) *Feminist
Psychotherapies: Integration of Therapeutic and Feminist Systems*, Chaplin's
(1988) *Feminist Counselling in Action*, Laidlaw et al.'s (1990) *Healing Voices:
Feminist Approaches to Therapy with Women*, and Worell and Remer's (1992)
Feminist Perspectives in Therapy – An Empowerment Model for Women, all

provide extremely adequate descriptions of a variety of feminist therapeutic models. However, it is this very *descriptiveness* which this text hopes to challenge. While the title of Enns' 1993 article, 'Twenty years of feminist counseling and therapy: from naming biases to implementing multifaceted practice', makes clear two important developmental shifts in feminist therapies, our suggestion is that there is a need for a *third* stage in the development of feminist therapies, one that involves naming biases *within* the profession, and adopting a reflexively deconstructive stance in clinical practice. In stating this, we are concerned to keep pace with the developmental shifts in feminist *theories* challenging the eurocentric and heterosexual biases which have come to dominate, and thus represent 'feminism', as singular (see Evans, 1995; hooks, 1982; Spelman, 1988; Tong, 1989; Weedon, 1987, for fuller discussions of developments in feminist theories). For example, Chapter 1 reviews the findings of a research project which scrutinized the philosophical and political ambiguities in the beliefs of feminist therapists (Marecek and Kravetz), while the final chapter, 12, by Bruna Seu, explores the use of language as ideological activity in psychotherapy, investigating the problematic implications of psychodynamic psychotherapy for feminist practice.

In thinking about, and writing about these issues, many of the contributors to this volume have agreed to step out of fairly comfortable positions as established therapists, even as established *feminist* therapists, in order to critique their work. In addition, most have agreed to step out of fairly comfortable social positions as white, eurocentric, heterosexual women, in order to think about the very ways in which not only psychotherapy, but also *feminist* theory, has acted to privilege and thus replicate these same universal notions of 'woman'. For instance, in Chapter 3, Aileen Alleyne makes clear the ways in which feminist theory has been the property of white women, functioning to exclude the multiple perspectives of black women. Vanessa Swan charts her experience as a feminist, confronting her racist assumptions about the therapeutic needs of Aboriginal women, and men, in Australia (Chapter 2).

As editors, we think this willingness represents a crucial and exciting shift of emphasis in the perspective of both feminists and psychotherapists, one which demonstrates a willingness to explore ambiguities, tensions and omissions, as opposed to a defensiveness or a tendency to locate 'problems' outside the subject. This builds on work by feminist researchers such as McLeod (1994), whose empirical conversation analysis of interviews of therapists and clients in a British women's therapy centre raised serious questions about feminist therapy's ability to consider other social inequalities as being equally as oppressive as gender. By engaging with these difficulties, the authors in this current text demonstrate that explicating the tensions inherent within, and between, feminisms and psychotherapies acts to open up the possibilities for further clinical and theoretical understandings of gender and 'woman'. As such, this offers a challenge to critiques such as Kitzinger and Perkins' (1993) *Changing Our Minds – Lesbian*

Feminism and Psychology, which dismisses these possibilities as completely incompatible.

Before detailing the contents of this book, we want to contextualize its rationale more fully, by locating it within a brief history of feminist therapy. Enns describes this history, in the United States, as spanning two phases, starting from the early 1970s. Initially, consciousness-raising groups provided a forum for a selection of women to develop links between their personal experiences of their gendered subjectivities, and the political context in which these were constructed. The ethos of consciousness-raising groups was that 'institutional structures and social norms, *as well as* individual attitudes and behaviors, provide the framework for analysis' (Kravetz, 1980: 269) (emphasis added). In addition, there was 'equal sharing of resources, power, and responsibility . . . generally leaderless and stress principles of sisterhood and the authority of personal experience' (Kravetz, 1980: 269). Some of these groups also took social and political action, offering both support and advice for other women around issues such as domestic violence, reproductive rights or mental health matters. However, despite the personal and political challenge of consciousness-raising groups, Enns reports that the most salient effect of these groups was an increase in women's *personal* insights and improved relationships *between* women. The wider political impact of 'C-R' groups was limited (Enns, 1993).

In spite of their turning away from the accepted expertise of the established professions, Enns points out that, paradoxically, one of the outcomes of consciousness-raising groups was the development of feminist *therapists*. She suggests that the wish of consciousness-raising groups for more effectiveness resulted in them turning to some of the therapeutic practitioners in their midst to provide leadership roles. Further, through their participation in consciousness-raising and self-help groups, many women *therapists* became radicalized in their attitudes to women, and attempted to integrate their feminist beliefs into their professional work. Through setting up 'women's' groups and 'feminist' supervision groups, both of which attempted to bring closer together the personal and the political aspects of gendered subjectivities, feminist therapy services for women, run by women, began to develop (Eichenbaum and Orbach, 1982; Heenan, 1986).

Alongside this grass-roots movement, many feminists working *within* the psychology and psychotherapy professions had begun to highlight sex biases and gender stereotyping in this field, marking the beginnings of feminist deconstructive psychology research, focusing 'on issues specific to women's needs' (Brodsky and Hare-Mustin, 1980: 407). One such issue involved redressing the myths and inaccuracies concerning the sexual abuse of women, as Moira Walker, in Chapter 4 of this book, makes clear. Worell and Remer summarize the dissatisfactions which feminists have expressed about traditional psychological and psychotherapeutic theories and practices (1992: 6). These include such things as: depictions of male development and behaviour as the norm, the desirability of sex-role stereotyping, a focus on the individual divorced from social context, blaming the victim, conflating gender with psychopathology and the increasing use of psychopharmacology as a treatment preference for women. They suggest six drawbacks to traditional psychological theories which have implications for women; that is, they are androcentric, gendercentric, ethnocentric, heterosexist, intrapsychic and deterministic (1992: 115–20).

One important contribution was Gilligan's (1982) *In a Different Voice*, in which she sought to put women's gendered attributes on the psychological map, in a more positive light. Gilligan expounded on what she described as *women's* way of dealing with moral issues, 'in a different voice'. She argued that women's 'different voice', relationship-orientated and concerned with care, becomes suppressed owing to the dominant culture's emphasis on logic and reasoning. In Chapter 5 of this text, Sesan and Katzman discuss some of the ways in which feminist therapists have made use of the centrality of 'connectiveness', in both theorizing about, and working with women's eating problems.

Like many other feminists, Gilligan was influenced by Jean Baker Miller's *Towards a New Psychology of Women* (1976), in which she sought to contextualize and valorize the kinds of personal qualities which she contended that women have, as a result of their social position. In particular she suggested that women's subordinate position in relation to men functioned to produce and maintain characteristics in women such as tenderness and vulnerability which are negatively valued in contemporary Western society, in comparison to attributes such as autonomy and independence, conflated with masculinity (Broverman et al., 1970). Baker Miller called for both women and men to embrace a wider range of emotional qualities. As such, she was arguing that social change could be facilitated through the adoption of androgynously gendered subjectivities.

While feminist therapy has been defined differently by many authors over the years (Brown, 1994; Dutton-Douglas and Walker, 1988; Enns, 1993; Laidlaw et al., 1990; Worell and Remer, 1992), Sturdivant's comments made clear its *political* aims. She argued that feminist therapy could further 'the goals of the larger feminist movement by facilitating change in the internalised psychological oppression of women and by increasing personal understanding in individual women of the effects of sexist social programming' (1980: 178). In this text, Sesan and Katzman (Chapter 5) outline the tenets of what has come to be known as feminist *empowerment* therapy – commitment to consciousness raising, to an egalitarian therapeutic relationship, to valuing women and to engaging clients in social action. Gilbert's definition of feminist therapy also made explicit its roots in humanistic theory. She stated that it 'not only incorporates an awareness of the effects of ideology and social structure on the behavior of women but also contains several principles considered essential to the development of autonomous and self-actualised women and to the eventual establishment of a social structure consistent with the feminist ideology of egalitarianism' (Gilbert, 1980: 247).

In attempting to develop a coherent model of feminist therapy, Worell and Remer make clear the theoretical bases of therapeutic interventions which meet the required criteria; these are 'gender-free', regarding socialization as the main reason for sex-role stereotyping; 'flexible', in that the concepts used allow for in-group as well as between-group differences; 'interactionist' which means they understand individuals within a social context; and finally, 'lifespan', a view which doesn't fix maturity at a particular age, nor does it prescribe its attributes (1992: 120–1). The main theoretical and therapeutic thrust of most of the empowerment models of feminist therapy deriving from North America focus on re-socializing clients' sex-role stereotypes through an amalgamation of cognitive-behavioural techniques which both 'raise the client's consciousness' and enable her to 'learn and practice new, more effective behaviors' (Cammaert and Larsen, 1988: 29). The theories and techniques drawn on in this project range from assertion training, to humanistic therapy, to cognitive-behavioural techniques, through to psychodrama and family systemic therapy (Dutton-Douglas and Walker, 1988; Worell and Remer, 1992). In Chapter 11 of this book, Elsa Jones discusses some of the dilemmas in taking a feminist perspective into family systemic therapy.

In addition to the specific aims of empowerment therapy, feminist practitioners are 'ethically obligated to be aware of new information and knowledge about the psychology of women', and 'a feminist therapist must be cognizant of the overlap of roles and must develop strategies to prevent any abuse of her power and privilege' (Cammaert and Larsen, 1988: 22). Further, feminist therapists are concerned not to reproduce the practice of pathologizing women through the use of diagnoses which are imbued with and skewed by gender norms (Brown, 1994). Worell and Remer (1992) outline a detailed feminist therapist code of ethics which has been adopted by various therapeutic institutions in the United States, not all of which are specifically feminist.

In contrast to the ways in which aspects of humanistic models of therapy have been deemed to be compatible with feminist goals, psychoanalysis and feminism have had a much more uneasy relationship, as Heenan's chapter (6) on feminist object relations therapy denotes. Interestingly, one of the ways in which psychoanalytic theory has become more acceptable to feminist therapists has been through the adoption of aspects of feminist object relations theory, which focused on issues of connectedness within the mother–daughter relationship. This theme arose from the writings of Nancy Chodorow (1978, 1989, 1994), and was taken up by the feminist therapists at the Stone Center (Jordan et al., 1991), in conjunction with the work of Carol Gilligan (1982). In contrast to humanistic empowerment models of therapy so popular in the United States, the founders of the first women's therapy centre in England, feminist object relations therapists Luise Eichenbaum and Susie Orbach (1982, 1983, 1987), chose this psychoanalytic framework for its therapeutic model. British object relations theory has also provided inspiration for feminist therapists working with women's eating problems (Bloom et al., 1994; Lawrence, 1987; Orbach, 1978, 1986). In addition, many feminist psychoanalysts regard Freud's work as containing the potential to enrich understanding of gender (Sayers, 1985, 1986a, 1986b, 1990), and in Chapter 7, Pam Trevithick makes clear Freud's belief in the need to make therapy accessible across class and educational boundaries. Further, aspects of Jung's analytic psychology have also appealed to feminists in the therapeutic professions, and in Chapter 10, Schaverien makes clear why this is so. Moreover, while Lacanian psychoanalytic theory has proved invaluable to feminists working in the field of cultural theory, as Adams indicates in Chapter 9, it also contains ideas which can enrich feminist therapeutic theory.

OUTLINE OF THE BOOK

We posed three questions to each contributor, asking 'which woman' was addressed by their feminist and therapeutic theories, 'which feminist beliefs' they adhered to, and 'which therapeutic model' they subscribed to. In their different and sometimes differing ways, the chapters follow on from each other in a fairly orderly, indeed one might say 'connected', way. However, despite the connections, each can be read in its own right. While, like other texts on feminist practice (Burman, 1990; Ussher and Nicholson, 1992), this book has been written in the main by practitioners, we start and finish with discussions of feminist therapy informed by the authors' very different research projects. In Chapter 1, Jeanne Marecek and Diane Kravetz, both well-established writers on the subject of feminism and psychotherapy, highlight the lack of critique of the inherent tensions between political theory and therapeutic practice, arising out of the work of practitioners, as opposed to academics. They are concerned to explicate these disparities, which have resulted in the conflation of 'neutrality' with feminism, in the belief that feminist therapy is a 'process', as opposed to an ethical or political stance, and in the equation of *woman-centred* practice with feminist therapy. At the same time, they are sensitive to the ways in which the theoretical divisions between feminist practitioners and feminist academics can act to close down, rather than open up, arenas for discussion.

The necessity of a willingness to address material differences between women, and between groups of people, is a theme in the next chapter. Vanessa Swan charts her journey through both feminism and therapeutic theory. She highlights the limitations of her 'knowing', in her position of privilege as a white feminist and therapist, when her authority was acutely challenged by Aboriginal peoples. Her frank account of the emotional and political dilemmas she experienced, when forced to acknowledge she did not *know*, had implications for both her feminist beliefs and her choice of therapeutic model. She argues for the adoption of a narrative model, as a deconstructive tool which avoids the reproduction of social oppressions within therapy. In Chapter 12, Bruna Seu takes a more critical stance on narrative therapy.

The implications of the lack of attention to the eurocentrism of feminist theory lead Aileen Alleyne, in Chapter 3, to clarify some of the reasons why many *black* women in Britain might resist being positioned as feminists. While denoting the historical, political and cultural differences which have contributed to this, Alleyne is also concerned with issues of division. However, her interests lie in the psychical divisions which can occur for black women and men, as a result of racism. Notwithstanding the multiple differences between black people, she argues that ideas from Winnicottian object relations theory, in particular his understanding of the 'true' and 'false' self, provide a therapeutic reference point for analysing the intrapsychic impact of racism. Moreover, she offers a unique analysis of how this 'cycle of events' could be taken up in therapeutic practice, given the clinician's commitment to grounding therapy in a social context.

In Chapter 4, Moira Walker turns to a different subject, and a different therapeutic model, in discussing the contribution of feminist political and object relations theory to expounding the gender biases inherent in psychoanalytic theories about sexual abuse. As such, she highlights different power imbalances which arise in the tendency both to blame mothers and to idealize fathers. This tendency occurs when analysing sexual abuse at a theoretical level, but it is also mirrored in the clinical material of incest survivors. Walker indicates the ways in which feminist object relations theory enables practitioners to work with the powerful tensions which arise at both a theoretical and a therapeutic level, owing to the position of mothers as central to child development. The need to work with this dynamic has particular implications for transference and counter-transference feelings in the therapeutic relationship, and Walker offers a woman client's account of her experience of a feminist psychodynamic therapy, as well as offering an analysis of the differing facets of this therapy.

Robin Sesan and Melanie Katzman, in Chapter 5, outline a different attempt to move feminist psychotherapy away from privileging gender, by focusing on more widespread power imbalances, as opposed to differences between men and women. Through examples of their eating disorders work in varying therapeutic modalities, they make clear the epistemological, political, and cultural bases of their feminist empowerment model of therapy. Their work marks a shift in the perspective of North American feminist therapists, from specifying interventions and goals, as outlined earlier in the introduction, towards an acceptance that compromise has become the present-day solution to dealing with the tensions inherent between feminist politics and clinical commitments.

Chapter 6 provides a critical review of feminist object relations theory and therapy. In addressing some of the themes central to this text, Colleen Heenan highlights the contributions made by Nancy Chodorow, Jessica Benjamin, and Luise Eichenbaum and Susie Orbach, towards analysing the social-situatedness of unconscious processes, and thus the impact on gendered, psychological development. By situating heterosexuality as problematic, the authors redressed an imbalance in psychoanalytic thinking which has skewed accounts of male and female subjectivities. At the same time, these analyses engender tensions in feminist theories which need addressing – issues such as essentialism, the reification of women, and the adoption of universalistic notions of 'woman'. One further contribution of Eichenbaum and Orbach, already highlighted by Walker, was their feminist psychodynamic therapeutic framework, and Heenan summarizes the key points from this, drawing on some of her own experiences as a feminist therapist, in critiquing this model.

While Pam Trevithick, in Chapter 7, also draws on British object relations theory, she offers a very different account of how aspects of Winnicott's theory of the 'facilitating environment' were adapted as a model for therapeutic work with working-class women. Trevithick's chapter contains a perhaps surprising account of Freud's writings on the need for psychotherapy to be accessible. She makes clear that psycho-analytic psychotherapy, if grounded in the emotional and material reality of the implications of poverty and urban decay, can offer the means to understand the dynamics which hinder change, as well as offering a framework which can support workers attempting to deal with the overwhelming impact of ongoing poverty. Womankind, a project for working-class women in Bristol, offers an example of the importance of responding appropriately to the emotional and material needs of women, responses which may well fall out of the remit of the usual boundaries imposed within a psychoanalytic model.

In Chapter 8 Chaplin reflects back on the particular journey which led her to develop the 'rhythm' model of feminist counselling (1988). Chaplin takes up the power imbalances between psychotherapy models and feminist beliefs and argues for a questioning of all, including feminist, hierarchies. She invites us to transcend dualisms and polarities and proposes meaning as fluid, thus finding useful similarities between her and the postmodern deconstructive project. However, although she celebrates difference and change, she also warns against the dangers of extreme relativism. Chaplin explores not only the ways in which humanistic counselling has been posited as inferior to psychoanalysis, but also how, because some feminists have integrated aspects of humanist theory in their clinical models, they have had to contend with accusations from postmodern feminists, with regard to their 'essentialism'. In contrast, Chaplin returns to the ways in which her rhythm model offers a challenge to the power imbalances within a psychoanalytic framework, as well as arguing for the *compatibilities* between a humanistic and postmodern framework.

Tessa Adams turns her attention, in Chapter 9, to the work of Kristeva and the creative feminine offered as an 'unrepresentable subversive dynamic challenging paternal signification'. In this scholarly piece of work, Adams argues that Kristeva's Lacanian analysis presents psychotherapists with a dilemma: as language is for Kristeva the foundation of social oppression, for women to enter rational discourse implies relinquishing the 'maternal relationship' and pre-verbal signification. In this way women are repressed by their entry into language, which is considered however a sign of psychological maturity. But to remain outside language would be to submit to psychosis. It is in this context that Kristeva suggests the artistic endeavour as the custodian of the maternal body, compensatory and productive. Adams raises some crucial questions like 'Is the feminist concern which seeks to deconstruct the socio-cultural positioning of male prerogative inevitably problematized by a psychodynamic analysis that proposes language as intrinsically patriarchal?', thus offering a fundamental challenge to feminist psychoanalysts. In explicating Kristeva's ideas, Adams contrasts these with aspects of the work of Klein and Milner on the creative impulse. In addition, she points out where Chodorow and Kristeva can be seen to be both in conflict and in agreement.

In Chapter 10, we return to psychoanalysis and feminism, although this time from the perspective of Jung's analytical psychology. Already well known for her work on aspects of psychoanalysis and art therapy, Joy Schaverien provides us with a succinct outline of aspects of Jungian theory relevant to a feminist approach to therapeutic practice. She chooses the metaphor of 'The Coniunctio', an image which Jung used for the meeting of the unconscious, in the psychoanalytic relationship. Schaverien makes clear, despite the scepticism some feminists may have about the heterosexuality of this theme, that by using Jung's imagery in an informed way, it is possible to make use of it as part of the feminist challenge to the dualistic bias of psychoanalytic theory – a point which Chaplin has raised in this book, and one which Jessica Benjamin sought to redress. In her chapter, Schaverien not only outlines some of the ways in which feminists have taken up aspects of Jungian theory, but offers two open and insightful clinical accounts which further illustrate the theoretical points she is making.

In the following chapter, 11, Elsa Jones explores another challenge which arises for feminists, that of working within the modality of a family, or couple situation, when the 'presenting problem' is that of male violence against women. While Swan has already touched on some of these tensions, Jones offers the reader a clear and concise outline of the contributions which feminist theory has made to systemic family therapy, a model which is at the roots of narrative therapy. By interweaving an account of therapeutic work with a heterosexual couple, in which the man's violence towards his female partner was the focus, with a critical analysis of theoretical developments in systemic theory, Jones is able to bring to life the challenges which face the systemic therapist, when attempting to keep the gendered nature of the relationship to the fore. At the same time, she does not lose sight of the gendered and political dynamics of the therapeutic relationship, issues which she has touched on elsewhere, in her writing on this subject.

Finally, in Chapter 12, Bruna Seu raises questions about both feminism and psychotherapy which have implications across the theoretical landscape of this text. In drawing on ideas from postmodern theory, in particular the emphasis on language as constructive as opposed to reflective, Seu questions the possibility of feminist therapy providing a neutral space within the clinic room. Seu's brief account of the postmodern 'turn to language' highlights the tensions in the claims of either feminist or psychotherapeutic theories to 'discover' meaning. Instead, through her discursive analysis of a woman's account of therapy, she makes clear the dangers of adopting an intrapsychic framework which, although it produces a sense of agency, positions the psychotherapy client as responsible. This becomes problematic when an exclusively intrapsychic reading might lead the woman to blame herself for events which a political or feminist analysis would deem to be outside her control. In her feminist use of postmodern theory, Seu indicates how the concept of discursive positions can provide a more socially constructed account of gender oppression than occurs through attributing language as gender-specific. While suggesting that ideas from postmodern theory can open up analyses, Seu argues against the possibilities of taking up a position of 'not knowing', and thus of the promise of a narrative framework for feminist therapy.

Feminist therapists are concerned with understanding the impact of power and dominance, and of the social construction of gender, on both psychological development and therapeutic practices. At the same time, as each of the authors in this book makes clear, feminists working in this area, whether as academics or clinicians, are no strangers to the tensions inherent in attempting to grapple with the political and therapeutic implications of focusing on individuals' difficulties, when the attention of feminist activists has been on generating much more widespread social changes. This collection of writings represents a further contribution to the development of relevant debates as opposed to being a relativistic celebration of feminists' models of therapy as inherently good and beyond critique. We hope the reader will find these discussions as stimulating and enjoyable, and as thought-provoking, as we have found them throughout the process of editing the book.

References

Baker Miller, J. (1976) *Toward a New Psychology of Women*. Harmondsworth, Middlesex: Pelican Books.

Bloom, C., Gitter, A., Gutwill, S., Kogel, L. and Zaphiropoulos, L. (1994) *Eating Problems: A Feminist Psychoanalytic Treatment Model*. New York: Basic Books.

Brodsky, A. M. and Hare-Mustin, R. T. (eds) (1980) *Women and Psychotherapy – An Assessment of Research and Practice*. New York: Guilford Press.

Broverman, I., Broverman, D., Clarkson, F., Rosenkrantz, P. and Vogel, S. (1970) 'Sex-role stereotypes and clinical judgements of mental health', *Journal of Consulting and Clinical Psychology*, 34: 1–7.

Brown, L. (1994) *Subversive Dialogues: Theory in Feminist Therapy*. New York: Basic Books.

Burman, E. (ed.) (1990) *Feminists in Psychological Practice*. London: Sage.

Cammaert, L. P. and Larsen, C. C. (1988) 'Feminist frameworks of psychotherapy', in M. A. Dutton-Douglas and L. E. Walker (eds), *Feminist Psychotherapies: Integration of Therapeutic and Feminist Systems*. Norwood, NJ: Ablex Publishing Corporation.

Chaplin, J. (1988) *Feminist Counselling in Action*. London: Sage.

Chodorow, N. (1978) *The Reproduction of Mothering: Psychoanalysis and the Sociology of Gender*. Berkeley, CA: University of California Press.

Chodorow, N. (1989) *Feminism and Psychoanalytic Theory*. New Haven, CT: Yale University Press.

Chodorow, N. (1994) *Femininities, Masculinities, Sexualities – Freud and Beyond*. London: Free Association Press.

Dutton-Douglas, M. A. and Walker, L. E. (eds) (1988) *Feminist Psychotherapies: Integration of Therapeutic and Feminist Systems*. Norwood, NJ: Ablex Publishing Corporation.

Eichenbaum, L. and Orbach, S. (1982) *Outside In, Inside Out: Women's Psychology – A Feminist Psychoanalytic Approach*. Harmondsworth, Middlesex: Pelican Books.

Eichenbaum, L. and Orbach, S. (1983) *What Do Women Want?* London: Fontana.

Eichenbaum, L. and Orbach, S. (1987) *Bittersweet*. London: Century Press.

Enns, C. Zerbe (1993) 'Twenty years of feminist counseling and therapy: from naming biases to implementing multifaceted practice', *The Counseling Psychologist*, 21 (1): 3–87.

Evans, J. (1995) *Feminist Theory Today – An Introduction to Second-Wave Feminism*. London: Sage.

Gilbert, L. A. (1980) 'Feminist therapy', in A. M. Brodsky and R. T. Hare-Mustin (eds), *Women and Psychotherapy – An Assessment of Research and Practice*. New York: Guilford Press.

Gilligan, C. (1982) *In a Different Voice*. Cambridge, MA: Harvard University Press.

Heenan, M. C. (1986) 'Leeds Women's Counselling and Therapy Service', in *Finding Our Own Solutions – Women's Experience of Mental Health Care*. London: Women in Mind Publications.

hooks, b. (1982) *Aint I a Woman?* London: Pluto Press.

Jordan, J. V., Kaplan, A. G., Baker Miller, J., Stiver, I. P. and Surrey, J. L. (1991) *Women's Growth in Connection – Writings from the Stone Center*. New York: Guilford Press.

Kitzinger, C. and Perkins, R. (1993) *Changing Our Minds – Lesbian Feminism and Psychology*. London: Onlywomen Press.

Kravetz, D. (1980) 'Consciousness-raising and self-help', in A. M. Brodsky and R. T. Hare-Mustin (eds) *Women and Psychotherapy – An Assessment of Research and Practice*. New York: Guilford Press.

Laidlaw, T. A., Malmo, C. and associates (1990) *Healing Voices: Feminist Approaches to Therapy with Women*. San Francisco: Jossey-Bass.

Lawrence, M. (ed.) (1987) *Fed Up and Hungry: Women, Oppression and Food*. London: Women's Press.

McLeod, E. (1994) *Women's Experiences of Feminist Therapy and Counselling*. Buckingham: Open University Press.

Orbach, S. (1978) *Fat is a Feminist Issue*. London: Paddington Press.

Orbach, S. (1986). *Hunger Strike*. London: Faber and Faber.

Sayers, J. (1985) 'Sexual contradictions: on Freud, psychoanalysis and feminism', *Free Association*, 1: 76.

Sayers, J. (1986a) *Sexual Contradictions: Psychology, Psychoanalysis and Feminism*. London: Tavistock Publications.

Sayers, J. (1986b) 'Sexual identity and difference: psychoanalytic perspectives', in

S. Wilkinson (ed.), *Feminist Social Psychology; Developing Theory and Practice*. Milton Keynes: Open University Press.

Sayers, J. (1990) 'Psychoanalytic feminism: deconstructing power in theory and therapy', in I. Parker and J. Shotter (eds), *Deconstructing Social Psychology*. London: Routledge.

Spelman, E. V. (1988) *Inessential Woman: Problems of Exclusion in Feminist Thought*. London: Women's Press.

Sturdivant, S. (1980) *Therapy with Women: a Feminist Philosophy of Treatment*. New York: Springer Publishing.

Tong, R. (1989) *Feminist Thought: A Comprehensive Introduction*. London: Routledge.

Ussher, J. and Nicholson, P. (eds) (1992) *Gender Issues in Clinical Psychology*. London: Sage.

Weedon, C. (1987) *Feminist Practice and Poststructuralist Theory*. Oxford: Basil Blackwell.

Worell, J. and Remer, P. (1992) *Feminist Perspectives in Therapy – An Empowerment Model for Women*. New York: John Wiley and Sons.

1

Power and Agency in Feminist Therapy

Jeanne Marecek and Diane Kravetz

Psychotherapy has been a site of feminist activism since the Women's Liberation movement of the 1960s. Feminists of the '60s charged that traditional clinical theories about women were little more than ideologically driven pseudo-science, and that therapists often privileged the interests of men, while urging women to accommodate to oppressive conditions in their relationships, families, and work places. Feminist therapy was born out of this oppositional spirit. Practitioners of various therapies – psychoanalysis, humanistic therapy, family and marital therapies, cognitive-behaviour therapy – drew upon their experiences as therapists to re-invent therapy in accord with their feminist ideals. Since that time, development has continued, but it has been uneven, reflecting differing modes of therapy and differing philosophies, politics, and principles associated with feminism.

We come to feminist therapy as theorists, not therapists. Seen from our vantage, the project of transforming therapy in accord with feminist principles is neither straightforward nor self-evident. Feminists who are therapists operate in a space of contradiction, ambiguity, and perhaps even incommensurability. As therapists, they are part of an elaborate professional culture that constrains what can be seen and what can be said. The assumptions, constructs, and values of modernist liberal individualism are deeply embedded in this culture. Indeed, psychotherapy may be the exemplar *par excellence* of both the modernist faith in technology and the liberal enthronement of the self (Cushman, 1995; Espin and Gawalek, 1992; Hare-Mustin and Marecek, 1990; Richardson et al., forthcoming). Therapy discourse typically centres on the construct of the private, autonomous self, a self that stands apart from history and culture. It assumes that free choice and self-determination are both possible and desirable. Authenticity and individual self-realization are taken as unproblematic goals of treatment and defining aspects of mental health.

In contrast, much of contemporary feminist theory has taken issue with modernism, liberalism, and individualism. Feminists have problematized the constructs of self, choice, personal control, and freedom. In place of the notion of a unitary self that is pre-existent and self-contained, current theorizing favours multiple selves, positioned within different social hierarchies and subject to ongoing revision. Moreover, when considered from the standpoint of women and other disadvantaged groups, self-determination and personal control appear not as universal human attributes, but as privileges granted only to some. Violence and victimization – both threatened and actual – constrain women's freedom in fundamental and far-reaching ways.

How, then, have feminist therapists – with one foot in the culture of psychotherapy and the other in feminism – negotiated these contradictory points of view? It is surprising to us that the extensive literature by North American feminist therapists rarely makes reference to difficulties of merging the two. Addressed primarily to practitioners and geared to providing information useful in the everyday practice of therapy, the writings of feminist therapists have been more concerned with practical utility than with theory-building or with philosophical foundations. The literature also contains remarkably little dialogue between writers, in which differing points of view are registered and competing ideas challenged and debated. Critical attention remains focused primarily on the inadequacies and flaws of conventional clinical theories and practices; critical analyses of feminist ideas and practices are comparatively rare. Lack of acknowledgement, recognition and acceptance from the mainstream professions remains a problem. It may be that as long as feminist therapy remains marginalized, feminists will defer critique of one another's work. Yet a reckoning of the points of convergence and divergence seems a necessary first step towards synthesizing the knowledge that has accumulated.

In the USA, the material and cultural conditions of the 1990s are posing additional challenges for feminist therapists. As members of the psychotherapy profession, they have been subjected to a sweeping re-medicalization of the mental health field, and a reassertion of biological models of disorder and treatment. In addition, the corporatization of health care has proceeded on a massive scale, imposing unprecedented demands for efficiency and cost-cutting. At the same time, feminist therapists are part of a movement that has developed divergent political and intellectual strands, leading to hybridized, 'hyphenated', and sometimes divisive feminisms. Even more problematic, American feminists must contend with a concerted backlash in the mass media and a broad societal shift toward social, political, and economic conservatism. Feminists who do therapy, we conjecture, confront these social trends more directly than academic feminists, like ourselves, who are shielded by the relative liberalism of university campuses.

How do feminist therapists negotiate the complicated strands of emerging feminisms? What accounts do they give of their feminism and its influence on their work as therapists? What practices have they devised to evade or transform therapeutic culture, even while they must necessarily remain part of it? Conversely, in what ways does psychotherapy culture and its characteristic discourse 'constrain what can be seen and said' even for feminists? What is it like to practise feminist therapy in a time of backlash?

Twenty-five practising therapists agreed to be interviewed for our study. In telephone screening interviews prior to the study, these therapists either identified themselves as feminist therapists or said they brought a feminist perspective to their work. The therapists were recruited from a variety of work sites, including state and private agencies, college counselling centres, and group and individual private practices. All were from the state of Wisconsin; most were located near Madison, the site of one of the largest state universities in the USA. Of the 25 therapists, 16 were psychologists (9 with doctorates), 2 were psychiatrists, and 7 were social workers. All were women and all had considerable experience as therapists (median = 14 years; range, 5–28 years).

The interviews were carried out by advanced social work graduate students. They were conducted in private, and at a time and place convenient for the therapist. The interview guide contained 19 open-ended questions, and the respondents were encouraged with prompts and probes to express their ideas fully. Most interviews lasted between one and a half and two hours. Interviews were audiotaped with the therapist's permission and the tapes were transcribed by professional transcribers.

THEMES OF FEMINIST THERAPY

The therapists in this study spoke with assurance about their competence and effectiveness. They were committed to working as therapists and they derived considerable satisfaction from their work with clients. Many spoke with conviction about the importance of feminism in their lives; several had participated in women's studies programmes, activist projects, and feminist social service agencies at earlier points in time. Yet, when we asked them to tell us how they actually brought feminism into their therapy practice, the picture that emerged became more ambiguous, and their answers reflected some ambivalence. From our outsiders' vantage point, it seemed as if the culture of therapy was hospitable only to certain limited strains of feminism. In what follows, we take up five themes that emerged in therapists' accounts of themselves and their work. We focus on the points of contradiction, accommodation, and resistance that emerged in therapists' accounts of their work.

Where is the Feminism in Feminist Therapy?

Feminists who have written about feminist therapy have usually pointed to its emancipatory goals for women as its most distinctive feature. Some writers, such as Alexandra Kaplan (1976) and Sandra Bem (1976), saw feminist therapy as a tool for 're-socializing' women. Others used the metaphor of a raised consciousness, that is, awareness of how personal problems are linked to larger systems of discrimination and hierarchy, to describe the goal of feminist therapy (Brodsky, 1973; Coleman, 1996; Gilbert, 1980). Yet others, like Miriam Greenspan (1983), included instigating women's anger at oppressive circumstances as a goal of therapy, along with engendering female solidarity and political participation as necessary goals of feminist therapy.

Against this backdrop, our respondents' account of their work surprised us. We asked the question 'What does it mean to you to say that your therapy is feminist?' Most often, the answers pointed to processes of therapy, not to goals. That is, most therapists did not mention re-socialization, instigation of anger, raised consciousness, or political change. Instead, what they reported as the distinctive element of feminist therapy was how a therapist 'does' the therapeutic relationship. For example:

> [I]t's softer . . . less critical, . . . less dualistic . . . less judgmental. It's a more open way of looking at an individual.

> That all people who come through the door would be treated with dignity and respect, and compassion and equality. That's the essence of it. Safety. I would add safety to that.

> So it's a kind of respectful approach to, a respectful manner toward both the concerns and the women's ways of doing things that feels different and characteristic of women.

> Humanness, nurturing, and support go to the very essence of feminist therapy.

> One of the big factors . . . would be that you be aware of power differentials between you and your clients and trying to minimize those.

> . . . a style of interacting with people . . . Probably a sort of basic respect for humanity.

> I bring to [a therapy session] that belief that we're in a relationship and that whatever happens in our time [in the therapy session] is about connecting and making some kind of new way in relationship with someone else.

This emphasis on process as the defining element of feminist therapy was repeated in other parts of the interviews. For example, when the interviewers asked respondents to describe 'a model of mental health in accord with your feminist principles', nearly all of them interpreted the question to be about how mental health services should be conducted, not about how mental health should be defined.

We also asked respondents to recount incidents when their feminist values and their professional training came into conflict. The respondents' answers again centred on processes in the therapy relationship, rather than goals or outcomes. The single area of conflict mentioned most frequently was feminists' willingness to overstep conventional client–therapist boundaries. A variety of examples were recounted – hugging or touching a distressed client; lending a client a piece of jewellery for a special occasion; permitting oneself to 'tear up' openly when a client cried; self-disclosures (such as revealing that the therapist was a survivor of childhood abuse or a lesbian); and letting clients read the diagnostic manual and take part in selecting their diagnoses.

Our respondents described these actions as deliberately undertaken to accomplish therapeutic ends specific to feminist therapy. Yet they remained uneasy about them. They were careful to insist that such incidents were infrequent and that, most of the time and in most respects, they were vigilant about maintaining conventional boundaries (e.g., 'But I don't let clients call me at home'). Many took pains to hide such practices from other therapists; otherwise, they feared, it would jeopardize their standing in the professional community. As if to underline this ambivalence, many respondents termed their actions 'boundary violations', a phrase that emphasizes their transgressive aspect.

In the texts of the interviews, two different rationales can be discerned for relaxing client–therapist boundaries. One involves reducing the hierarchy between therapist and client. The other focuses on creating a therapy environment in which clients experience care, support, and nurturance. These rationales reflect two distinct models of feminist therapy, and perhaps two different ideas about how therapy helps women change. Often, however, they were blurred together in respondents' discussion. Tracing out the implicit theories of change and the intended and actual consequences of 'boundary violations' is an important area for further study.

For most of our respondents, it was the quality of the relationship and the style of interaction – respectful, kind, informal, and nurturing – that made feminist therapy distinctive. In characterizing that style, many respondents drew on contrasts and opposites that set a strong moral tone. Whether intending to or not, they projected a view of conventional therapy as a monolithic practice that is negative and harmful – judgemental, critical, disrespectful, 'stone-cold', distant, and even inhumane. Yet we must note that respect, humanness, and warmth – though perhaps not always achieved in actual practice – hardly constitute radical departures from contemporary professional norms. Stepping back from such polarities might create a space in which therapists' ambivalence about boundary issues could be aired and in which productive dialogue could take place.

Many respondents described the feminist style of therapy interaction in terms that closely mirrored stereotypic feminine traits. Indeed, in their accounts, it was sometimes hard to disentangle whether feminist therapy proceeds as it does merely because the therapist is a woman or because the therapist has self-consciously adopted a feminist model. As we shall see, the conflation of woman and feminist was a theme that recurred in the interviews.

Gender Essentialism

and the picture that came out of this, which was completely unconscious, looked almost identical to a woman's reproductive system. It is *so* amazing! (a therapist describing a diagram she had drawn of feminist clinical supervision)

Many respondents drew upon constructs of femininity and womanliness to describe how they brought feminism into their therapy practices. Often their choice of words posited an essential female nature:

> [I]t's to understand in a theoretical way the essence of being a woman, and to understand in a very individual way how the person across from me . . . how that is manifest in the woman.

> [I]t's an example of deep therapy because it means trying to unearth the feminine character.

> We talk through everything. That's part of the beauty of being a woman.

Many respondents framed their thoughts in terms borrowed from the work of the Stone Center,[1] which they understood as invoking an inevitable and universal female nature, and celebrating the 'connectedness' and 'relationality' inherent in all women. Other strains of feminist thought (and most strains of feminist psychology) have opposed the division of labour based on sex and sex-based prescriptions regarding psychological traits and qualities. But the popularized version of Stone Center theory, as our respondents reported it, reinstated gender dichotomies and encouraged women to seek fulfilment in womanly roles and femininity.

This kind of dichotomous thinking and gender essentialism is a powerful rhetorical device, one that is pervasive in popular media and a staple of self-help culture. No doubt it is familiar to many therapy clients, and thus affords easy communication and rapport. But many feminist theorists have pointed out that it leads into political and interpretive quagmires, and can easily be twisted into support for a conservative sexual politics (Bohan, 1994; Brown, 1994; Hare-Mustin and Marecek, 1990). Consider, for example, the best-selling *Men are from Mars, Women are from Venus* and its endless sequels and reiterations (Gray, 1992). Drawing on gender dichotomies, Gray informs his female readership that men and women, like alien species, are inevitably different and mutually incomprehensible. The book preaches forbearance and passive accommodation to objectionable behaviour by members of the other sex. Conflicts between spouses or partners are framed as simply personal issues, unrelated to the larger system of gender inequality and female subordination.

By focusing on the ways in which all women are supposedly the same, the rhetoric of gender dichotomies and gender universals sidesteps differences of culture, class, ethnicity, and sexuality; these are differences that generate hierarchies of power, status, and material resources among women. Moreover, when our respondents employed the rhetoric of gender universals and gender dichotomies, men and so-called male behaviour often figured as little more than signifiers for all that is not womanly, and hence undesirable (cf. Hare-Mustin and Marecek, 1994). But although many of our respondents drew upon such totalizing rhetoric at some points, they offered observations that unwittingly contradicted it at other points. For example, when we asked whether men could practise feminist therapy, all but one respondent answered in the affirmative. Many cited examples of male therapists (or other men in their lives) who embodied the qualities of 'caring' and 'nurturing' ascribed to womanhood.

Self and Choice in Feminist Therapy

Therapeutic culture – whether professional theorizing or self-help discourse – presupposes a unitary, authentic, pre-existent self that resides out of reach of the influence of society and culture. This true self was a prominent feature in many respondents' accounts of their therapy practice; some added the further twist that this interior, true self was gendered. Their metaphors of 'going back' to the true feminine self, 'unearthing' it or 'finding' it in some inaccessible and heretofore unknown location implied that the true self could be retrieved by peeling away layers of falsity built up by a lifetime of exposure to cultural norms, social dictates, and even personal relationships. For many respondents, the course of therapy was a journey of discovery and acceptance of an intrinsic woman-self.

You have to work that through and confront that so that they can get to being able to find their real self . . . It's easier working with women, talking woman to woman about finding your true self.

. . . that trajectory of learning about myself as a woman that for me is the edge right now, is going back to my true selfhood: Who am I as a woman?

I think that there is sometimes a denial of one's feminine self because it's devalued sociologically, so in therapy we re-value the feminine self.

. . . self-journeying around to explore my womanhood.

Once one presumes that there exists an inner, authentic, true self, then therapy becomes a matter of helping clients to make choices in accord with the wants and needs of that self set free from external influences.

I think I give them choices. It's all about really allowing them to be who they need to be – and I think that's the beauty of feminism. It's not confining; again, it goes back to being kind.

The political aspect [of feminist therapy] [is] the radical nature of helping people become themselves.

What I try to do is I . . . get them to move towards being the best they can be, in terms of their own definition of that.

I let women choose, my job is not to tell people what is best for them. I just expand the range of options.

[A feminist model of mental health is] a real openness towards people's individual process as [they] try to carve out some uniqueness.

The notion that it is possible to adopt a position outside society, and thus to act as the author of one's own subject, has come under heavy criticism in academic circles, as has the very concept of a true self. The scholarly attention now focuses on devising more plausible accounts of how selves are constituted and re-constituted in ongoing social relations. But our respondents did not move in scholarly circles; they accepted the notion of an authentic self uncritically, and that notion played a pivotal role in their understanding of what does and should transpire in feminist therapy. What possibilities for feminist practice are enabled and what possibilities are constrained by this presupposition?

In keeping with a strong tradition of liberal feminism, our respondents valued free choice and self-determination for women. They reported that they devoted much energy in therapy to fostering women's ability to choose for themselves. Yet, the value they placed on free choice seemed to us incompatible with the belief in a pre-determined feminine self. If such a universal template of female psychology did exist, then rather than being free to become whatever she chooses, a woman could only become who and what she was already destined to be. Thus, ultimately, choice is an illusion; a woman can only – to echo a phrase repeated frequently in the interviews – 'become herself.'

The construct of a self that stands outside its engagement with culture implies that every person is (and should be) free to define her own subjectivity. This led to a paradox when respondents discussed the ethical stance of feminist therapists. For many of them, clients' autonomy, and hence therapists' value-neutrality, was a core ethical principle of feminist therapy. The therapist's role then was to 'validate the client's experience', to 'honour' clients' values, characteristics, and life-style choices. As one respondent put it, 'where a client is at is where she needs to be.' But the ideals of unconditional acceptance and value-neutrality had clear limits in actual practice. For instance, many respondents had definite ideas regarding the proper ways of being a woman; encouraging clients to conform to these ideas was a key aspect of feminist therapy:

> . . . in therapy we re-value the feminine self.

> [Feminist therapy] conveys a kind of honoring of the characteristics that women . . . bring into the office.

An even clearer instance of the actual limits of value-neutrality could be seen in respondents' ideas about working with violent men. Nearly all the respondents refused to work with men who were sex offenders and incest perpetrators; some also refused to work with men who physically abused women. Their reasons dwelt on their moral abhorrence of the men's behaviour. For example:

> I refuse to work with someone who has hurt women. Or who has hurt children.

I don't work with rapists . . . my feelings get in the way. I'm too sure of my own negative feelings about whatever they've done.

I'm not confrontative enough.

Moreover, several respondents recounted confronting clients directly about behaviour that was abusive or harassing.

In sum, respondents invoked an extreme moral relativism as an ideal connected to feminism, and they seemed to endorse untrammelled free choice as a matter of feminist principle. But when the topic turned to actual situations, they articulated strong feminist values and a set of ethical commitments grounded in their feminism. Feminist critics of psychotherapy have always begun from explicit value positions and demanded ethical accountability (for example, Brown, 1994; Hare-Mustin, 1983; James and MacKinnon, 1990; Kitzinger and Perkins, 1993; Lamb, 1996). It is ironic that so many of our respondents felt that feminism compelled them to disavow an ethical stance in theory, even while it operated in their therapy practice.

In terms of a feminist politics, therapy goals of self-transformation and self-fulfilment are limited, even diversionary. They imply that the emancipatory project of feminism is personal fulfilment through a process of private discovery, without regard to social or political change. As Ruth Waterhouse and others have noted, therapy cannot 'transform the public and private worlds which serve to oppress women' (1993: 68). The discourse of self-fulfilment, as Waterhouse asserts and we concur, is one that co-opts feminist therapists by falsely equating personal change with feminist change.

The Trouble with Power

Power has been the central problematic in feminist social theory. Psychology as a discipline (and feminist psychology as part of that discipline) has had relatively little to say about power, despite its centrality in contemporary social theory. Moreover, what psychology *has* had to say, as Celia Kitzinger (1991) notes, is striking in its naiveté and in its failure to engage with ongoing debates about power elsewhere in intellectual life.

Although our respondents made frequent references to issues of power throughout the interviews, they seemed to have trouble finding a comfortable language for talking about it. The interviews are peppered with circumlocutions: 'feelings of empowerment', 'moving the client into a state of empowerment', and 'empowering the "woman's voice"'. The following exchange is a good example of the hesitancy that threaded through the interviews:

> [Interviewer: How do you define power for yourself?] Well, I guess empower. I guess that's what I'd say. It enhances. Well, I guess it can be positive or negative. To me a positive way of experiencing power, viewing power, is one of empowering. It's viewing someone's strengths, sort of looking at their resources, what they have inside, their own expertise.

Other respondents also grappled with differentiating good kinds of power from bad kinds. For one respondent, the good kind of power was 'power-to'; the bad kind, 'power-over'. For another, the good kind of power was 'power-with', that is, 'balancing the dimensions of power with involvement'. Yet another articulated good and bad in terms of an explicit gender dichotomy:

> . . . a woman wielding masculine power can be as screwed up as a man would [be]. . . . The difference is in the connectedness and depth. The next step . . . is women's reaching for a deepening, a kind of spirituality and a wisdom.

To our ears, a strong note of wariness about power sounds through these statements. The speakers introduce the question of different kinds of power and take upon themselves the struggle to locate and delimit a kind of power that is acceptable. Power that implicates other people seems always to be dangerous and morally suspect. Wielding such power can be corrupting (e.g., it 'screws up' people), unless it is accompanied by personal connection and emotional involvement. Power that seems safe is power that remains self-contained, that is found 'inside' and 'deep'. Instead of power, speakers prefer to think in terms of expertise, psychic resources, and wisdom. Indeed, the speaker in the last excerpt seems to argue that, at least for women, spirituality and 'reaching for a deepening' should take the place of power altogether. It seems as if respondents got around their discomfort with power by re-locating it away from the arena of social relations and into the private realm of the psyche. Phrases like 'feelings of empowerment' and 'becoming empowered' seem to bespeak a mental state more or less equivalent to self-confidence, improved self-esteem, or self-knowledge. They serve to transform power into something private and static, instead of something necessarily transactional and always under social negotiation.

Once power is located wholly within a woman's psyche, empowerment can occur within the confines of the psychotherapy relationship, in isolation from ongoing personal relationships or social systems. Indeed, in some respondents' accounts, therapy 'empowers' women simply by helping them find the inner power they already have:

> My work is a lot about trying . . . to facilitate women having as much of their power and range and their self as they can.

> We work a lot about her getting connected with her power source and her center, following her own knowing.

Concerns about excess or misused power re-emerged in the context of discussions about the power dynamics of the therapy relationship. In the words of one respondent:

> I think the potential for even well-meaning and well-intentioned and really skillful therapy to inadvertently abus[e] a client exists just through the power dynamic.

Thus, many respondents emphasized that they, as feminist therapists, ceded power to their clients.

> . . . from a more feminist perspective, that continual kind of awareness especially with women of how much they come into our offices and kind of hand over power. And we have to continually empower and empower and give that message very strongly.

Strategies for empowering clients included: offering respect, unconditional approval, and acceptance; self-disclosures by the therapist; creating an informal atmosphere in therapy sessions; 'letting' clients direct the process of therapy; letting clients read the diagnostic manual and participate in choosing their diagnosis. One therapist avoided the labels *therapist* and *client* in an effort to subvert hierarchy.

In the accounts of the therapy relationship, the prevailing metaphor was an economic one. Power was figured as if it were a quantifiable and readily transferrable currency akin to money. The therapy relationship was viewed as a self-contained and closed system, a zero-sum game, as the commonly used phrase 'equalizing the client–therapist power differential' implies. If the therapist relinquished (some of) her stock of power within the relationship, then the client's stock necessarily increased. Moreover, it was assumed that whatever differences in status, material resources, and social background existed between therapists and clients could be left outside the therapy office. The power to be redistributed in therapy was that which arose solely within the therapy relationship.

This way of talking about the power dynamics of therapy seems to offer only a limited and mechanistic view. We can question whether all kinds of power are the same, and hence whether power is readily transferable from one party to another. We can also question whether all therapy clients (or even all women in therapy) are (or feel they are) powerless *vis-à-vis* their therapists or in their lives outside therapy. We question as well the idea that the client–therapist relationship can be 'equalized' at the will of the therapist. When one party gives over power to another, parity can be achieved only at one level. At a meta-level, it is the giver who remains in control of the situation, as the statement 'I let her direct the process' illustrates. One more question must be asked, and that is the question of whether and how being granted power in the therapy relationship produces changes in clients' lives in the real world.

As feminist therapists, the respondents' commitment to helping women was enacted within the private space of therapy. In that setting, helping women *feel* efficacious is perhaps the best that can be done. But many respondents were well aware that promoting feelings of empowerment is not the same as rectifying social injustice. Once the topic of conversation shifted away from feminist *therapy* and to the feminist *movement*, respondents spoke eloquently about injustice, domination, and oppression, noting that power and privilege were not distributed fairly in the world outside of therapy, not even in such intimate social systems as relationships and marriages. Some respondents were angry and disappointed that the feminist movement had, in their view, turned a blind eye to the ways that class, ethnic identities, education, and other material resources were implicated in power. But they did not bring this same critique to bear on feminist therapy. Instead, they drew a clear line between political work and clinical work. Working for social change was seen as an important task but one that was unrelated to the practice of therapy. To quote one respondent, '. . . when I think about quitting therapy, I think I would do social change stuff'.

Secret Identities: Feminism by Another Name

In the USA of the 1990s, the mass media has captured the term 'feminist' and imposed on it negative meanings unrecognizable to most feminists: man-haters, whiners, 'femi-nazis', bluestockings, enemies of the family, and political extremists. The backlash has put feminists in a discursive predicament. To speak about feminism necessarily means speaking to and from the narratives about feminism in the culture at large. Producing a positive identity as a feminist in the context of this cultural backlash presents a rhetorical challenge.

For many of our respondents, feminism was a central part of their personal history and identity. Some had been identified with feminism for their entire adult lives. Some practised in feminist-inspired agencies. Yet many were reluctant to use the label 'feminist' in public settings. Only one called herself a feminist therapist in public communications (e.g., in the telephone directory and on her business cards). Some avoided the term in speaking with clients; they soft-pedalled or disguised their feminist values. Some invented alternative names for feminist therapy:

> If I met someone who was labeled capital-F feminist, it would give me pause . . . as to what that person was about.

> I would probably refer to it as 'woman's therapy', since feminist therapy is . . . It's a turn off to [men], so I have a tendency to *not* use that word.

> About identifying myself as a feminist therapist? I don't think I ever do . . . In fact, I'd be surprised if many people kind of go around the community or, as people call, say (assuming a falsetto, singsong voice), 'Well, I'm a feminist therapist.'

> I wouldn't say 'I'm so-and-so and I'm a feminist therapist.' I don't hide it . . . except I would if I were doing something for a client like testifying in a custody hearing and it would work against her best interests.

Since the early 1970s, feminists have continually assailed conventional psychotherapists for not owning up to their values. Writers on feminist therapy have always claimed this as a cornerstone of feminist therapy; feminist therapists would 'come clean' about their values at the onset of therapy, thus assuring clients' right to informed choice about their therapist (e.g. Hare-Mustin et al., 1979). But in the anti-feminist climate of the 1990s, most of our respondents deliberately concealed their feminism from their clients, some to a greater extent than others. Some respondents justified this practice on blatantly pragmatic grounds: if they revealed their feminism, they would lose business. Others justified disguising their feminism by claiming that a forthright stance as a feminist would compromise their credibility and effectiveness, and thus impede clients' progress. Still others justified their silence in the face of clients' anti-feminist statements by psychologizing those statements as indications of, for example, 'an unconscious survival strategy', 'false consciousness' or 'being in denial'. Although we sympathize with the difficult position of being a feminist in a time of backlash, we find such justificatory practices troubling. They run the risk of dishonesty, of patronizing women, and of disrespecting clients' ability to think for themselves.

Another response to the anti-feminist backlash is to dissociate oneself from the portrayals of objectionable feminists by portraying oneself as an acceptable feminist. Thus, several respondents were careful to distinguish themselves from anti-feminist stereotypes. For example, one respondent, asked if her clients ever guessed that she was a feminist, replied with a self-congratulatory air, 'Nope. I mean, I'm pretty gentle.' Another, having affirmed that she was a feminist, quickly added 'But *I* don't stuff it down people's throats.' Yet another respondent, though she considered herself a feminist therapist, took the occasion of the interview to discuss 'appalling' feminist therapists she had known. These manoeuvres can be seen as efforts to produce a positive feminist identity in the face of cultural backlash. However, they have the unintended effect of confirming the negative stereotypes, by saying in effect, 'There *are* harsh, confronting, and appalling feminists, but I am not one of them.' Thus they contribute to the backlash. In contrast to a collective political strategy of disputing the stereotypes, private solutions set feminists against one another, diminishing possibilities of political solidarity.

Practices of concealment and distancing may assuage an individual feminist's worries about her public image. But such strategies surely undermine feminism as a whole. Under the onslaught of media vilification, the feminism of our day, a movement that began with Betty Friedan's (1963) discovery of the 'problem that has no name' seems at risk of becoming the 'movement that has no name'. Furthermore, if most feminists elect to go underground, then distorted images of feminism can be promulgated without fear of contradiction.

CONCLUSION

We began this study with a vision of feminist therapy as a practice that brought the feminist commitment to social and political change to the practice of therapy. Our reading of the interviews, however, suggests that this was a simplistic and overly optimistic view. Among our respondents, the professional identity as a therapist was the primary one, and they positioned themselves within the professional culture of psychotherapy. It was that culture that set the terms of discourse; elements of feminism were incorporated into their work insofar as they were compatible and furthered therapy goals. Thus, like conventional therapists, our respondents privileged private meanings, feelings, and ideas. The focus of their therapy was the autonomous self, and the core constructs identified with their feminist approach – womanly 'relationality', self-empowerment, self-discovery, self-fulfilment – all were centred on this individual self. Our respondents held strong opinions about the political and social changes necessary to accomplish gender equality. Yet, as therapists, they worked within existing gender arrangements and social institutions and did not overtly challenge systems of power operating in society.

Our goal in conducting this study was not to produce a representative survey of feminist therapists, something we believe could not be done. Rather we wanted to examine at close hand how a small set of experienced feminist therapists managed to put feminism into practice in their work. The question remains whether the members of this study were an idiosyncratic group of feminist therapists. Indeed, when colleagues read earlier drafts of this paper, a frequent response was to offer to put us in contact with therapists who would be better exemplars of feminist therapy. However, there is little reason to assume that our respondents were atypical. Most practised in a progressive, politically liberal community that had been a national centre of political organizing during the Women's Liberation movement of the 1970s; they lived in close proximity to a university well known for its women's studies programme and its mental health training programmes. Moreover, as a group, our respondents had more training than psychotherapists in general. Based on our screening interviews, we preferentially selected therapists with PhDs and MDs. We did this not because we expected them to be better feminists or better therapists, but rather because we expected that they would be more fully part of the professional establishment, and thus in a better position to address the question of how professional culture and feminist principles could be joined.

Beyond our choice of a sample, other aspects of our methods deserve comment. In retrospect we see how certain choices shaped the results of the study in ways we did not anticipate. First, we often regretted that we had not carried out the interviews ourselves. Too often, as we pored over the tapes and transcripts, we wished for a chance to probe more deeply or to follow a therapist's thought to its full conclusion. Sometimes we wondered what would have happened if the interviewer had challenged the therapist's views. On the other hand, there were some advantages of having social work students as interviewers. The presence of students inclined respondents to be somewhat 'teacherly' in their interviews; they elaborated on their ideas and took pains to supply needed context. Also, they shared biographical information that they might not have mentioned otherwise. Nonetheless, using interviewers meant that we, as researchers, could not be in dialogue with our respondents. We lost opportunities to test our emerging interpretations against respondents' realities.

We also wondered whether we should have given the questions to respondents ahead of time. Would this have produced fewer instances of contradiction? Would the contradictions have been recognized and worked through? Would respondents have produced fuller accounts of the ways that feminism inflected their work? (Some therapists were interviewed in two sessions and so they could have prepared for the latter session. We note that none of them did so.)

One additional aspect of the study's method deserves comment. We deliberately chose to study practitioners 'out in the trenches', not clinicians working in academic settings or the experts who have formulated feminist therapy theories. We wanted to know how feminism is played out away from academic settings and we wanted access to practice knowledge arising from clinical experience. The discrepancies between how feminists write about feminist therapy and how our respondents talk about it are striking and instructive. At the very least, they recommend further attention to feminist therapy as it actually takes place.

For the therapists in our study, professional culture seemed to exert a greater pull on their feminism than vice versa. Indeed, several described themselves as more moderate in their feminist views, less activist, and less angry than they had been earlier in their lives. Whether this reflected professional acculturation, the impact of cultural change, or (as many believed) simple ageing, we cannot say. We screened several feminist therapists who had no professional training, but we chose not to interview them. Had we done so, their interviews might have revealed a feminist practice in which feminism, not psychotherapy, provided the guiding framework and master discourse.

To a large extent, our respondents seemed to operate in isolation from other feminists. Doing any type of therapy without a supportive network seems difficult. Therapists experience at close hand others' emotional pain, feel the pressure of clients' expectations, and constantly face the uncertainty of how best to help. Without the emotional sustenance of a peer group, it is easy to be tempted by simplistic formulas and fads that promise instant cures. Without the intellectual sustenance of a peer group, it is difficult to sustain critical consciousness. None of our respondents mentioned such ongoing peer groups, nor did they mention participation in feminist professional organizations, or involvement in the women's community. Few seemed to have access to the professional literature on feminist therapy or the academic literature of feminist psychology, feminist social work, or women's studies. Occasional attendance at workshops and training institutes (such as those of the Stone Center) seemed to afford their only exposure to new developments.

Feminist therapy has for the most part developed outside the academy and, as Laura Brown (1994) pointed out, this separation has produced benefits as well as losses. Among the benefits, Brown believes, have been the freedom to experiment and willingness to take risks. A negative consequence is intellectual isolation. Our respondents had little knowledge of ongoing scholarly debates about the very theories that formed the foundation of their practice. Moreover, they were unaware of the current outpouring of feminist writing about issues raised in their work – for example, men and masculinity, child sexual abuse and recovered memory, cultural diversity. In the face of such intellectual isolation, the easy slide into the prevailing conservatism seems nearly irresistible.

Feminist therapists constitute a significant block of feminist activists in the community and a significant proportion of feminists in psychology. Their perspectives are needed in discussions about the relation of feminist theory and feminist practice. Moreover, their work as therapists affords them a unique purchase on the workings of patriarchy in personal life: this knowledge could add to feminist thought in important ways. The task for feminists in the privileged setting of the academy is to seek ways to collaborate with practitioners that both support them in their work and bring them into ongoing dialogues.

NOTES

We acknowledge with thanks the following individuals, who responded to earlier versions of this chapter: Laura Brown, Maria J. Coleman, Steven E. Finn, Ian Hacking, Rachel T. Hare-Mustin, Patricia Kurtz, and the editors of this volume. They did not always agree with our ideas, but their insights and critical commentary gave us much food for thought. An earlier version of this chapter was presented at the meetings of the American Psychological Association, August 1996, Toronto, Ontario, Canada.

1. The Stone Center publicizes its work primarily through conferences, training institutes, and audiotapes. Our respondents learned about the Stone Center's ideas through such oral presentations. See *Women's Growth in Connection* (Jordan et al., 1992) for a representative collection of lectures given at the Stone Center.

REFERENCES

Bem, S. L. (1976) 'Beyond androgyny: some presumptuous prescriptions for a liberated sexual identity', in J. Sherman and F. Denmark (eds), *Psychology of Women: Future Directions*. New York: Psychological Dimensions.

Bohan, J. (1994) 'Every answer is a question: feminist psychology on the brink'. Paper presented at the annual meeting of the American Psychological Association, Los Angeles, CA, August 1994.

Brodsky, A. M. (1973) 'The consciousness-raising group as a model for therapy with women', *Psychotherapy: Theory, Research, and Practice*, 10: 24–8.

Brown, L. S. (1994) *Subversive Dialogues: Theory in Feminist Therapy*. New York: Basic Books.

Coleman, M. J. (1996) 'Nomadic tracings'. Unpublished doctoral dissertation, Union Institute, Cincinnati, OH.

Cushman, P. (1995) *Constructing the Self, Constructing America: a Cultural History of Psychotherapy.* Reading, MA: Addison-Wesley.

Espin, O. M. and Gawalek, M. A. (1992) 'Women's diversity: ethnicity, race, class, and gender in theories of feminist psychology', in L. S. Brown and M. Ballou (eds), *Personality and Psychopathology: Feminist Reappraisals.* New York: Guilford Press. pp. 88–107.

Friedan, B. (1963) *The Feminine Mystique.* New York: Dell.

Gilbert, L. A. (1980) 'Feminist therapy', in A. M. Brodsky and R. T. Hare-Mustin (eds), *Women and Psychotherapy.* New York: Guilford Press. pp. 245–66.

Gray, J. (1992) *Men Are from Mars, Women Are from Venus.* New York: Harper Collins.

Greenspan, M. (1983) *A New Approach to Women and Therapy.* New York: McGraw-Hill.

Hare-Mustin, R. T. (1983) 'An appraisal of the relationship between women and psychotherapy: 80 years after the case of Dora', *American Psychologist,* 38: 593–601.

Hare-Mustin, R. T. and Marecek, J. (1990) *Making a Difference: Psychology and the Construction of Gender.* New Haven, CT: Yale University Press.

Hare-Mustin, R. T. and Marecek, J. (1994) 'Feminism and postmodernism: dilemmas and points of resistance', *Dulwich Centre Newsletter,* 4: 13–19.

Hare-Mustin, R. T., Marecek, J., Liss-Levenson, N. and Kaplan, A. G. (1979) 'Rights of clients, responsibilities of therapists', *American Psychologist,* 36: 1494–505.

James, K. and MacKinnon, L. (1990) 'The "incestuous family" revisited: a critical analysis of family therapy myths', *Journal of Marital and Family Therapy,* 16: 71–88.

Jordan, J. V., Kaplan, A. G., Miller, J. B., Stiver, I. P. and Surrey, J. L. (1992) *Women's Growth in Connection.* New York: Guilford Press.

Kaplan, A. G. (1976) 'Androgyny as a model of mental health for women: from theory to therapy', in A. G. Kaplan and J. P. Bean (eds), *Beyond sex-role stereotypes.* Boston: Little, Brown.

Kitzinger, C. (1991) 'Feminism, psychology, and the paradox of power', *Feminism and Psychology,* 1 (1): 111–29.

Kitzinger, C. and Perkins, R. (1993) *Changing our Minds: Lesbian Feminism and Psychology.* New York: New York University Press.

Lamb, S. (1996) *The Trouble with Blame: Victims, Perpetrators and Responsibility.* Cambridge, MA: Harvard University Press.

Richardson, F. C., Fowers, B. J. and associates (forthcoming) *Renewing Psychology: Beyond Scientism and Constructionism.* New York: Jossey-Bass.

Waterhouse, R. L. (1993) ' "Wild Women Don't Have the Blues": a feminist critique of "person-centered" counselling and therapy', *Feminism and Psychology,* 3 (1): 55–71.

2

Narrative Therapy, Feminism and Race

Vanessa Swan

This chapter is not a critical analysis of narrative and deconstructive therapy from a feminist perspective. Nor is it an exploration of the critique of feminism by women of colour. Nor do I consider all aspects of my privilege, for example that afforded to me by my sexuality. Each of these would be a worthy project, but are not the focus of this text. This chapter is an account of a personal journey to the edge of my experience, a journey during which I began to see my own racist practices and the ways my feminism contributed to maintaining them. This process was complex, for not only did my focus on gender oppression blind me to the differences between women but conversely it also held the key to opening myself to look at my racist ways. Aldrecht and Brewer emphasize the significance of such a process:

> We want to reiterate how important it is that women come to alliances on equal footing with each other; however, it is critical that women who have privilege come to terms with the implications of it. (1990: 9)

In this paper I will describe the process by which my awareness of my own racial privilege has been raised. The setting for this was a project involving Australian Aboriginal families in which I took part. The theoretical context was the framework of narrative and deconstructive therapy and a personal commitment to feminism.

Before I begin to write about my experiences, it is important that I situate myself. I came to this project as a middle-class, white, heterosexual woman. I have experiences of gender oppression which led me to my feminism. I have an Arabic mother whose presence in my life has increased my race awareness, to some extent, and sensitized me to the occasions when white anglo feminists use simplistic descriptions of Arab women's experiences as examples of their own oppression. These discussions are complex. I have found it difficult to disentangle the feminism from anti-Arab racism, the notions of right and wrong from issues of cultural difference and self-determination.

During my training as a social worker, I became interested in therapy. However, I found it very hard to reconcile my feminism with therapeutic practice. By the mid-1980s I was convinced that practising therapy meant abandoning my values and reproducing the worst of patriarchal, anglo culture. My dilemma was that many of the women who came to me as a therapist had been convinced by their experience of life that they were neurotic or mad or worthless. Feminism went part way to engaging them in other possibilities but the sting of pathology seemed often too potent to allow these possibilities to take hold. In my experience, women who are convinced they are inadequate find it very difficult to believe their voices are worthy. It was from this discomfort, and the desire to find a bridge between individualized self-evaluation and political awareness, that I came to narrative therapy. As an approach, I believe, narrative therapy has space for my feminism and a balm for the sting of pathologizing practices. It is through my involvement in this therapeutic approach that I have come to look more closely at my feminism and views about myself and the world that it gives me.

NARRATIVE AND DECONSTRUCTIVE THERAPY

Narrative and deconstructive therapy has been developed very consciously as a political project by Michael White (1988, 1989, 1991) and David Epston (White and Epston, 1989). Many of the key authors of narrative therapy have backgrounds in systemic family therapy and other, pur-portedly politically 'neutral' family therapies of the 1970s and 1980s. It is as a result of this backdrop that the location of narrative therapy is within the very baggy and ill-fitting category of family therapy. However, in direct contrast to many other family therapies, narrative therapy is inten-tionally a political implement.

So what are the ideas that underpin and influence this approach? The fabric of the so-called 'scientific' project of psychology has been frayed by postmodern writings that contest modernist notions of reality and truth. This unravelling has created enough space for the weaving of new ideas about the social construction of the self and reality. In keeping with the Derridian notion of the self, personhood and the context of our lives are not seen as two separate entities. Rather, they are seen as something which is imposed and constituted by language formulated in relationships with others (Derrida, 1974). These relationships are saturated by the discourses within our communities which act to reproduce certain prac-tices of power and imbue aspects of people's lives with particular meaning (Foucault, 1973).

The process of how discourse and particular practices of power act to construct certain meanings around our lives and the events which take place in them can be understood in terms of stories and narratives we have about ourselves. What we remember, what we forget or dismiss as chance, how we understand our experience, what it means to us, for ourselves, for our relationships with others and for our futures are all considered in the metaphor of storied lives. A child catches a cold. The mother scolds herself for her negligence in allowing her daughter to go to school without a coat. The event of a child catching a cold has many possible meanings which would have a place in other possible stories about a person's life – chance, tiredness, the onset of winter. However, the mother's story of failure and neglect about herself is the story which dominates. This is not a story which the mother individually selects, but one that has been informed and constructed by her lived experiences in the community she is part of. There are layers upon layers of stories about what it is to be a mother, what it means to nurture as a woman, ideas about sickness being invited in by individual action. These stories serve to support the mother's notion of negligence and make her blind to all of the times her daughter has been warm at school – more insidiously, make her blind to the beliefs about women, mothers and the expectation of their role in the community that construct and support her story about herself.

In a narrative framework, the therapist's role is to bring to a person's awareness these taken-for-granted stories and the ideas and beliefs which support them. For example, the idea of women as nurturers who must strive ever harder to meet all of the needs of those around them is a notion in most cultures. People are invited actively to consider the impact of these ideas on their lives, the lives of others and on what they want for themselves. For some women the identification of cultural imperatives to nurture is a freeing process by which they are able to critique this as merely an idea and not an invisible truth against which they must measure their lives. These seemingly free-floating ideas act to maintain structures and relationships in very particular and oppressive ways. Through a process of deconstruction, mechanisms of social control can be recognized.

Deconstructions of conversations name these ideas and unravel their history and impact on people's lives, and invite them to consider the effect of these ideas on what they want for their lives and the lives of others around them. White says:

> . . . deconstruction has to do with procedures that subvert taken-for-granted realities and practices; those so-called 'truths' that are split off from the conditions and the context of their production, those disembodied ways of speaking that hide their biases and prejudices, and those familiar practices of self and of relationship that are subjugating of persons' lives. Many of the methods of deconstruction render strange these familiar and everyday taken-for-granted realities and practices and objectify them. (1991: 27)

The process of deconstruction erodes the power of these dominant stories in the lives of those it touches. It makes it possible to highlight alternative meanings. In the lives of women where themes of 'not good enough, not wise enough' have dominated, narrative works to separate these stories from who they are as people, exposing these notions as ideas and not truths about them as women. It acts to provide space for other, over-shadowed knowledges and meanings to appear from the margins of these women's lives. This can constitute the beginning of conversations about the times in their lives when they succeeded, times when they were guided by their intellect and knowledge of the world, times when they may have dismissed their own achievements as luck or attributed them to the efforts or others. These times are now coated with the flavour of their own strength and agency in their lives. Alternative stories of strength and trusting their own judgement begin to speak to them more of who they are as people, alternative knowledges that work for them rather than against them in their lives. This does not come from a process of the therapist imposing and insisting on 'better' ideas and ways of being, but through questioning which solicits ideas about the person's preferred ways of thinking, living and interacting with themselves and others in their lives.

The therapist then works with the person to identify an audience or community of persons in their lives who are supportive of these developments in their sense of self. It may be people from their past who have always known this about them, or present relationships with people who view them with confidence, or possible future relationships based on their preferred sense of self.

Through this process, a person's alternative knowledges of themself, their strength and abilities are exposed and made apparent. The location of the problem is also made apparent. It is in the ideas and beliefs which circulate within our community and not within the person or their individualized experience of emotions or thoughts. Heather Elliot points out:

> This approach to therapy does not see the person as the problem but rather the internalisation of certain ideas about the self which circulate within a given culture. (1997: 58)

Preferential ideas about particular gender, sexual orientation, class, race and colour are some of these ideas about the self which circulate within our culture. These are often the shading of stories about the self that influence our lives and our relationships with others. Certain meanings, certain ways of connecting ideas, form the discourses which inform this. When these ideas become problematic in people's lives, the process of narrative therapy works to expose these unhelpful networks of ideas. A person comes to realize that these are simply someone's ideas, not irrefutable truths and absolutes about themselves and the world.

And so the beliefs, the politics and the ethics of this approach are distilled and made evident. The process of deconstruction, the techniques of externalizing the problem from the individual (White, 1991), are not only informed by experiences of the person seeking therapy and the issues they identify as problematic in their lives, but also by the beliefs and ethics of this approach implemented by the therapist. For example, a heterosexual couple seek counselling regarding conflict in their relationship. The man has been violent towards the woman on a number of occasions. I must use this approach to clearly name and maintain the man's responsibility for his violence. I will use methods to support him to be different within the relationship but this is not achieved through any compromise in the identification of his responsibility which is his (Jenkins, 1990). In keeping with this, if the situation were reversed, and it was the woman who was violent towards the man, I would not look to the woman's responsibility in this same way, for the power difference is great. She acts in a wider context of gender oppression; therefore although we would still look at other ways she would prefer to respond in the relationship, a knowledge of her lesser power would inform the ways this conversation went. The nature of their relationship would be focused upon. I act with the politics of relations of power in mind. Similarly, the process of deconstruction occurs with these ethics in mind. One would not ask questions such as 'Where did the idea that violence in a relationship is a bad thing come from?' Such questions and directions in this work would serve to support and strengthen oppressive and abusive practices in our community. The aim of this approach is the opposite. It is consistent with Michel Foucault's words:

> . . . to give one's self the rules of law, the techniques of management, and also the ethics, the ethos, the practice of self, which allow these games of power to be played with the minimum of domination. (1988: 18)

These and the beliefs about the ways in which dominant cultural ideas and practices are reproduced in people's lives raise an important question. How do we as therapists, with particular gender, class and sexuality, often working in the very structures which formalize and maintain these relations of power, work against our own reproduction of these oppressive ways in our lives and our work?

The Family Centre in New Zealand have developed a narrative approach, 'Just Therapy' (Tamasese and Waldegrave, 1994), which attempts to reverse the societal bias against particularly dominated cultural groups and women. Through a process of caucusing or speaking in privacy in 'like' groups and a structure which involves accountability of the dominant to the less powerful, the reproduction of the oppression of dominant culture begins to be avoided.

> The unique aspect of this approach is the reversal of usual modes of accountability. Because management and decision making is commonly exercised primarily by men or white people, the patriarchal and racist assumptions in society simply permeate the therapeutic community. Our reversal consists of full recognition of dominated groups to be self-determining, and a requirement of the dominant groups to check out aspects of their orientation and projects with the other groups. (1994: 59)

It has been the application of these ideas to the everyday workings of narrative therapy which has been the focus of much energy in recent years. My own personal journey into this work around the issue of race began two years ago through my involvement in a project called 'Reclaiming Our Stories, Reclaiming Our Lives'.

CAMP COORONG

From June through to September 1994, I was part of a small team of counsellors, both men and women, Aboriginal and white, who worked with Aboriginal families using a narrative and deconstructive approach. This counselling project implemented one of the recommendations made by the Australian Royal Commission into Aboriginal Deaths in Custody (November 1987 to December 1990). The project involved consulting family members of persons who had died in custody regarding their knowledge and experiences, providing counselling at a five-day camp on which we lived together on Aboriginal land, following up these people regarding their experiences at this gathering, documenting this process and providing narrative training for those family members who were interested.

Some Aboriginal people chose narrative therapy to be the framework for this project. The counsellor's experience in using the approach was the reason our involvement was requested. The aim of the project was to bring forth the marginalized stories of strength and survival of Aboriginal people that are frequently hidden by white Australian culture. The words of the written report describe the narrative and deconstructive approach used at the camp:

> . . . this project recognises the importance of Aboriginal people taking the primary role in the telling of their stories, and the importance of an exploration of these stories so that their special knowledges and skills relevant to healing processes might be honoured and re-empowered. As well, the project aimed at providing support for Aboriginal people to take further steps to break free of the destructive stories that have been imposed upon them by dominant non-Aboriginal culture, including the ideas of health and well-being that are so often imposed by mainstream services. ('Reclaiming Our Stories, Reclaiming Our Lives', 1995: 20)

Before the gathering, we consulted with all of the families involved, to seek their advice about the camp and the content of the discussions. We used their guidance to plan the topics of conversations to be conducted at the camp. The themes that were chosen by the families were Naming Injustice, Caring and Sharing, Healing Ways, Remembering, Journeys, and Talking to our Young People. We followed a process of accountability to the Aboriginal counsellors, to Aboriginal people on a steering group and to the families. Aboriginal people caucused separately from the white people. The framework of narrative therapy was the therapeutic approach we used for the counselling at the camp and the group discussions. The stories of racism and attempted genocide were told. Racist ideas and ways of talking of stereotyping and minimizing, of dismissing and telling only certain stories, were named by the families and made evident for what they are – methods of control and oppression. Aboriginal healing knowledges were shared. The stories of survival and strength against white domination were recounted and honoured. Their significance for future generations was acknowledged.

The counselling team followed the directions of the families. The Aboriginal counsellors facilitated the sessions, providing questions that drew out some of the less told narratives. The whole counselling team formed a listening group or audience that reflected back what we heard:

> . . . Aboriginal people commented that hearing their own stories reflected back in this way enabled them to see themselves differently, and to reclaim a pride in who they were. (ibid.: 19)

As a result of my involvement in this project, through conversations with Aboriginal people and other people of colour and by reading the challenges of black feminists, I have been thinking about my work, the approach I use and the issues I must face as a middle-class, white woman. In my description of this process and the dilemmas I am considering, I do not want to give an impression that I now speak from a position of having reached a place of wisdom. I have merely been taught just a little about seeing beyond the familiar. I will tell you about how this happened, about what I have begun to face.

CHALLENGES AND DILEMMAS

In keeping with 'Just Therapy' notions of accountability and the ethics of narrative therapy, the white women counsellors invited a group of Aboriginal feminists to meet with us. We wished to hear some of their views about what we were about to be part of and to hear what they felt we should know and do, before we embarked on the consultation with the Aboriginal families. I went to this meeting with pen and paper, with an expectation of recording issues, ideas about what to do next and pieces of information: the implements I would use to begin this process of understanding and 'knowing about'. I remember how angry the Aboriginal women were: how dare we presume to do our research and to then 'know'? It was our middle-class, white privilege which sought to colonize their experience. How dare we spend a few hours with them, thank them politely, using the best of our middle-class eloquence, and from then on claim to 'know about'? What I began to learn at this meeting was not about Aboriginal people's knowledges of themselves, information I had no right to, but about their knowledge of white ways in relation to their experience. I learnt to direct myself towards becoming more comfortable with 'not knowing about'. This was the beginnings of separation from my middle-class professional views that drive me towards a self-satisfied sense of 'clarity': this expectation of 'understanding' that claims and colonizes, that presumes to know and evaluates others' worlds and experiences. I learnt about what it is like to stay with listening, to privilege 'asking and hearing about the effects of my practices' over 'understanding and knowing about others' ways'. I began to think about the importance of asking and hearing about my use of privilege. And I began to learn about some of the depths of a relationship of account-ability, one of the key political tools of narrative therapy.

Accountability is not a process of acquisition of information, but an ongoing commitment to learning and changing. Through these experiences I began to challenge my behaviour, not just in a series of a few meetings but as part of a longer-term commitment. The focus is on self, not other. There is not a particular volume of information which I must consume to stand on the moral high ground of being rid of racism. I must come to an acceptance of the ways my privilege will continue, at times, to blind me to my oppressive practices, and I must therefore commit myself to an ongoing relationship of accountability, just as women would be horrified by men who challenge their own sexism and then believe they will never behave in sexist ways again. Although one would hope that these men would have better judgement and would not make the same mistakes, the mechanisms of dominant culture mean they will continue to be, at times, susceptible to ways of patriarchy. The ways of racism are similar.

I have found this journey towards accountability enlightening of my racist ways: I am ashamed to say, ways that were invisible to me until these conversations and others like them. I have found this process immeasurably important and yet difficult and very treacherous. Although my class and race privilege drives me towards consuming and acquiring others' experience, in contrast to this, I also have knowledge of other ways; my experience as a woman has been in deferring to others. Much of my gender training has been about listening to men and to children. I have learned to defer to men's knowledge and to take postures of not knowing and not understanding. A childhood with parents who supported my confidence, opportunities in education and a feminist realization about my world have provided me with other lessons in listening to my own voice. It seems to me that the hard-learned, feminist-supported counter to the gender-flavoured 'don't speak because how would *you* know?' that many women find whispered into our ears can be presented with a megaphone in the process of being awakened to our class and race privilege. My challenge has become – how do I open myself to the views and critiques of people of colour, be comfortable in not knowing and yet hold on to what I do know, which I must to survive in a patriachal world? And how do I encourage a critique of my conversations, ideas and values by oppressed groups, but not pale into invisibility as a woman with the momentum of this gender-enlarged self-doubt?

I was, at times, frozen by self-doubt and uncertainty. I wondered and struggled. I listened, I talked and I began to learn. Time and time again I was directed back to the skills I had been asked for in the first place. I was asked to share my knowledge as a therapist in a model that had been judged by some in the Aboriginal community to be useful to them. I was asked to use the techniques I and the other therapists had to bring forth the families at the camp's healing knowledges, the naming of the practices of racism in the white society and the identification of the ways these knowledges were undermined and negated.

There were times in this process, when stories of terrible atrocities were shared with us, when I would be determined to take action about an issue and to protest and enlist the support of others. Through the conversations of accountability with the families and black workers, I heard frequently that I was not being asked to take up a cause 'on behalf of'. I was being asked because I had specific skills that, at this point in time, were needed by Aboriginal people. Knowing of my preparedness to take action about these issues was useful if they chose to take this path; however, deciding to take my own action was patronizing and arrogant. This seems all so obvious in retrospect but, at the time, was a salient lesson in collaboration. I learnt more about 'working for and with' and not 'doing to and on behalf of'. Some of these lessons I already knew, but the awful weight of the injustices, and my wanting to take responsibility for my white racism, slowed my memory.

Through the questions and the dilemmas, I began to wonder about my feminism. I began to wonder about how my own experiences of oppression as a woman fitted in this process. Could my feminism serve to strengthen my resolve to challenge the ways I oppress others or would it misdirect me?

Reynolds (1996) spoke of two ways in which she abdicates responsibility for her white privilege, one being class and the second (preferred) tactic gender. The homogeneous catch cry – 'We as women . . .' – highlights our oppression and connectedness as women, but makes us blind to the privilege some of us have, maintaining the visibility of those of us who also act to oppress others. Reynolds (1996) recounted the experience of a black, male friend:

[He] . . . was reading an article about a particularly brutal racist incident involving Vancouver police. He was feeling attacked by racism and a caring white woman co-worker asked what was up. When he shared the story she chose to connect to the story 'as a woman'. So she said something like 'Cops and men are always abusing women too.' Her comment re-positioned [the man's] racist experience into a context of gender; not only was his experience invalidated, but now he, as a man, was repositioned as the oppressor.

This clearly identifies part of my dilemma. How do I make sense of my experience of oppression and understand this in relation to my role as an oppressor? When I think in terms of the modernist construction of dualities this cannot coexist – I am one or other, never both. What does this mean for my connection to other women? How do I join with other women to demand gender equity and yet focus on my participation in abusive tactics of power over some?

In conversation with other white feminists working on this project, we began to think about how we could have our experiences of oppression work for us in this project, not against us. We began to think about how we raise issues of gender inequality and what that experience is like. When are we most likely to do this? What are some of the common responses to such issues? How do we feel when these occur? We embarked upon this exercise with awareness of the danger of empathic exploration in regard to the experience of other cultures, the danger of using eyes that are blinded by our own culture and processes of understanding which are limited by our own constructions of meaning. We therefore understood its validity was limited and only relevant if we sought the views of people of colour in regard to our thoughts. In doing this we began to think about some of the common criticisms and silencing strategies we have experienced as feminists. We began to consider the subject of how an issue is raised. Frequently when someone from a marginalized group raises a complaint about oppressive practices of a person or group, the appeal and defence of the perpetrator is often in regard to the way in which the issue has been raised. 'There was no need to yell and shout about it' or 'It was inappropriate for it to have been raised in such a public context' or 'Why didn't you tell us about this sooner? It didn't seem an issue for you last year.' So the emphasis goes away from the content of what has been raised to the process issue of the way in which it occurred, thereby placing the responsibility on the person from the oppressed group to take care of the perpetrator(s) of the oppression. The guidelines for the conversation begin to look entirely moulded by middle-class niceties. The mechanisms by which defensiveness operates are made invisible and the responsibility for change is handed to those experiencing the oppression and not the perpetrator of the action.

We began to think about the many and varied ways that are used to hold the focus on the person experiencing the abuse. For example, dismissing the sexist statement as '. . . only a joke'; attempting to highlight the intent rather than the actual event. ('. . . I didn't mean it like that, I'm not like that'); methods which problematize and pathologize the person experiencing the abuse, suggestions that they are humourless, pedantic and have limited understanding. And so we began to use our experiences as women to support our challenge to our racism. We learnt to listen for content, to honour and respond in the spirit in which the challenges were raised; information given to facilitate our relationship with Aboriginal people.

These were some of the beginnings of the lessons that I learnt. This journey I have embarked upon is one I could nonetheless choose to leave at any time. Privilege affords the capacity to stop and be blind again. And so again I return to a commitment to particular ethics, values and beliefs. It is my commitment to feminism that maintains my passage on this journey. For without a commitment to justice for *all* women, what is feminism?

IMPLICATIONS FOR THERAPY

These are the implications for my feminism of learning about racism. What are the implications for the ways I practise therapy? I have learnt that being a culturally appropriate therapist to other communities is not a matter of learning a sufficient volume of information. What is important is a commitment to engage in practices of accountability until outside involvement is not needed. In New Zealand, white family therapists have been asked for an undertaking by Maori therapists not to work any longer with Maori families. Australia is not at this stage yet. However, I believe there are important practices, in keeping with a narrative and deconstructive approach, we can engage in to minimize the harm we do as white therapists.

At the women's health centre where I work, an example of these practices occurred recently. The centre was asked by a government institution to provide counselling for Aboriginal women resident within this institution. A consultation occurred with the Aboriginal women prior to the request for our involvement. The women asked for counselling and the majority asked that the therapist be a white woman. I believe I should not argue against this with individual clients, but there are ways I can structure in accountability and open space for Aboriginal therapists in a situation such as this. I remember the early days of the women's health movement. Many women were reluctant to see women doctors about gynaecological matters, saying they felt more comfortable with male doctors. However, this was not simply a mandate for maintaining the proportions of male doctors, or a clear sanction for not changing the practices of male doctors. It perhaps represented women's comfort with what was familiar and our training in deferring to male judgement. I would not presume to interpret Aboriginal women's experience. But what I learnt from the project was that I would reproduce oppressive ways, and therefore I must structure in accountability. I approached a group of Aboriginal narrative therapists and asked them to be involved in this project. They were familiar with structures of accountability and they immediately took on the responsibility for the project, giving me instructions about what they wanted me to do. The project would be run and organized by Aboriginal women and at the same time counselling would be available to women by a white worker if they wanted this.

CONCLUSION

No longer can I look at the shaved heads of the right wing, or the other extreme examples of racist positions, and think that is racism and I am not. Of course it is me, as Reynolds (1996) said:

> When I'm faced with owning my own racism, and my participation in racist processes, I get overwhelmed, numb and paralysed. But we as white people have a choice – we can throw up our hands in guilt and despair, or roll up our sleeves.

This is a task I have just begun; my sleeves must stay 'rolled up'. I continue to live within my own cultural experience, within the privilege given to me because of my skin colour, my sexuality and class, and with the experience of oppression my gender affords me. I must therefore continue to engage in processes of accountability if I wish to minimize the ways I oppress others. I must continue to examine critically the ways I act, the ways I practise therapy and my feminism. I do not believe it is a matter of dealing with my oppressive ways and thereby becoming enlightened. It is an ongoing commitment to be accountable.

I hope that I have become more aware of the ways of racism and that there are certain practices I will not engage in again. I believe that, given my location within our culture, there will be other oppressive things I will do. Commitment to processes of accountability will minimize the harm that I do and I hope that, in time, the strength of racism will be eroded. However, in a personal way I have just begun. As Greene states:

> Women who consider themselves feminists are not free of the many troublesome attitudes and struggles that all other human beings face. Aspiring to the ideals of feminism and making a commitment to the struggle this inevitably entails, however, makes as good a starting point in this undertaking as any. Perhaps that is a good place to begin. (1995: 312)

REFERENCES

Aldrecht, L. and Brewer, R. M. (1990) *Bridges of Power: Women's Multicultural Alliances.* Philadelphia, PA and Gabriola Island, BC: New Society Publishers.

Derrida, J. (1974) *Of Grammatology.* Chicago: University of Chicago Press.

Elliot, H. (1997) 'En-gendering distinctions: postmodernism, feminism, and narrative therapy', *Gecko: A Journal of Deconstruction and Narrative Ideas in Therapeutic Practice,* 1: 52–71.

Foucault, M. (1973) *The Order of Things: An Archaeology of the Human Sciences.* New York: Vintage Books.

Foucault, M. (1988) 'The ethics of care for the self as a practice of freedom', in Bernauer, J. and Rasmussen, D. (eds), *The Final Foucault.* Cambridge, MA: MIT Press.

Greene, B. (1995) 'An African perspective, on racism and anti-semitism within feminist organisations', in Adleman, Jeanne and Enquidanos, Gloria M. (eds), *Racism in the Lives of Women: Testimony, Theory and Guides to Antiracist Practice,* pp. 303–13.

Jenkins, A. (1990) *Invitation to Responsibility: The Therapeutic Engagement of Men who are Violent and Abusive.* Adelaide: Dulwich Centre Publications.

'Reclaiming Our Stories, Reclaiming Our Lives' (1995), *Dulwich Centre Newsletter*, 1.

Reynolds, V. (1996) 'White'. Address presented at the Narrative Ideas and Therapeutic Practice Conference, 23 February.

Tamasese, K. and Waldegrave, C. (1994) 'Cultural and gender accountability in the "Just Therapy" approach', *Dulwich Centre Newsletter*, 2–3.

White, M. (1988) 'The process of questioning, a therapy of literary merit?', *Dulwich Centre Newsletter*, Winter.

White, M. (1989) 'The externalizing of the problem and the re-authoring of lives and relationship', *Dulwich Centre Newsletter*, Summer.

White, M. (1991) 'Deconstruction and therapy', *Dulwich Centre Newsletter*, 3.

White, M. and Epston, D. (1989) *Literate Means to Therapeutic Ends*. Adelaide: Dulwich Centre Publications. (Published by W.W. Norton in 1990 as *Narrative Means to Therapeutic Ends*.)

3

Which Women? What Feminism?

Aileen Alleyne

This chapter will start by highlighting some important differences for black women in the debate on feminism. It will then explore the author's thesis which is presented within the 'Cycle of Events', and which is seen as intrinsic and central to black women's experience of oppression. The chapter ends with a look at some particular concerns raised within the Cycle and its implications for psychotherapy practice.

The use of the term 'black' will be confined to women and men with *known* black African ancestry. The author is aware of other sections of the 'black' community who share similar experiences of racism and cultural oppression. This chapter will not be able to address these important nuances and will therefore focus on a few areas pertinent to the black experience.

WHAT CONSTITUTES BLACK FEMINISM

First of all, it is important to acknowledge that there are areas of commonality amongst all women. It would be true to say however that the term 'feminism' clearly carries different meanings for black and white women. Although we might agree with the main tenets which, broadly speaking, relate to the debunking of female gender stereotypes and the continued struggle for equal rights and opportunity with men, feminism for black women has at its core a historical importance which is borne out in black/white relationships. This crucial history for black people has created a transgenerational transmission of trauma, which is heavily compounded by our present-day experiences of cultural oppression and racism. The links with the living past affect our present and threaten to shape our future. I am suggesting that from an intrapsychic perspective, this dynamic has become the main psychological pivot for all our actions and the factor which underpins a main part of what feminism is about for the black woman.

Being a feminist is a label which most black women in Britain seem reluctant to own and wear in the same way as their white female counterparts. The reasons for this are probably as diverse as the differences that exist between black people; but in the words, quoted by Jolly, of Grace Mera Molisa in her speech to the First National Conference of Vanuaaku Women on Efate, in 1978, we might get a bit closer to what is felt and expressed about feminism by many black women.

> Women's liberation or Women's lib is a European disease to be cured by Europeans. What we are aiming for is not just women's liberation but a total liberation. A social, political and economic liberation. Our situation is very different to that of European women. Look around you and see, especially in town. Hundreds of our women slave every day for white women. They cook, clean, sweep, and wash shit for crumbs from European women. European women thought up Women's Liberation because they didn't have enough to do, and they were bored out of their minds. They wanted to be liberated so they could go out and work like men. They were sick of being ornaments in the house. They hate their men for it. That's not our position at all. Our women always have too much to do. Our women never have the leisure to be ornaments. Our societies are people oriented so we care for one another. Our situation also affects men. (Jolly, 1991: 4)

Molisa's views might not be fully embraced by all black women; however, the essence of her speech will ring familiar bells for many black women living in British society today. No black person has been spared the effects of racial oppression, and as a consequence, we start, consciously or unconsciously, from this important historical premise in our struggle for personal freedom. When we reflect on the goal of feminism, which is the acquisition of equality and personal autonomy for all women, we can begin to put into context the chapter's question: Which women? What feminism?

To examine these questions more closely, the first acknowledgement which must be made is the fact that black women's fight for liberation predates white feminist thought and literature. We have carried in our collective and individual psyches a history of enslavement and racial oppression through the generations. This powerful intrapsychic experience has profoundly influenced our relationships with ourselves and with the white other, and has shaped our determinism. White feminism does not address this history in which its subjects – white men and women – have played a part and by which they have also been powerfully affected. The tendency to believe that our shared history had devastating psychic effects on black people only is a myth. My philosophical standpoint is that both blacks and whites carry different emotional burdens and responsibilities for this history which we must own as part of our respective intrapsychic makeups. From this position, I as a black woman am put more in touch with how intimate black/white relations are, as if tied together by an important historical umbilical cord. The use of this analogy will play an important part in the discussion to follow.

The *fundamental* difference for me therefore between black and white feminism is that the black woman's struggle has been born out of a strong conscious recognition of this important history which has shaped her relationship to the white other. As a consequence, we must see the black woman's needs for personal freedom and autonomy in the context of the bigger struggle, *a black people's struggle*. Black feminism parallels this struggle in the work black women strive to address in their relationships with black men, with each other, and with white society as a whole. The difference highlighted here between black and white women's struggle presents a challenge in the debate on feminism and psychotherapy and the recognition for fuller understanding of black intrapsychic and inter-personal issues which must be understood within a historical, social context. As stated earlier, history has left black/white relations with a unique, intimate, and pathologically ambivalent attachment amongst its peoples that distinguish it from other race relations dynamics. The dis-courses operating within our unequal and incongruous object relations have been more rigorously examined by black American writers. Drawing on aspects of black feminist thought advanced by black American women, bell hooks, a scholar and writer of black women's issues, suggests that we first of all shift from statements like 'I am a feminist' to those such as 'I advocate feminism.' Such an approach could 'serve as a way women who are concerned about feminism as well as other political movements could express their support while avoiding linguistic structures that give primacy to one particular group' (1984: 30). Her view on feminism is a popular one which might be embraced by many black British women.

> To me feminism is not simply a struggle to end male chauvinism or a movement to ensure that women will have equal rights with men; it is a commitment to Western culture on various levels – sex, race, and class, to name a few – and a commitment to reorganise American society so that the self-development of people can take precedence over imperialism, economic expansion and material desires. (hooks 1981: 194)

Other views on black feminism have been notably expressed by Patricia Hill Collins (1991) who offers a collective definition taken from the ideas of Anna Julia Cooper, Pauli Murray, bell hooks, Alice Walker (1982, 1983, 1988) and other black women intellectuals. Black feminism is seen as 'a process of self-conscious struggle that empowers women and men to actualise a humanist vision of community' (Collins, 1991: 39).

Alice Walker (1983) prefers the term 'womanist', a term she defines thus: 'womanist is to feminist as purple is to lavender'. She clarifies this position from the standpoint of being 'committed to the survival and wholeness of entire people, male and female'. She goes on to say that a womanist is 'not a separatist, except periodically for health', and is 'traditionally universalist, as in "Mama, why are we brown, pink, and yellow, and our cousins are white, beige, and black?" Ans.: "Well, you know the coloured race is just like a flower garden, with every colour flower represented"' (1983, xi). Collins (1991) notes that Ms Walker, by redefining all people as 'people of colour', creates a solidarity within the collective human experience while recognizing the need for individuality and self-determination.

One of the few books on black women's lives in Britain, *The Heart of The Race* (Bryan, Dadzie and Scafe, 1985), notes the fact that black women had challenged the white influence of the women's movement back in the early 1970s. They reflect on the fact that they and other black women were much more influenced by what was happening in black liberation movements in Africa and America and not by what the British voice of feminism, Germaine Greer (1971), and other white middle-class feminists were fighting about here in Britain. Issues which related to black women then were their economic dependence on men, childcare, women's role in the work place and racism affecting black people generally. They felt these were not burning issues for white feminists, who were more concerned about abortion and wages for housework. This situation has not changed much over the years.

From these expressed views we can draw the conclusion that what underpins black feminist thought and experience is our history of oppression and the ways we have chosen to handle its effects on our lives. These views also highlight the ever present links in black/white dynamics. An aspect of this complex relationship can be studied more closely in Figure 3.1 (Alleyne, 1992) which highlights crucial dynamics within the black person's intrapsychic journey. I am suggesting that these stages have to be negotiated in order to achieve a sense of freedom and personal empowerment. From this diagram also, a route out of our internalized oppression is suggested, which requires work on the self with the inclusion of the family and collective. Liberated feminists therefore, and the role of psychotherapy in black people's lives will have to take on board all that this work will entail.

In this diagram of the *Cycle of Events*, I am arguing the points that through the generations it was possible for us to perpetuate certain false-self traits by carrying internalized negative patterns of cognition about ourselves, particularly in relation to the white other. I believe this complex internal process, which starts at the pre-verbal stage and which can be seen in the example of the black mother rejecting her dark-skinned baby, can lead to internal disturbances and *false*-self traits in that child as it finds ways of coping with the rejection from its parent. The relevance of the *false-self* concept to feminism and psychotherapy thus becomes an important construct in understanding the black woman's struggle for individuation and her healthy negotiations in a predominantly white society. Furthermore, I am arguing that as it is not possible to erase history from our experiences, its facts and consequences then become crucial lessons which we must analyse and learn from in order to be able to move on with our lives. The psychological effects of black/white historical attachments, coupled with the virulence of present-day racism, have affected this *moving-on* process, preventing full emergence of the black potential. Within this arrested state, I am suggesting that negative self traits develop within a

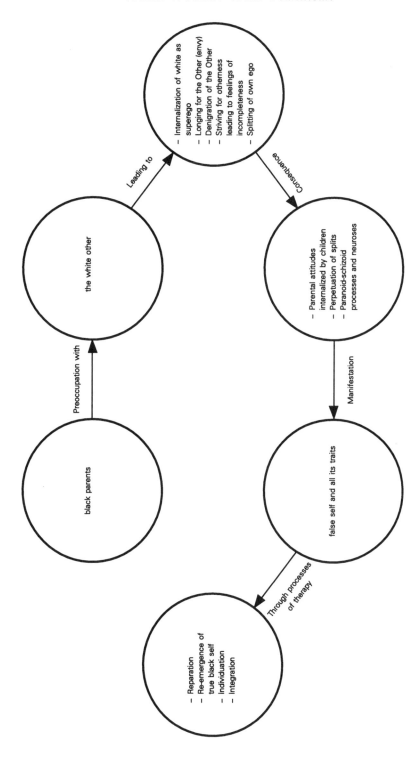

Figure 3.1 *Cycle of Events (Alleyne, 1992)*

dependent *false* persona, suppressing a *true* identity and independent self. The thrust of the thesis is in the belief that a psychological metamorphosis is a necessary process in the black person's journey which has to be negotiated effectively with the support and cultural expertise of the therapist providing that pyschotherapeutic help.

Views on the *true* and *false* self, and truth and authenticity, are highly contentious issues in counselling and psychotherapy, and many readers would immediately declare having problems with them. However, I am taking a stance by embracing Winnicott's (1958) view on this important concept of identity in which he distinguishes the *true* and *false* self by viewing the latter as being a defensive structure, a 'false' *adaptation* to an *environment* which has not met the needs of the *'true'* self during formative months of infancy. He further suggests that, during psychoanalytic treatment, patients with a *false* self must regress to a state of dependence on the analyst during which the latter can respond to his emergent true self (Rycroft, 1972). Winnicott's (1958) emphasis on 'good enough' mothering in transcultural terms is met through the 'holding' from the biological maternal source, the social environment, and the 'mother country' with which most black people with colonized backgrounds have had close ties. Our shared history and its effects may show that where Balint's (1989) concept of the Basic Fault has occurred within these settings, therein lies the development of false-self structures for both racial divides. Additionally, observations from my own clinical practice suggest that it is not just an accident or coincidence that many black clients in therapy refer very naturally to the terms *'true* and *false* self' without much pre-knowledge of analytic or psychological understanding. This is very difficult to explain and may be a phenomenon which can provide some insights into the contents of the black archetype and its tendency to organize towards healing. The need for black people and black women to negotiate this particular psychological journey – the Cycle – is crucial, and dictates the discourses within feminism and psychotherapies. I hasten to add that what is not shown in Figure 3.1 and can't be explored fully within the remit of this chapter, but which must be a consequence of black/white attachments, is the white person's own unconscious preoccupation with the black other and all that is symbolic of blackness.

Depending on where we have had our upbringing, whether here in Britain or back in the Caribbean or Africa, it is my belief that we have all been exposed to various kinds of edicts which have been geared to elevating the white person. I am suggesting that this indoctrination for black people has contributed to a white internalized superego which has also been heavily influenced by colonized parental introjects. Few of us have escaped this experience which has shaped our adaptation to our environment. The differences in adaptation are as varied as the countries and home environments from which we come.

Additionally, if we were to think of black/white attachments as either parent/child or sibling relationships, I would further suggest that black people's conscious and unconscious preoccupation with the white other produces powerful feelings of ambivalence similar to those felt towards one's siblings and/or parent. These feelings can manifest in our longing for the other in ways, such as, our envy of the ease with which whites are accorded opportunity and access in society. Alongside feelings of longing, envy, and even love for the white other are opposing feelings of denigration, anger and hate. Within this ambivalence, there is a need to manage these contrasting emotions in healthy ways which protect against the temptation to constantly react in an angry fashion or survive through striving for otherness. Some black people may try to cope by employing powerful defences, such as disassociating, splitting, projecting and withdrawing from the impingements of a hostile, white discriminatory world. The effects of the latter defensive structure – withdrawal – can be seen where the black person completely loses the battle to maintain emotional equilibrium and the ability to affirm her centredness. This situation most often leads to a deep sense of ontological insecurity with emotional disturbance and mental health presentations. This particular brand of mental ill-health is most observed in the splitting of the ego and feelings of incompleteness. Perpetuation of these internal dynamics is witnessed along generational lines, leading to repetition of parental attitudes being internalized by black children and the continuation of *false* self traits being observed in the new generation. The effects of internalized oppression on each generation are obviously shaped also by current social realities. White practitioners using traditional eurocentric approaches to treatment misunderstand these presentations in their full cultural contexts, and black people are frequently diagnosed as schizophrenics with inappropriate drug therapy and other medical interventions.

To illustrate the impact on the self of the above discussion, the following two letters from a popular leading black magazine, *Ebony* (1990), and a brief clinical vignette from my private practice, are included to illustrate the workings of the *false* self from different sections of the black community.

> I am white woman happily married to a Black man for 10 years. We have two beautiful children, ages, 2 and 5. It sickens me to think that as my children grow up, they will not have the decision to be who they want to be but that society will determine that for them. They can't even be proud of being both Black and White because society will not allow them. If my son, who looks completely White wants to be considered Black, who will accept him? . . . Unfortunately, racism is here to stay. I tolerated it when I married my husband but cannot tolerate it where my children are concerned. Should they be treated differently because two people who love each other very much wanted children? I think not. (*Ebony*, 1990)

This letter illustrates several points relating to the chapter topic. We can empathize with the concerns of this white mother who is aware of the tensions and conflicts within black/white relationships which will have a direct impact on her mixed-race children. Her awareness of *racism* from whites, and the *racial prejudice* from blacks towards her children, and particularly her son, is very much heightened no doubt by the intimate, close and loving attachment to a black man, her husband. Her commitment to help her children develop an awareness of external realities, whilst enabling them to chose freely their own identity in a hostile world, identifies her as a *true* feminist and humanist, who will certainly play a crucial role in her children's individuation process by providing them with an environment which fosters cultural education for critical consciousness and acquisition of personal agency.

★ ★ ★

I am a proud African-American woman of African Native American descent. I have never, nor will I ever, apologize for my ethnic background. My hair, eyes, and complexion are God's creation. To apologise for not being black enough is to make an apology for God . . . (*Ebony*, 1990)

The first point about this letter is in this woman's description of coming from 'African Native American descent'. This description tells us that her African heritage is black and the Native part, American Indian. We are left to work out that this black woman is probably pale to light brown in complexion, with eyes and hair revealing her mixed heritage. I think we are introduced to an individuated black woman who is affirming her own identity and difference, whilst firmly addressing an aspect of this identity which causes confusion for both blacks and whites who might feel she is not *black enough*. The question of being not authentically black, or false, may stem from our (black people's) difficulty in embracing differences amongst ourselves, and, more to the point, not being able to recognize aspects of internalized racial oppression in ourselves which stem from a unilateral position to pressure a monolithic black self. The emotional elements of this struggle are tied up with powerful feelings of envy, hate, love and shame, which in turn create a 'schizoid' transference (*not schizophrenia*), with the white other. From the diagram depicting the Cycle of Events, it is clear to see how this kind of inner conflict can suppress the emergence of a *true* creative and emaciated black self.

THE CASE OF PATRICK

Patrick is a 38-year-old black man who is in a relationship with a white woman. He holds a senior post in one of the caring professions and is currently completing his PhD thesis. Born to African parents who emigrated to England, he is now coming to terms with aspects of his upbringing which he feels have strongly affected his sense of identity and self-esteem. Patrick was fostered out from the age of four to a number of white adoptive parents. He now realizes that as a direct result of internalizing parental colonized ideas as a child which had left him feeling 'inferior', he subsequently went out of his way to prove his worth to his white foster parents. His 'survival techniques' were manifest in his obsession to be the best at everything, and to be appreciated for his intellect which he over-nurtured to the detriment of an emotionally impoverished self. Patrick would intellectualize his emotional pain as a way of avoiding having to deal with feelings.

In our work together, a peculiar aspect of the transference-resistance was observed in the way he upheld the 'Queen's English' with a reverence that became both a coping mechanism and his trap. Patrick's pursuits of mainly white ideals (e.g. golf, opera, theatre), alongside a romanticized link with his 'mother country' in Africa, had produced a splitting of the ego and a false, compensatory self. Patrick's work in therapy focused on him being able to negotiate the Cycle (as depicted in the diagram) in order to work through the psychological consequences of his identity crises. By re-discovering a positive black identity that he could own, he was able to embrace both the symbolic black and white aspects of his self, without splitting his real desires for academic aspirations, individuality, personal autonomy and a sense of true belonging to the black collective. A separation and subsequent split from his white female partner seemed inevitable as she held the brunt of his anger and rage toward his natural and non-biological parents. In couples work they both came to a deeper understanding of the nature of their bi-racial attachment which perpetuated paranoid-schizoid processes in Patrick's thinking and relating. A contracted period of working together with this couple had also enabled them to examine and understand how the processes of projective identification had locked them both into a very unhealthy situation which had become both intractable and destructive.

From the above examples, it is not difficult to see how intimately the historical links are bound up in black and white peoples' lives. What is presented as a major challenge for all therapists, including black and white feminist therapists, is the awareness and confidence to identify and work with opposites, that is, the symbolic black and white within each and every one of us. Within this shadow side, race and all its primitive representations are ever-present.

To summarize the hypothesis within the Cycle of Events which I have tried to bear out in the 'cases' presented, I am suggesting that in order to find the *true* self, a self which is not to be idealized, but to be presented diversely with all its flaws and foibles, the black person *must* find ways of separating out emotionally and spiritually from the white other who has become the white parental imago. This imago which has operated over time has developed to a point where it functions like a filter through which the black experience is shaped and felt and sometimes acted out. I am claiming that this process arrests the development of the superego (as opposed to Freud's (1924) resolution of the Oedipus complex), leaving the black person in a perpetual state of *adolescence*, dependent and always judging her/his worth in relation to the white other. According to Fanon, 'the black man stops behaving as an *actional* person' in this state of unhealthy attachment and dependence (1986: 154).

Within the practice of counselling and psychotherapy, one of the most important tasks is to address issues of dependence upon the therapy and therapist in order to achieve a proper separation that is necessary before letting our clients/patients go. This is an important rite of passage which must be negotiated and worked through in all therapeutic alliances where the transference neurosis has been carefully fostered and developed. In a similar way, I am suggesting that a culture-specific transference neurosis does exist in black/white relationships. Our shared history has created a state of dependence on both sides of the black/white divide. This dependent relationship, when coupled with the *real* transference in the therapy, will be doubly intensified, requiring skilful handling by the culturally competent practitioner. It is my concern that this expertise is a rarity and frequently resisted in psychotherapy practice, leaving yawning gaps in the white practitioner's repertoire of skills and experience. Sadly, the black client's journey is stultified, which in my view is another form of cultural misappropriation, raising important questions about what is cure and how we measure it.

It is important to note that the process of separating out and working on *false*-self traits can be done through means other than traditional counselling and psychotherapy in order to achieve the goal of individuation. This reparative work – which, for example, is undertaken in black women's groups, various spiritual and alternative pursuits, and the more notable Black Men's march in America which was celebrated as a day of atonement for 1 million black men – can allow the space for therapeutic healing and growth.

The rest of this chapter will briefly highlight some of the issues at the heart of black feminism which have further implications for the Cycle of Events and the implications for counselling and psychotherapy practice.

CORE THEMES IN BLACK FEMINISM

Black Women's Relationships with Black Men

Black British women as a group reflect diversity at many levels, socially, culturally, politically, economically, sexually and spiritually. Many would agree that within this heterogeneity can be felt a dynamic force which is expressed by black women achieving at a fast pace in many areas. 'Sisters' are basically doing it for themselves by occupying influential positions in the job market, pursuing personal ambitions for higher education and academic achievements and investing in their personal and emotional development with a renewed passion. The same cannot be said for most black men in Britain today. Although similar diversities can be identified within the black male population, full expression of the potential that we know to exist amongst our men is not realized in similar ways. This situation has created an atmosphere of concern, verging on a state of crisis, as to the future direction for black men in British society. This concern includes those men who are our grandfathers, uncles, fathers, brothers, partners and sons who face the brunt of racism in this society. What affects them will certainly affect us as women. However, the crisis goes largely unseen in the wider community as we fail to give this important issue the deserved public attention and proper acknowledgement it needs.

From my observations, the far-reaching consequences of this crisis have created huge splits between black men and black women where feelings of jealousy, rivalry and competition are felt by black men towards their women who are forging ahead. Some are able to cope, whilst others reluctantly resign themselves to the situation, which invariably changes their relationship status to their partners. Changes experienced in these partnerships produce conflicts with gender identity and problematic issues of power and worth between the sexes. Within the black community there is a sense of estrangement from each other which brings with it feelings of isolation and loss. These are the dilemmas the black woman faces amidst her own struggle through white oppression, and as we can see, her relationships with black men (not exclusively those that are heterosexual and intimate) are important to her life and add a crucial dimension to the debate on feminism and its therapies.

Intimacy and Trust

The theme of intimacy and trust is commonly presented in the work with most clients who seek help with relationship problems, abuse of one kind or another, and issues of loss and change. This theme does present in similar ways for black women. However, if we reflect on some of the areas discussed earlier in this chapter, namely, black women's relationship with black men, their relationship with white society and their relationship with themselves, it is not difficult to see how the themes of intimacy and trust can influence patterns of relationship dysfunction in these configurations. Difficulties in getting too close (intimacy) and the ability to let go (trust) can be understood in the context of black women choosing at an unconscious level to protect themselves from hurt. The *strong black woman* image, although complimentary, can also create problems for her in letting go, showing vulnerability and feeling able to ask for help. The work of the counsellor and psychotherapist in managing this theme is to enable the woman to feel trusting enough to talk about those issues that really matter to her and where *race* might be ever-present. Allowing the therapeutic dialogue to be conducted when necessary in the client's native patois, Creole or slang if she so wishes, can aid the processes of fluency, fluidity and trust in the therapeutic alliance. The therapist who is able to engage authentically in reciprocal ways can help with the building of trust and bridge the cultural gaps much more quickly than the one who isn't. A more relaxed 'conversational' style of therapy, which is able to interpret (not in an overzealous way) the client's defences whilst allowing space to address and truly understand the realities of the external world, is going to be far more enabling to the client when addressing culture-specific matters relating to the client's life.

The baldness of the classical approach to therapy has proved time and time again to be stiff, inhibiting and disabling for the black client. This is perhaps one of the reasons why there are so many premature endings within transcultural alliances and one which also contributes to the crisis regarding the scarcity of black clinicians who themselves have to undergo treatment for training.

Shame

The theme of shame is perhaps the single most important variable over-arching much of what is understood to be happening in the psyche of black women and men in British society today. The word itself requires some explanation. Shame is described as the action of covering, of veiling, of hiding. It resembles emotions like jealousy, envy, spite, love, hatred, and pride. It might be related to feelings such as 'I cannot see myself as I want others to see me.' This would become an introjection, that is, taking in judgement and punishment by others.

Shame has been described as 'a reaction formation to exhibitionistic wishes' (Jacobson, 1964: 100). In this sense it is a rigid defence structure built into the character and used against the risk of being humiliated; a risk viewed as continually present in cultural oppression.

Shame is interwoven with issues of narcissism, though the two realms are by no means identical. It is the veiled companion of narcissism. Shame stems from internalized conflict with an external authority (society) and guards against the boundary of privacy and intimacy. Shame in this sense protects the innermost vulnerable bits of the self and defends against anxiety which threatens to destroy an integral image of the self.

Shame threatens our individual relationships with each other in the black community in forms where we act out our feelings of indignation, rage, and frustrations at other black people. Sadly, the acting out of these feelings is often done to those closest to us and destroys our relationships with each other. The effects of shame can be seen in our relationship with our children who face fierce criticism from black mothers and fathers whose intention to 'discipline' becomes synonymous with demanding obedience. The need to control invariably leads to aspects of parenting which destroy the full development of the black child's self-confidence, autonomy and creativity.

Shame has played a major part in creating difficulties for our group in sustaining social, economic and political collective efforts. Many a group effort has ended prematurely or aborted because we have lost faith in each other and ourselves. In this sense, shame leads to cultural isolation, which is the withdrawing from other black people and sometimes turning to the white world which is not as welcoming. We also act out our hurt, embarrassment, fear, dislike and mistrust by dividing ourselves into subgroups of separatists ('anti-white'), anti-blacks ('coconuts'), racial hybrids, and so on. Shame has left us with *complexes* about skin colour and accepted concepts of beauty, for example, and about maintaining a comfortable sense of one's individuality within the black collective.

Cultural shame and its resulting isolation from other black people is one theme that can present both white and black therapist alike with immense difficulty, as it touches so deeply the night side of love, that is, that part of our souls which reminds us of our own mortality. The rule of thumb in beginning to address this sensitive area is to be alert to the temptation to over-interpret, which can lead to devastating consequences of re-shaming the shamed. The overzealous therapist can become a danger to the client's progress.

IMPLICATIONS FOR THERAPY

As human beings we have a tendency to look for logical maps to offer knowledge and meaning to the unknown and the unfamiliar. The terrain of inter-cultural therapy carries no such maps or recipes; no formulas and no particular scientific psychological techniques. Instead, what we have are guidelines for dealing with the illogical and irrational. The following six principles urge (a) that we pay attention to our *approach* to the therapy which must create a synthesis between extra- and intrapsychic factors, (b) that the *philosophy* underpinning feminist/transcultural practice must create room for the inclusion of work on issues of racism and its influence on the development of a racial and self-identity, (c) that we acknowledge the full *context* in which black women (and men) live their lives in a predominantly white society, (d) that we strive to be more skilful in *identifying culturally specific phenomena* which impede growth, (e) that we need to be committed to *sustaining the transcultural journey* with the black client to its mature end, and (f) that we re-evaluate yardsticks for *measuring effective outcome and cure*. Transcultural competence demands a rigour from the therapist to understand these principles and appropriately embrace them into the therapy.

Working towards a *resolution of the Cycle of Events* is one of the very important tasks of black British feminist therapy. The basic therapeutic skills for working in this mode are no different from other forms of therapeutic work, but the demand for the therapist to be authentic with the black woman is one that cannot be manufactured; it has be acquired through a slow reciprocal process of understanding one's own racial identity development and its complex relationship with the other. In my other work as lecturer and trainer working with issues of Difference and Diversity in psychotherapy practice, it is a common expectation of white practitioners from various therapeutic persuasions to want to assimilate this complex area of learning in one swoop; usually half a day's session's worth of training, or a day if that much. The ability to contain, hold and bear what is difficult for the client, as well as for ourselves as practitioners, is a key factor in this debate. Likewise for the black client/patient, her ability to truly engage in the work with various split-off parts of herself will require a similar kind of risk-taking. We can clearly see in this situation of the cross-cultural dyad, two cautious and equally nervous people whose ancestral relationships will certainly be re-awakened in the therapy with all their powerful feelings and consequences. Neither will be able to ignore the inner disturbance and its powerful primitive effects of making it inescapable to re-visit the living past which has to be re-worked into the living present.

REFERENCES

Alleyne, A. (1992) 'The re-emergence of the true self . . . the black experience in relation to the white other'. MA dissertation, University of Hertfordshire.

Balint, M (1989) *The Basic Fault*. London: Tavistock/Routledge.

Bottomley, G., De Lepervanche, M. and Martin, J. (1991) *Intersexions*. Sydney, Australia: Allen & Unwin.

Bryan, B., Dadzie, S. and Scafe, S. (1985) The *Heart of The Race, Black Women's Lives In Britain*. London: Virago Press.

Collins, P. (1991) *Black Feminist Thought*. New York/London: Routledge.

Cooper, A. J. (1982) *A Voice from the South; by a Black Woman of the South*. Xenia, OH: Aldine Printing House.

Ebony (1990), 46(2), December.

Fanon, F. (1986) *Black Skin, White Masks*. London: Pluto Press.

Freud, S (1924) *The Dissolution of the Oedipus Complex*, vol. 19. London: Hogarth Press.

Greer, Germaine (1971) *The Female Eunuch*. London: Paladin.

hooks, b. (1981) *Ain't I A Woman – Black Women and Feminism*. Boston, MA: South End Press.

hooks, b. (1984) *Feminist Theory: From Margin to Centre*. Boston, MA: South End Press.

hooks, b. (1989) *Talking Back: Thinking Feminist, Thinking Black*. Boston, MA: South End Press.

hooks, b. (1993) *Sisters of The Yam – Black Women and Self-Recovery*. Boston, MA: South End Press.

Jacobson, E. (1964) *The Self and the Object World*. New York: International University Press.

Jolly, M. (1991) 'The Politics of Difference: Feminism, Colonialism and Decolonisation in Vannatu', in G. Bottomley, M. De Lepervanche and J. Martin (eds) *Intersexions*. Sydney, Australia: Allen & Unwin.

Murray, P. (1970) 'The Liberation of Black Women', in M. L. Thompson (ed.) *Voices of the New Feminism*. Boston, MA: Becon. pp. 87–102.

Rycroft, C. (1972) *A Critical Dictionary of Psychoanalysis*. London: Penguin Books.

Walker, A. (1982) *The Color Purple*. New York: Washington Square Press.

Walker, A. (1983) *In Search of our Mothers' Gardens*. New York: Harcourt Brace Jovanovich.

Walker, A. (1988) *Living by the Word*. New York: Bantam.

Winnicott, D. W. (1958) 'Primary maternal preoccupation', in *Collected Papers*. London: Tavistock Publications.

4

Feminist Psychotherapy and Sexual Abuse

Moira Walker

Working with abuse survivors[1] is a demanding, important and increasingly large part of any counsellor's or therapist's work load. Workers need to be clinically experienced; resilient, with a sound understanding of the effects of abuse on the child and on the adult underpinned by a theoretical base that clarifies rather than confounds. This is not always the case. As Burstow notes in her book on working in the context of women and violence:

> Feminist counseling literature has not provided the concrete guidance needed. The literature is divided between weak theory with detailed practice suggestions on one hand and powerful theorizing with only general remarks and examples about how to put it into practice on the other. This deficit is a sizeable one. (1992: xiv)

In my experience it is sadly true that this can be a real difficulty for practitioners. Much of the 'powerful theorizing' alluded to above mystifies and intimidates rather than clarifies and encourages. Whilst practitioners in this field need to be flexible and prepared to explore new methods of working, they also need the security of a reasonably stable theoretical base. It can be a minefield, with the internal splits that frequently exist within the abuse survivor also reflected in theoretical disputes which, for many practitioners, bear little relationship to their work with clients.

I write this as a psychotherapist and counsellor with many years of experience in working with abuse survivors, and in training and supervising others in this field. I describe myself as a feminist psychodynamic therapist and will attempt to give the reader some sense of my understanding of the context of abuse; its history; how it is understood and explained societally; and the impact of feminism and feminist therapy upon it. Two aspects of work with survivors, the blaming of mothers and the idealization of fathers, will be given particular attention, as these are frequently raised in both supervision and training. These will be discussed in the context of aspects of feminist object relations theory that provide valuable theoretical and clinical insights. An interview with an abuse survivor in which she discusses her own experience of feminist therapy will also be included to ground the discussion and to give a voice to the person who matters most – the client. The discussion inevitably will not be complete and it will fail to be a neat theoretical package. I make no apology for this: it is not a neat field and I invite readers to use this chapter as a basis for their own discussions and ideas.

SEXUAL ABUSE: THE CONTEXT

In any discussion of sexual abuse it should be remembered that abuse extends beyond the sexual and that all forms of abuse are harmful. Children are abused psychologically, physically and sexually, and many suffer forms of all three. There are no neat distinctions to be made. The acknowledgement of sexual abuse as a serious problem has always been resisted, and still is, although this resistance takes different forms at different times. Sexual abuse is now in the public gaze, but its history has been marked by denial and a general sense that it is beyond credibility. It should also be noted that boys as well as girls are sexually abused, and that although the research points to the great preponderance of men as perpetrators, women also sexually abuse children. Acknowledging that women also abuse, especially sexually, is very difficult for many feminists. As Young points out:

> Examining the reasons for the feminist resistance to acknowledging female abuse realistically provides us with clues to society's denial of the wider problem. The reason, as those working in the field know, is to do with maintaining a status quo that is recognisably fragile. (Young, 1993: 108)

It is difficult to estimate accurately the number of children who suffer sexual abuse: this partly depends on the definition used, and partly on the research methods employed. Retrospective studies on adults always indicate a higher level of abuse than cases actually reported and formally identified in children. This, of course, reflects the large numbers of children who suffer but are never identified and never receive help. Abuse remains a carefully kept secret in many families. Finklehor stated (1986: 16), 'The reality is that there is not yet a consensus among social scientists about the national scope of sexual abuse.' This remains the case but whilst accurately defining and measuring the extent and nature of a problem is always important, the difficulty of doing so should not distract us from serious enquiry into the problem. It is sufficient to know that an enormous number of children from all social classes suffer horrific treatment, and that these children grow up into adults carrying appalling secrets and terrible pain.

WHAT IS ABUSE?

Measuring the extent of sexual abuse is problematic, and defining it is similarly fraught with difficulty. One such difficulty is whether sexual abuse involves only actual contact or whether non-contact events should be included. Another is the age of the perpetrator: a current concern relates to older children abusing younger – what age gap is necessary before one child can be deemed to have abused another? Or can a child of for example ten abuse another child that age? Or would this be harmless 'playing' or 'experimentation'?

I would suggest the following as a broad working definition of sexual abuse. It is essential to recognize as crucial elements the misuse of power and authority, combined with force or coercion, which leads to the exploitation of children in situations where adults, or children sufficiently older than the victim to have greater strength and power, seek sexual gratification through those who are developmentally immature and where, as a result, consent from the victim is a non-concept. Such gratification can involve explicit sexual acts – anal or vaginal intercourse, fondling, masturbation – or may involve invasive and inappropriate actions not directly involving contact: watching a child undress, bathe, use the toilet, in order to gratify the perpetrator rather than meeting the needs of the child; forcing a child to watch adults having sex or making them watch pornographic videos. What is central is the exploitation of the child; the denial of their rights and feelings, and the essential gratification of the abuser through the child, the child being regarded solely as an object for the perpetrator's use and to meet their needs.

Inevitably any discussion on any aspect of sexual abuse triggers strong feelings. It is an irony that reflects the strength and the power of these that in the 1970s and 1980s feminists often accused therapists, particularly those informed by psychoanalytic theory, and in many instances quite correctly, of denying the reality of abuse, thereby silencing thousands of victims. At the same time social workers were often attacked in the media for removing children from actually or potentially abusive homes without sufficient cause. These were not easy years for therapists who went against the tide of disbelief: a colleague of mine who, like myself, was identifying abuse in these years and working with survivors, recalled how she was described as 'a dirty old woman'.

In the 1990s the pendulum has swung the other way. Therapists are now being attacked for being overzealous, and accused of planting ideas of abuse where none exists – 'false memory syndrome' as it is popularly called. In fact, many survivors enter therapy or counselling with clear memories of abuse, whereas others may recover these whilst in therapy. Recovered memories is a highly contentious area that I have written about elsewhere (Walker, 1996) and I can do no more than allude to here. However it is clear that therapists should take enormous care not to be suggestive to their clients and not to use hypnosis inappropriately: abuse survivors and victims of other traumas are suggestible, and memories have to be carefully handled:

> Although hypnosis does not necessarily involve any compromise of the patient's autonomy, it always carries the potential for being perceived as intrusive, controlling, manipulative and so on and thereby grossly distorting the transference relationship. I would caution against the use of hypnosis for penetrative exploration of the patient's mind and certainly it is unwise to use hypnosis for uncovering repressed memories because of the dangers of creating pseudo memories. (Mollon, 1996: 155)

Whichever way the argument goes, the crux is that it is all in someone's mind: either the mistaken client's or the unscrupulous therapist's — someone must be fantasizing somewhere. A convenient escape route for the perpetrator, with the counsellor and therapist all too often becoming a handy fall guy, and another avoidance of the real issues of recognizing the extent of abuse and the seriousness of its effects.

THE HISTORY OF ABUSE: THE STRUGGLE FOR BELIEF

Sexual abuse is not new and neither is its recognition. However, the pendulum of recognition and acknowledgement versus disbelief and denial has swung backwards and forwards over the last century. Denial is weighty and swings into full force whenever there is a danger of abuse being taken really seriously. So acknowledgement has been intermittent, and it is only in recent years that the reality of sexual abuse has taken on a more solid identity that is too large to be dismantled and swept away. As I will show later, this is largely thanks to the insistence and persistence of feminism.

Historically the misuse of children both sexually and physically has been well documented, particularly with regard to working-class children who all too often were a burden and an unaffordable expense to their families. Many became servants at a very young age and were exploited mercilessly:

> Another very vulnerable group in the nineteenth century was the servants. The habit from slavery days of men considering women household workers as being at their disposal for sexual services continued after slavery. If a servant girl became pregnant, there was no recourse when the mistress of the household turned her out. Many prostitutes were forced into the profession via that route. (Boulding, 1992: 200)

From the 1870s in London female activists petitioned the British Parliament against the sexual abuse of girls. Around this time Freud was developing his ideas and theories. He recognized the immense significance of childhood experience and began to identify the existence of sexual abuse, only to vacillate on this thereafter. In 1895 in *The Aetiology of Hysteria* Freud proposed a direct causal relationship between childhood sexual traumas and later adult difficulties, although he later retracted this.

Without a detailed analysis of his writings, which are many, it is not straightforward to distinguish the patterns and movements in Freud's own thinking from the selective use made of them by other professions and a wider society. Many held, and still do, the family as sacrosanct, and selectively extracted from Freud and other early theorists in order to support what was acceptable and comfortable to them. However, there is no doubt that his theory that memories of infantile seduction could be fantasy dominated much thinking, particularly in the psychiatric literature, and reflected a powerful resistance to believing in the reality of sexual abuse.

Understanding sexual abuse as fantasies arising from unresolved Oedipal issues tragically served to silence many survivors. However, in terms of Freud and the Oedipus complex, the problem is twofold. Firstly, the centrality of the Oedipal stage in Freud's thinking, combined with his own uncertainty about the reality of abuse, conveniently fuelled the flame of denial, which has burnt so strongly since. Secondly, the Oedipus complex itself has been misused and interpreted to suit the interpreter rather than fit with the client's own history and experience.

It is not only Freud's work and its interpretation that is problematic in this context. The work of Melanie Klein, extremely influential in Britain, is also highly significant. Melanie Klein explored and highlighted the significance of very early stages of development in the child, and the importance of the mother–baby relationship. Her contribution to psychoanalytic theory is profound, but her emphasis on fantasy and the inner world of the child has been another factor that has shifted the spotlight away from the actual behaviour of others towards the child. Hence what she interpreted as fantasies of a sexual nature would now be likely to be understood as abusive experiences. Nowadays in reading examples of her work with children her interpretations can appear worryingly unsubstantiated and highly suggestive, although of course, in Klein's eyes she was interpreting unconscious desires and wishes.

Legal changes were also occurring, and incest was made illegal in 1908 in England and Wales with an acknowledgement by the Lord Chief Justice of the time that fathers assaulting their daughters was not an infrequent occurrence. In 1932 Ferenczi presented what is now recognized as a most significant paper, although this was not published until 1955 (Ferenczi, 1955). This confirmed Freud's early views that hysteria in adults could be traced to childhood sexual trauma, and also identified splitting as a defence mechanism. This was not a popular move, and led to an extraordinary reaction against him:

> He was promptly dropped by Freud and by his so called friends. Leading cadres of the Psychoanalytic Association like Ernest Jones and others went so far as to continue to libel him after his death. He was bluntly called psychotic, although the famous psychoanalyst Michael Balint could testify to the fact that he wasn't. As far as I know, however, Balint did nothing to rid the world of these infamous lies. (Miller, 1991: 45)

TRADITIONAL EXPLANATIONS FOR ABUSE

Historically, various explanations have been offered for sexual abuse, all of which attempt to minimize its extent or significance one way or another. Until relatively recently a popular argument was that abuse is extremely rare. Another was that sexually abused children have particular characteristics that render them at least partially, if not considerably, responsible. This conveniently focused on the child, and the perpetrator somehow faded into the background. A well-known study by Bender and Blau in the 1930s posed this argument:

> These children undoubtedly do not deserve completely the cloak of innocence with which they have been endowed . . . we might have frequently considered the possibility that the child might have been the actual seducer, than the one innocently seduced. (Bender and Blau, 1937: 509)

Readers who hope to comfort themselves with the belief that in more modern times attitudes must surely have changed may find the following considerably disillusioning. In 1983, nearly fifty years after the Bender and Blau study, Judge Brian Gibbens passed a two-year sentence on a man convicted of raping a seven-year-old with the comment:

> No force was used. It is one of the kind of accidents that can happen in life, although of a different kind, and could almost happen to anyone. This was a momentary lapse. (*The Times*, 20 Dec. 1983)

The attitude reflected in these words essentially sees the male perpetrator as temporarily, and almost unfairly, tempted and unable to resist. The innocent child victim becomes transformed into a knowing seductress and the totally culpable and powerful adult male assumes the mantle of hurt innocent. It is the most extraordinary denial and transformation of the reality. Many more explanations have focused on the mother: either blaming a pathological mother understood as acting out her Oedipal wishes via her daughter, or viewing her as a helpless dependant, as colluding with the perpetrator, or as a victim herself. Placing the responsibility in these ways both avoids deeper questioning that may challenge existing social structures, and neatly and conveniently takes the responsibility away from the perpetrator:

> The notion of the 'collusive' mother who manipulates her husband and daughter into incest in order to fulfill her own unconscious desires is merely a mechanism for transferring agency away from the father; the father is rendered innocent. (Waldby, 1989: 91)

Traditionally, another interpretation of child sexual abuse concentrated not solely on the mother, but regarded the child's family as essentially dysfunctional, therefore requiring the treatment of the whole family. This again shifted the emphasis away from the perpetrator.

What is clear is that for a long time pockets of recognition occurred only to be quickly repressed or re-defined, a process that was similarly repeated in relation to the acknowledgement of domestic violence. In that area too, myths abounded that served to move the responsibility away from the perpetrator to the victim.

THE IMPACT OF FEMINISM

It is indisputable that feminism played a key role in identifying violence to women and children and in challenging and systematically dismantling the views described above. Feminism has always explored and recognized the connections between the experiences of the individual and social and political issues, and feminist research and methodology has always placed the actual experiencing of women at its centre. Feminist scholarship in the last two decades has changed and developed – it has conflicts of its own – so it is not possible to talk about *the* feminist perspective as there are many. However it is possible to extract key ideas and themes that have been vital to publicizing the previously private world of sexual abuse. It is certainly true that the feminist's radical challenges and questions of the 1960s and 1970s, focusing as they did clearly on the unequal position of women in society, in the family and in relationship to others, opened the lid on much that had been previously firmly buried:

> Further disclosures of men's domestic violence against women, of their sexual coercion and abuse of children in the home, and general control over resources and decision making, all continued both to feed feminist calls for a woman centred orientation in the social sciences and to fan feminist fears of the potential dangers of family life for women and children throughout the 1970's, so firmly hidden in the all pervasive familial ideology of the satisfactions of hearth and home. (Segal, 1995: 252)

Feminists forced into the public arena the previously private life of the family and, owing to the feminist movement, in the 1970s and 1980s the issues of rape and assault on women and children became a socio-political issue. Abuse to women and children came out of the closet; shame and secrecy began to move into sharing, openness, anger and demand for action. Much of this action was organized by women for women, reflected in the massive growth of Rape Crisis Centres, self-help groups and other organizations set up to work with women abuse survivors. This breaking of the secrecy should not be underestimated in its impact and significance. As Emily Driver states, 'when incest survivors break that circle of secrecy we begin to wield a great political power which has for centuries lain dormant' (Driver, 1989: 171). The work of Burgess and Holmstrom (1974), Brownmiller (1975) and Russell (1984) have all been very influential, as have the many personal accounts written by abuse survivors, for example Jacqueline Spring's account (Spring, 1987).

The work of feminists such as these provided the language and the concepts that established the framework for the discussion of sexual abuse. It seemed that perhaps for the first time in history sexual abuse had found a voice that would not be silenced. Feminism made sexual abuse visible and audible and provided an ethos and an analysis that was too strong to be ignored, and resonated too deeply with the experience of too many women to be easily denied. Its emphasis both on gender relations and power in the context of a deeply patriarchal society, and on the validating and conceptualizing of personal experience, proved a powerful combination. Feminist pressure was crucial in placing both domestic violence and child abuse on the political map. Bell (1993) uses the work of Foucault to examine in detail a number of theoretical issues and questions surrounding a feminist understanding of abuse, in particular those relating to sexuality and power. She notes that:

> The feminist position is not just about highlighting the sexual damage suffered by girls and women but simultaneously forms a fundamental critique of the family, of the construction of gendered sexuality, of the 'normality' of incestuous abuse. All this pertains to the abuse of girls and boys. The specific contribution of the feminist perspective is that it locates the problem of incest within the normal practices of sexuality, of power and of practices of 'not-hearing'. Its task has been to show the gendered quality of these practices. (1993: 17)

THE IMPACT OF FEMINISM ON THERAPY

The Challenge to Traditionalism

Feminist practitioners such as Judith Herman (1981) and Elizabeth Ward (1984) argued that all traditional explanations of sexual abuse systematically ignored the effects of power relationships and patriarchy, thereby misplacing responsibility. Feminist analysis has instead presented the experience from the point of view of mother and daughter in order to understand the central role played by power relationships in the family, whilst linking and connecting this with wider societal structures.

It is evident that these ideas represent an enormous challenge to a world frequently marked by an over-allegiance to, and an over-simplification of, an outmoded and essentially phallocentric theory. It is also clear that the psychoanalytic preoccupation with theories of infantile sexuality and the subsequent conceptual leap into the child's fantasies of sex, as opposed to actual abuse, was a grave mis-service to abused children. Nowadays, although a blinkered attachment to outmoded ideas may exist in some areas of practice, many have moved beyond this, although it should be noted that this is not always so in relation to recognizing power issues:

The most significant difficulty in the encounter between feminism and psychoanalysis remains the refusal of the analytic world to recognise the role of power in male female relations. Although gender and sexual identity are currently highly fashionable topics in psychoanalytic circles, I am often astonished to hear these discussed with barely any mention of the power differences between the sexes. (Maguire, 1995: 226)

Object Relations Re-Visited

Although attitudes may be hard to shift in some quarters, analytic and psychodynamic feminist therapists have attempted to re-formulate rather than demolish the existing theoretical base. Object relations theories in particular have been radically reviewed. Although object relations theory has tended to reinforce the sexism of traditional psychoanalytic thought, a feminist re-interpretation of this approach provides a theoretical base that incorporates a political understanding. The work of Nancy Chodorow (1978) has been particularly significant in this re-working and re-definition. She has focused on the significance of mothering in the child's development whilst linking the structural characteristics of bringing up children to the father's role in economic production. As Jacobs states:

> In identifying the relationship of structural forces to family dynamics and psychological development, feminist analysis of object relations theory counters the tendency toward reflexivity without undervaluing the role economic forces play informing and maintaining gender relations. (Jacobs, 1994: 21)

Such re-conceptualizing has been essential in relation to feminist therapeutic approaches to sexual abuse. Dorothy Dinnerstein (1976) used Kleinian theory to explain the misogynist nature of society by the fact that all children raised by women internalize a picture of women as both all-good and powerful on the one hand and all-bad and withholding on the other. I have noted earlier in this chapter the tendency for society to blame mothers but it is evident clinically that victims too often tend to blame their mother. The re-interpretation of object relations theory through a feminist perspective throws some light on this, focusing as it does on the centrality of the early mother–child relationship:

> Child development, as it is understood within a feminist framework of object relations theory, is not based on the adequacies or inadequacies of the mother, but on a structural arrangement of family relations that locates the mother in a central position with regard to the affective realm of personality formation. (Jacobs, 1994: 22)

Blaming the Mother: Fantasy versus Reality

As a consequence of this centrality mothers are open to both blame and idealization which can be reflected in how abused children view them: the idealized expectation can distort the reality, leading them to blame mothers for knowing or not intervening even when they did not and could not know. The belief in an all-powerful and all-knowing mother places an impossible burden on mothers, often in absolute contradiction to the realities of their world.

In therapy with survivors, it is crucial not to collude either with mother blame when this does not reflect the reality of the abuse, or with a refusal to recognize abuse by mother when this is so. Recognizing that both false blame and real abuse are possible, and understanding their source, can be central in helping the therapist to deal sensitively with these areas. As in all other work with abuse survivors this is done in the context of the greatest respect for the client and for their defences, and always recognizing the anguish that lies beneath. To be patient, to take care, to take time, to really listen and always go at the client's pace are of the essence. A feminist object relations understanding provides a valuable theoretical framework that informs the therapist and facilitates further exploration with the client.

Burstow captures the dilemma that can be created for the feminist therapist:

> Misogyny often figures heavily in survivors' readiness for anger and for the respective degrees of anger they feel towards the different people involved in the abuse. Survivors tend to 'understand' male perpetrators and to loathe female perpetrators. What is more significant, many survivors are positively livid at the women who indirectly facilitated the injury by doing nothing and are much less angry at the men who actually abused them. As feminist counsellors we are faced with a dilemma. On the one hand, we do not want to collude with misogyny. We know that lateral oppression and internalized oppression are at the core of the special fury felt towards women. On the other hand, we also know that survivors have a right to be angry and indeed need to be angry at everyone both directly and indirectly involved. (1992: 133)

Although, as Burstow notes, survivors blaming mothers is a common occurrence, this may seem to be in direct contradiction to the dynamic noted by Eichenbaum and Orbach, of mothers and daughters creating an alliance against father:

> Women often express contempt and disdain for their fathers because they are involved in mother's anger. Indeed, the daughter often carries her mother's rage. Once again daughter and mother share an experience. Both feel disappointed with father, both feel disdain. And thus they tighten their unspoken bond. (1985: 65)

However this is not the contradiction it appears to be. Daughters are drawn to their mothers in a profound way but sexually abusive experiences break into this bond and, as Burstow describes, drive a wedge between mother and daughter. If the abuser is father or stepfather this wedge will be greater, only preventable if mother is told and acts both to stop the abuse and to support her daughter. There is not space to explore why so often mother is not told but for a more detailed discussion on this see Walker (1992). In this scenario the abused child becomes a psychological orphan: father is abusing her and mother is not protecting her. She feels betrayed by both. Both mother and daughter are humiliated and subordinated by the abuse, and the power of the abusive man smashes the mother–daughter attachment. The earlier the abuse, and the closer the relationship with the abuser, the greater the damage to the child. She is left without safe attachment; her parents as 'good enough' good objects have been destroyed. This, of course, is further intensified if both parents are involved in the abuse, and even more so if the parents are implicated in an abuse ring.

It is important for clinicians to understand the origins of mother blame if they are to be able to work with this central aspect of the loss of a good person to relate to, to trust, to depend on. Abuse attacks these crucial developmental tasks. At the same time it has been crucial for feminists to dismantle society's tendency to blame the mother who becomes unfairly a useful dustbin for all the blame. Feminists have rightly exposed the largely male misuse of power and placed incest within a generalized theory of patriarchal power and sexual violence. Understanding and working with the first does not militate against the second – they both have an important place in furthering the debate and working with survivors.

There is a balance to be struck here and it deserves further enquiry: mothers should not be blamed directly or indirectly for the sexual abuse of their sons or daughters when clearly another has been indisputably and directly responsible. However, many remain reluctant to accept that women can independently abuse their children. This causes enormous distress to survivors abused by women who then find themselves disbelieved by those in the caring professions. Abuse by women contradicts the mythology of both motherhood and the family and we may yet discover this problem is underestimated as so many aspects of abuse have been in the past.

In this context we do need to remember that in some senses women do have considerable power over children. Both Dinnerstein and Chodorow recognize the crucial influence of the first few months and the first few years of life, and discuss the far-reaching implications of women having almost exclusive care of the child. Women do currently have real and substantial responsibility for (and thereby power over) children. In the context of a capitalistic and patriarchal society, this is in some senses essentially *insubstantial* (although it will not feel that way to the child) but it should not be so surprising if this responsibility and power is open to misuse:

> She sees the world around her as non-existent in a supportive way. It is then that she falls back on her own inappropriate and perverse behaviour; this, in turn, makes her feel powerless. Simultaneously and paradoxically she experiences her perverse behaviour as the only power available to her through her exclusive emotional and physical authority over her baby. (Welldon, 1988: 83)

If, at the same time, as Welldon discusses, a woman can experience her child as part of herself, at times indistinguishable from her, an attack on the child can be an attack on herself, both self and child being treated as part objects. These factors can be a potent combination and coexist in a world in which the paradoxes around motherhood abound: motherhood is both revered and idealized whilst simultaneously being starved of real support, recognition and resources.

Idealization of the Father: Fantasy versus Reality

A feminist understanding of object relations also provides valuable insights in relation to the need of the abused daughter to idealize the perpetrator when this is her father:

> Contemporary feminist theory has stressed that the idealization of the father is enhanced by his absence from the emotional and social life of his daughter. With the incestuous father, however, it is the dangerous presence of the perpetrator that intensifies the need for idealization. For abused daughters in particular the need to believe in the ideal father is especially strong as the extent of his control and the threat of his abuse violate the basic needs of trust and security upon which healthy psychological development relies. (Jacobs, 1994: 34)

Jessica Benjamin (1988) in another contemporary feminist analysis of psychoanalytic theory also argues that fathers in patriarchal cultures are the idealized identificatory parent, although she extends this argument to include boys as well as girls, suggesting that the same psychological pattern of idealization operates for both. These are valuable insights, providing a theoretical underpinning that informs a particular aspect of clinical work. In my practice it is evident that for some women abused by their father, separating psychologically from him, and accepting the reality of his abusive behaviour, is complex and painful. The internalized idealized image of a good father is tenaciously retained, the perceived loss of this being so great that it cannot be faced. One survivor described this to me:

> The worst thing in going through all of this was actually really facing what my father had done. It meant letting go of him, letting go of the hope that he'd ever be the father I wanted and needed him to be. That was quite devastating. It felt somehow easier to blame my mum for not doing anything, and now I do recognize that she really didn't know. And when I believed that it must have been my fault it wasn't quite so bad either in a funny way – because that at least made me feel that I could have changed it by being different if only I'd chosen to; that I did have some control. I've had to face that I couldn't have done anything – that I was entirely powerless. That has been very, very painful although now I can say that it was worth it, but it didn't feel like that at the time.

In my own clinical experience this situation is more evident when the father is the abuser; and less so if the perpetrator is the stepfather or another man. Then the idealized father can be held intact: the survivor holds the hope and the fantasy that their real father would be different. In some instances of abuse by fathers the survivor will fantasize that he is not her real father. Acknowledging, accepting and working through abuse by the father, and giving up the hope of the ideal father, is deeply painful and problematic as the example quoted above indicates.

For the client quoted above it was almost preferable to see either her mother or herself as responsible. In the former the innocent, unknowing mother could be blamed and raged at in a desperate psychical attempt to retain the idealized father, whilst the latter enabled the maintenance of the fantasy that there was some control or choice, when there was none. These complex unconscious strategies are not straightforward and are further reinforced by the sense of badness created by abuse. The abuser in denying responsibility effectively projects this responsibility into the child both by their abuse and by the accompanying verbal messages: 'you made me do this'; 'you want this'; 'you like it'; 'it's your fault'; 'you're bad, you deserve this' are frequently cited. Abusers are ruthless in their denial of their essential and absolute culpability. The idealization of father, accompanied by the introjection of the aggressor, becomes a powerful combination that leaves no psychological choice for the victim but to believe that she was bad and at fault. The introjection of the aggressor can result in self-harm, depression, suicidal behaviour and addictions although it can also be acted out against others. Powerlessness can also become internalized and, combined with idealization of the perpetrator, can lead to re-victimization.

Transference and Counter-Transference

There are other key concepts used by feminist psychodynamic therapists in their work with abuse survivors. Transference and counter-transference are central and the work of Herman on traumatic transference and traumatic counter-transference is invaluable (Herman, 1994: 136–47). Understanding and working with transferential aspects is particularly important because of the demanding and complex nature of the work. As Herman states:

> Re-enactment of the dynamics of victim and perpetrator in the therapy relationship can become extremely complicated. Sometimes the therapist ends up feeling like the patient's victim. Therapists often complain of feeling threatened, manipulated, exploited or duped. (1994: 147)

Working with the transference can be mistakenly misunderstood and criticized as denying the real relationship with the client, or the reality of their abuse. This need not be so. All practitioners working within the feminist framework, whatever their theoretical base, will be striving to work co-operatively with their client; to show her the greatest respect;

to value her and validate her experience; to acknowledge their own role within the relationship; to be constantly aware of the significance and impact of wider worlds and structures on both therapist and client.

However, analytic therapists have been criticized, for instance by Robert Langs (Smith, 1996), and sometimes rightly so, for interpreting as transferential material, client's comments that are actually coded references to the therapist's bad practice. Therefore references made by the client to their current and real relationship with their therapist are perceived as belonging to past relationships influencing the client's current experience of the therapist. This can be a very real denial of abusive practice in which the client, as with her abuser, cannot win: her reality is denied, with the danger that whatever she says reinforces the therapist's perception. This is not acceptable and it is vital that all therapists monitor in themselves, with their clients and with their supervisors, the possibility of abusive and repressive practice, and take responsibility for their own part of the relationship. However, this type of practice should not be generalized to all who work on the basis that the past can be repeated in present relationships, and that present relationships can become overwhelmed by past experiences to the extent that they become indistinguishable until explored in that context.

Feminist Psychodynamic Therapy in Practice

The crucial question arises: how does feminist psychodynamic therapy work in practice with abuse survivors? It should be emphasized that whatever the theoretical perspective of a feminist therapist, the client's needs and wishes come first. This is particularly significant with abuse survivors – in their childhood and often in adulthood these have been consistently ignored or destroyed. Essentially, the approach of the therapist should match what the client wants, not the other way round. This may mean that sometimes our feminist understanding of abuse informs our understanding but is not brought directly into the work – the individual may make it clear (if she is able to feel sufficiently safe) that she does not wish to work in this way and, of course, we should never enforce a perspective on her that is unwelcome.

The following account is taken from a lengthy interview with an abuse survivor describing the help she has been given.

Tina was a 42-year-old white woman, who had been in a lesbian relationship for the past three years. She had two grown-up children. She was sexually abused by her father as a child and physically abused by her mother. She had had eating difficulties all her life and had overdosed on several occasions; on one occasion this was nearly fatal. Previous help had proved unsatisfactory. The therapist she now describes worked in a local counselling and therapy centre offering a range of approaches within a feminist framework, including the psychodynamic.

Tina's Account of her Therapy

It felt different straightaway from the help I had received before: just little things – it was a really nice friendly building to go into. The staff all seemed relaxed, and you couldn't really tell who was who: you didn't feel you sort of stood out because you were a client. The first session was very different. I felt very welcomed, and taken seriously. Sue [the therapist] listened carefully but also explained how she worked and that there were other options available including groups. I had never been given any choice before but I knew I wanted to see someone individually, I wanted someone just for me.

She explained that her approach was psychodynamic; that she felt the past was very important to the present, and that it got repeated in ways for all of us that we were not consciously aware of, and that we could work to understand them. It really made sense to me. She explained that understanding did not provide easy solutions but could provide choices. She said we would work together on the eating; that she would not try and make me eat, that we'd try and make sense of it. She also told me that it wasn't going to be an easy journey but that she would guarantee to be with me at the same hour each week for an hour, in the same room; that she would do her very best and that we would be in it together. It was an entirely different approach from help I had been offered before.

She also said that our relationship would be important, and might tell us something about my other relationships, and that it might help to understand my abuse and the eating in terms of how women were treated more widely in the world. She also told me the time was for me and she hoped I'd say if I wasn't happy with anything although she recognized how difficult that might be. I'm quite sure I didn't take it all in then but it felt good – I really liked the idea that at last someone would take me seriously, and that what happened to me as a child really did matter. We carried on talking about how we could work together, it wasn't just sort of said and then forgotten about – it was part of the whole thing, if that makes sense. Even that first week I left feeling better about myself, it was a real sense of us working together, and I felt sort of bigger and taller when I left.

I saw her for two years and it was very good but very hard. We decided together when to end. I'm not saying everything now is fine, but it is much better. I have bad days, but now I understand them and feel in control of it, rather than it being in control of me. I do eat OK now but I know eating will never be entirely straightforward. But it's manageable. I haven't overdosed since I started seeing her and I have stopped sabotaging all my relationships. That's the one I really sorted out with Sue. You see I nearly did it to her as well. I had to recognize that because I felt so bad, and so frightened of trusting anyone, and so angry at what I'd lost as a child, that I just couldn't accept good things. It was like having a lethal cocktail of feelings and if anyone got too close or I began to trust them I would just put the boot in. I've lost a lot of people that way.

That was a really important part of the therapy because I really did not understand what I was doing – I just saw Sue as another betrayer, another monster, and I just wanted out and I saw her as thoroughly bad. Eventually I understand that when anyone got too close I threw a blanket of badness over them, the same as had been done to me, and it was nothing – or very little –

to do with that person. Then I'd often lose them and then I felt it was just another person who hadn't cared enough, but I had no understanding of where that was all coming from. I also began to recognize that I would get angry with anyone who offered me anything because it could never be the everything that I'd always wanted from my mother. I also worked on my own destructive feelings that I had towards my parents. It was all very complicated. Well, I didn't lose Sue and slowly the light dawned of what was happening. It was like a light slowly being turned on.

It was very, very painful because I really had to go into the pain of what had happened rather than avoid it and fling it around me. For a long while my fury with my mother took centre stage – that had always been an issue for me and the few friends who had known were sometimes quite shocked at how angry I was with her. I felt they expected me to be angrier with my father because he sexually abused me. But physical abuse is dreadful too. I was able to sort some of that out but it was such a relief to be able to be angry about my mother. I now feel they were both sort of trapped by things they couldn't control in different ways although that doesn't take away their responsibility, but it does put it in place more. I do have a little contact with both and therapy helped me to be able to be much firmer in my boundaries with them. I decided in therapy not to confront either of them – I don't need to and that recognition has been such a release.

Things started to improve after I'd dealt with all that – I really felt much better – but I suppose the other really important part was starting to make sense of it all in a sort of broader way – for me it wasn't enough just to look at it for me, although I do know other survivors who just want that. The timing was important because before that I'd have felt just ignored again, as if she was somehow saying I wasn't important because so many others had suffered too. But later it was a real help to think how the world is structured, how women get treated and respond, about power issues and how that gets muddled up with sexual issues for both men and women. Those sorts of issues had always been in the therapy from the beginning, but as time went on I wanted to turn the spotlight on them and to really try and look at women's issues within a wider structure. I think even nowadays most therapists wouldn't do that and that's where seeing a feminist therapist is really different. It did become really important to make sense of how my body had been misused and how that made me in turn misuse it, but it was more than that – it was beginning to see that in terms of how women and their bodies are seen and misused in this society more generally.

Some people when they finish therapy want to leave it behind them. I wanted to take it on and I have. I write about it, especially in newspapers because that's where it reaches people, and I'm a contact person for survivors who want to talk to another survivor and not a counsellor or therapist. And I talk to people like you who are writing about it. The more who hear the better and I'm appalled by the treatment so many survivors receive, particularly if they end up in the psychiatric system.

So what really helped? If I had to pick out the most important element it would be the feeling that my therapist was on my side with me; that we were in it together, and working alongside. I felt she fought for me and yet I saw her as essentially just another woman and that was very good. It wasn't just cosy because as I've said I felt I hated her for a while. And she could be challenging and she certainly had to take a lot from me. Being given a choice was vital; a good relationship with my therapist and her withstanding the onslaught whilst understanding what it was about, and for me moving to a political level. But I know from my own contact now with survivors that some women do not want, for whatever reason, to be politicized, and they must never feel that they have to be – they have had too much enforced on them before.

How Did This Approach Differ?

So, in what ways was this approach different from others not based in feminism? As with feminist therapy itself definitions of what it actually constitutes are bound to vary. The following is my attempt to draw out features which seem to me to be central.

Feminist therapy of any theoretical orientation values women, welcomes women and aims to provide settings that are essentially user and staff friendly. Women are respected, and underpinning the organization of the setting is a concern to provide from the start a warm and safe environment – clearly experienced as such by this client.

Feminist therapy also recognizes that women need choices and that an individual approach suits some and not others. Feminist therapy is explicit about what it provides and explains its approach without patronizing by over-simplicity or overwhelming with jargon and technical language. In the extract above it is clear that the therapist was explaining her framework without claiming it as the only or best method. The importance of the client as an equal partner in the therapy was stressed, as was the quality and significance of the therapeutic relationship itself. As Burstow (1992) notes:

> Statements that clarify the importance of co-investigation and mutual knowledge should be made from the very beginning because they set the stage for co-responsibility and for dialogue. From day one, the client should be provided with the information she needs if she is to make informed choices and is to play an active role in shaping the therapy. From day one, correspondingly, it is important to truly engage her in dialogue. (1992: 42)

There is a dialogue from the beginning and an explicit recognition that the client and therapist are equally important. However this recognition, although welcome, is often not straightforward for any woman, but particularly if she has been abused. A history of abuse in childhood does not lead to easy assertiveness in adulthood and the concept of choice and saying no may not be initially part of her emotional vocabulary. So apparent agreement may reflect a history of enforced compliance; fear of stating one's own needs, or the inability to even recognize these. Feminist therapy recognizes how low women's self-esteem often is; how women tend to defer and comply. It continually works both to acknowledge these and to boost the former and reduce the latter by very careful attention to their own style and to the process overall.

Abuse survivors have been stripped of their dignity and have been psychologically and physically invaded, and often learnt in childhood that compliance was one way to avoid or decrease the severity of the abuse. Any attempt to say no led to worse abuse. This dynamic can repeat in the therapeutic relationship, with the woman being frightened of saying no, and as feminist therapists we always hold this firmly and clearly in mind. We recognize that a client's ability to disagree or challenge has to be encouraged, that their right to do so must be continually stated, and that a woman's ability to really state her case and lay a claim to her own self may come only later in therapy.

In Tina's therapy the significance of external and wider issues was introduced in the first session without invalidating the client's individual experience, and further exploration of these was a response to the client's wishes. The client's needs remained central. As Tina herself noted, the theme of issues beyond herself was there throughout but did not move into the spotlight until she was ready. Timing was essential; and, as Tina stated, not all survivors want to explore further, and the choice must be their own. Survivors of abuse have a long history of being forced and coerced – feminist models of therapy must never repeat this.

For Tina, becoming aware of other political and structural layers that underlay and underpinned her own individual experience of abuse was empowering and enabling. The opportunity of using her own personal experience in a broader context was enormously important for her. For her it would have been insufficient to have explored only her own experience no matter how skilfully this had been done. She needed and wanted help as an individual with another individual but did not want an approach that only individualized. Essentially, feminist therapy with survivors never demeans or diminishes the individual's own experience, but additionally offers the structural and political understanding that reconnects them with the corporate experience of women. Instead of standing alone and isolated in their own suffering they are invited to join with, identify with, a wider world of oppressed women in the context of understanding how power and sex become inter-related.

In her therapy Tina needed to be angry with her mother, and was then encouraged to explore and understand this both in relation to her own experience and in a broader context. Her previous experience had been that this was not acceptable and of course it is not only friends of survivors who have this difficulty – so do some counsellors and therapists. However, feminist therapy is generally alerted to recognizing women's difficulty with anger:

> Women's unease with acknowledging or expressing their anger creates a situation in which they fear it is enormously powerful. They fear it could alienate at least, annihilate at most, the person towards whom it is directed. They fear they will lose what little they have. (Eichenbaum and Orbach, 1987: 55)

For Tina, a therapist who could work with her anger was clearly crucial in several respects, and extended beyond her mother and connects to my next point, that of the psychodynamic aspects in this piece of work.

Readers may be wondering what were the specifically psychodynamic features in the therapy. As described by Tina, the therapist made clear several important underpinnings of psychodynamic work: the significance of the past; repeating patterns; her belief in the unconscious, and in the significance of the unconscious being rendered conscious. Boundaries and maintaining a clear therapeutic frame are also important in the psychodynamic approach, and this is reflected in the therapist's clarity about timing, length and place of sessions.

Tina's own description of her therapy gives us a clear example of psychodynamic working. She vividly describes her anger with Sue – a powerful description of the negative transference discussed earlier in this chapter. Sue's ability to withstand this was clearly crucial: as Eichenbaum and Orbach have reminded us, women are frequently scared that their anger will destroy what little they have. However, surviving the rage would not have been sufficient. It was crucial that Sue understood and worked with the complexity of unconscious messages and meanings that were being expressed. Recognizing how the effects of abuse are re-enacted unconsciously, spilling into other relationships, is crucial for clients and enables pieces of the jigsaw to fall into place. As Tina expressed, this time is extremely painful but potentially liberating.

In the example given by Tina, her feelings towards Sue at this point seem clearly transferential. However a feminist therapist working with abuse survivors also needs to recognize when anger towards her has a reality base. Interpretations can be deeply repressive if they are used as a way of avoiding difficulties in the real relationship. Indeed, it is very noticeable from this account, the enormous value Tina placed on the real relationship with her therapist. She selected this as the key to the success of the therapy and a very real, warm sense of these two working together emerged. It was clearly important for Tina to see her therapist, at one level, as being just another woman, although it was also crucial that she had the therapeutic skill to work with Tina to make sense of the very rocky times they also shared.

CONCLUSION

There is no doubt that the key contribution made by feminists has been forcing abuse into view and this time around in history keeping it there. The feminist theorists and practitioners coming from an analytic and a psychodynamic perspective who have re-assessed object relations have also made a key contribution.

It is impossible to do adequate justice to either abuse survivors or those who work with them in explaining the complexities that exist for both.

Perhaps it is these complexities that deserve the last word: there is much we do not know; much that many people do not want to know, and there is a responsibility on us all to keep the spirit of enquiry open. Abuse is widespread, its effects are enormous, and feminists and feminist therapists – of whatever theoretical persuasion – should keep the issue where it belongs: in the open, under scrutiny, asking questions, always with the awareness that our knowledge is horribly incomplete.

NOTE

1 Readers will note that the term 'survivor' is used throughout. This is not to deny the awful reality that children who are sexually abused are 'victims'. This is incontrovertible, and for many children further victimization pursues them into adult life. Indeed, the struggle to move from victim to survivor is enormous. The term 'survivor' marks the successful struggle of the many who bravely contend with the legacy of victimization. Those who have suffered from childhood abuse often dislike and resent the use of 'victim', feeling it continues to label them inappropriately. Therefore 'survivor' is used to respect and applaud their struggle.

REFERENCES

Bell, V. (1993) *Interrogating Incest: Feminism, Foucault and the Law*. London: Routledge.

Bender, L. and Blau, A. (1937) 'The reaction of children to sexual relations with adults', *American Journal of Orthopsychiatry*, 7: 514–15.

Benjamin, J. (1988) *The Bonds of Love*. New York: Pantheon Books.

Boulding, E. (1992) *The Underside of History: a View of Women through Time*, vol 2. London: Sage.

Brownmiller, S. (1975) *Against Our Will: Men, Women and Rape*. New York: Simon and Schuster.

Burgess, A. W. and Holmstrom, L. L. (1974) 'Rape trauma syndrome', *American Journal of Psychiatry*, 131: 981–6.

Burstow, B. (1992) *Radical Feminist Therapy: Working in the Context of Violence*. Thousand Oaks, CA: Sage.

Chodorow, N. (1978) *The Reproduction of Mothering*. London: Yale University Press.

Dinnerstein, D. (1976) *The Mermaid and the Minotaur: Sexual Arrangements and Human Malaise*, New York: Harper and Row.

Driver, E. (1989) 'Positive action', in E. Driver (ed.), *Child Sexual Abuse: Feminist Perspectives*. London: Macmillan.

Eichenbaum, L. and Orbach, S. (1985) *Understanding Women*. London: Penguin.

Eichenbaum, L. and Orbach, S. (1987) 'Separation and intimacy: crucial practice issues in working with women in therapy', in S. Ernst and M. Maguire (eds.), *Living with the Sphinx*. London: Women's Press.

Ferenczi, S. (1955) 'Confusion of tongues between adults and the child', in *Final Contributions to the Problems and Methods of Psychoanalysis*. London: Hogarth Press.

Finklehor, D. (1986) 'Designing new studies', in D. Finklehor (ed.), *A Sourcebook on Child Sexual Abuse*. Beverly Hills, CA: Sage. pp. 192–223.

Herman, J. (1981) *Father–Daughter Incest*, Cambridge, MA: Harvard University Press.

Herman, J. (1994) *Trauma and Recovery*. London: Pandora Books.

Jacobs, J. (1994) *Victimized Daughters: Incest and the Development of the Female Self*. London: Routledge.

Maguire, M. (1995) *Men, Women, Passion and Power: Gender Issues in Psychotherapy.* London: Routledge.

Miller, A. (1991) *Breaking Down the Wall of Silence.* London: Virago.

Mollon, P. (1996) *Multiple Selves, Multiple Voices: Working with Trauma, Violation and Dissociation.* Chichester: Wiley.

'Report from the trial of Watson-Sweeney', *The Times*, 20 Dec. 1983.

Russell, D. (1984) *Sexual Exploitation: Rape, Child Sexual Abuse, and Sexual Harassment.* Beverly Hills, CA: Sage.

Segal, L. (1995) 'Feminism and the family', in C. Burck and B. Speed (eds), *Gender, Power and Relationships.* London: Routledge.

Smith, D. L. (1996) 'Communicative psychotherapy', in M. Jacobs (ed.), *In Search of Supervision.* Buckingham: Open University Press.

Spring, J. (1987) *Cry Hard and Swim.* London: Virago.

Waldby, C. (1989) 'Theoretical perspectives on father–daughter incest', in J. Campling (ed.), *Child Sexual Abuse: Feminist Perspectives.* London: Macmillan.

Walker, M. (1992) *Surviving Secrets: The Experience of Abuse for the Child, the Family and the Helper.* Buckingham: Open University Press.

Walker, M. (1996) 'The Recovered Memory Debate', in *New Directions in Counselling.* London: Routledge.

Ward, E. (1984) *Father–Daughter Rape.* London: Women's Press.

Welldon, E. (1988) *Mother, Madonna, Whore: The Idealization and Denigration of Motherhood.* London: Free Association Books.

Young, V. (1993) 'Women abusers – a feminist view', in M. Elliot (ed.), *Female Sexual Abuse of Children: the Ultimate Taboo.* Harlow: Longman.

5

Empowerment and the Eating-Disordered Client

Robin Sesan and Melanie Katzman

Orientation? Feminist. What does that really mean? How does one provide feminist treatment? As self-defined feminists in the field of eating disorders we are often asked to provide the feminist view as if there is some unified doctrine of feminist understanding of eating disorders. Initially perhaps there was. The goals for a feminist treatment of eating disorders were clear: 1) acknowledge that eating disorders are a gendered disorder, 2) in asking 'why women?', incorporate what we know about the psychology of women, 3) bring our knowledge of physical and sexual abuse in this population forward, and 4) put women into positions of power in the field. The intertwining of feminist principles with treatment for eating-disordered women made intuitive and logical sense.

However, it appears to us that as the field of feminist therapy moves into its young adulthood, the eating-disorder treatment field is just approaching its adolescence. In recent years feminist theoreticians and clinicians have received more of a respected platform, influencing and guiding the understanding and treatment of eating disorders. As feminist approaches to eating disorders become articulated and debated, opportunities for clarification and differentiation emerge. As is true for many phases of development, the progression toward maturity involves a questioning of what is, a looking back at what has been, and a looking ahead to the possibilities of what could be. Adolescence brings with it a period of challenge and a movement toward self-definition. This often involves a differentiation of the self from the ideas of the dominant culture. In this case the dominant culture is second-wave American feminism which includes theories related to radical feminism, cultural feminism, socialist feminism and the challenge of the postmodern perspective (Evans, 1995). In attempting to answer the question 'What is a feminist approach to the treatment of eating disorders?' we begin the process of deconstructing feminist therapy and its application to eating-disordered clients. The mere use of the words 'disordered' 'treatment' and 'client' reflect a choice. These terms have been eschewed by many as an oversubscription to a medical model; however, we elect to retain them as we feel they are descriptive and can be used as a bridge between feminist thinking and biomedical theorizing. As professionals in 'mainstream' academic departments offering help in a 'managed care' environment we believe that re-defining every term can be alienating and obstructive to the very communication that is required for feminists to have an expansive influence. In addition, we are concerned that modifying the terms may inadvertently cloak the very power imbalances we want to address. In this chapter and in our work we strive for alternative pathways for change, not novel nomenclature.

As contributors to this volume, we have been asked to address the inherent tensions between feminism and psychotherapy by drawing on debates which arise when working with the notion of empowerment in therapy. By focusing on current feminist treatment models for eating-disordered clients prevalent in the United States we raise questions about not just the parameters of treatment delivery but the feminist technology which inspired them. As a result, in this chapter we question what we perceive to be the prevailing conceptualizations of feminist treatment for eating-disordered clients in the States. We also attempt to refine and specify the parameters of treatment delivery while still operating within a feminist-inspired technology.

Although there is great variety in feminist theory and in the practice of feminist therapy within the United States, American feminism is essentially pragmatic and individualistic. Across many disciplines, including psychology, sociology, anthropology, history and core sciences, feminist theorizing regarding women's ways of knowing, women's struggles for equality, and women's search for an authentic voice have materialized. Feminist therapy, principles and actions, have followed a similar pragmatic paradigm. As practising feminist therapists, we tend to do what works, attempting to remain true to our individual beliefs about women's strengths, recognizing the many cultural constraints against women's growth, and modelling relationships which minimize hierarchy and help to empower women who have been disempowered by the culture. These core beliefs are central to feminist empowerment models of therapy.

FEMINIST THERAPY AS EMPOWERMENT

Empowerment, defined as authorizing, delegating authority to, enabling or permitting, is often a central goal in feminist treatment. Inherent in this definition is a belief that one has the power or the free will to act on one's own behalf and to make choices. Although it is important to relinquish the idea of a unitary, modernist subject in order to explore women's differences (Hare-Mustin and Marecek, 1988), modernist concepts such as progress, self-improvement, and self-determination remain essential to the theory and practice of North American psychotherapy and feminist therapy. The belief in the individual's capacity to make choices predates postmodernism and is reflective of American culture, beliefs and values. Based on these assumptions and definitions, Worell and Remer (1992) describe an empowerment model of therapy in which both internal and external contributions to women's personal distress are recognized. Women in therapy are helped to differentiate between cultural causes of their distress and internally imposed restrictions. Such an analysis minimizes feelings of being sick, dysfunctional, or wrong, and reduces women's feelings of powerlessness and hopelessness. Women are thus 'empowered' to make different choices. An empowerment model assumes that power can be reclaimed once lost and that power can be given or taught to someone. It also assumes that power to make choices, to speak for oneself and to determine one's course or direction is a positive attribute. This is congruent with our beliefs and with the way in which we work with both male and female clients.

The Guiding Principles of Feminist Empowerment Therapy

Empowerment models of therapy draw from several different feminist therapy perspectives (Rawlings and Carter, 1977; Gilbert, 1980; Butler, 1985; Lerman, 1986; Travis, 1988; Brown, 1994), resulting in approximately four key principles of feminist therapy that tend to unite feminist therapists. They are as follows:

1   Commitment to a consciousness-raising treatment approach in which clients are encouraged to explore the role of sexism and oppression and examine contradictions in prescribed sex roles. Women are helped to recognize the high incidence of victimization of women and how this contributes to emotional distress.

2   Commitment to working towards an egalitarian therapy relationship and minimizing hierarchy between client and therapist. Power differentials between client and therapist are openly examined and explored.

3   Commitment to a woman-valuing process whereby women's strengths are recognized and weaknesses are re-framed as strengths. Demeaning language towards women is challenged and women are encouraged to value connections with other women.

4   Commitment to engaging clients in social action/social change helps to empower women to examine and change systems which are harmful to them and those they love.

Crisis and Connection in Women's Lives

Work on the psychology of women has enhanced the empowerment model described above, and added to our understanding and treatment of eating disorders (Gilligan, 1982; Surrey, 1991). Increased respect for women's development challenged traditional conceptualizations of eating disorders which characterized anorexia nervosa and bulimia nervosa as failed attempts at separation-individuation. Therapists/clinicians such as Steiner-Adair (1986), Fallon et al. (1994) and Kearney-Cooke (1991) have presented an alternative model which recognizes women's need for social and emotional connection along with the fear that these connections may be severed as one matures in a society in which female adults are not taught to compete, let alone excel. In other words, eating-disorder pathology develops as a response to the confusion and 'crisis of connection' that girls experience around the loss of their relational world as they come of age within a culture that does not value these types of connections with others. Eating disorders emerge at the time when girls are most vulnerable as they psychologically resist the demands of an unkind culture and stop knowing what they know about direct expression in relationships. The self of the teenage girl goes underground for safety and protection, leaving her vulnerable to losses in self-confidence, psychological distress and eating disorders. She becomes cut off from herself and from her body. She no longer knows herself or her needs.

Empowerment therapy is a connected therapy – the relationship and connection between therapist and client is actively explored and experimented with. It challenges our notions about remaining distanced and detached in our therapy relationships. The concept of therapeutic neutrality is questioned as we model authentic (rather than therapeutically 'staged') relationships with women. The model holds interdependence, as opposed to autonomy, as a goal for adulthood, and demands that the therapist and client engage in a relationship in which there is mutuality and acknowledgement of the individual's sense of self, her need for connection and her need to care for others as well as to be nurtured. Therapy thus becomes a collaborative process which includes a two-way dialogue between client and therapist, helping to demystify the therapy and therapy relationship. Such a model allows a client to rely less on the authority of others and more on her own inner authority, the voice which went underground when the eating disorder appeared (Steiner-Adair, 1991).

EATING DISORDERS AS DISORDERS OF POWER

Feminist perspectives on the aetiology of eating disorders have focused on issues of gender inequality and the socio-cultural influences of the media, fashion business and diet industry that perpetuate a cultural mandate towards slenderness (Chernin, 1981). Striegel-Moore (1995) highlights the fact that because women in our culture have less access to power they feel a stronger need to conform to social norms. These norms are gender-specific and relate to appearance standards and behaving in typically feminine ways. There are great social sanctions against women who do not conform to the culture's norms, leaving them feeling separated from others, hopeless, and powerless. The body becomes a battleground for these feelings. Similarly, Kearney-Cooke (1991) identifies the cultural silencing of women as a power problem for women. Women who take the initiative, act on their own behalf or assert themselves in public domains are described as unattractive, selfish, or masculine. A retreat to eating-disorder pathology may be the only response that makes sense to a woman challenged by our culture's sexism. Eating disorders have thus been viewed as gender-based appearance disorders. The meaning of women's conformity or resistance to the cultural mandate for femininity has been a focus of treatment (Steiner-Adair, 1992).

However, a perspective that privileges gender and sexism over other forms of oppression, such as racism, heterosexism and poverty, may be limited in its explanation of eating-disorder aetiology and limiting for women in general. Tension exists between 'gender feminists' who identify gender as the sole factor in women's oppression and 'equity feminists' who take a broader look at issues of social inequality and social injustices (Sommers, 1994). Thompson (1994a, 1994b) suggests that taking a 'gender feminist' stance and confining our understanding of eating-disorder pathology to the drive for thinness may mask women's real concerns about access to power and the limited avenues available to them for self-expression. Food refusal may be one of the few globally employed attempts to free oneself from another's control (Katzman and Lee, 1997). This behaviour is not gender-specific or ethnocentric. Orbach (1986) likens the self-starvation of anorexia to a hunger strike, exerting one's power and control over a dominant force. Feminism has limited our view of eating pathology by its emphasis on gender and sexism. A broader perspective allows us to better understand the powerlessness the African-American teenage girl feels in her white affluent school because she is not white. It helps us recognize her food refusal and drive for thinness as an attempt to be white; as an attempt to have access to power. Her anorexia is not related to cultural standards of beauty, but rather it is related to the lack of power she has in a white culture and her need to assimilate. Viewing eating disorders as disorders of the powerless allows us to recognize the shame felt by a white overweight single mother on welfare, who binge-eats at night after her children go to bed to drown in her food the sorrow and terror she feels as a result of her poverty and loneliness. Similarly the 14-year-old who 'diets' away any female curves following sexual abuse by her father is building an anorexic fortress against future sexual abuse advances when she feels powerless to defend herself through alternative means.

Eating pathology is not confined to the socially privileged white women in our culture, yet feminist models focusing on issues of gender and sexism have not focused interventions on the diverse group of women disenfranchised by our culture and disenfranchised by feminism. By widening our view of the aetiology of eating disorders as disorders reflective of power imbalances within relationships, families, and culture, we are able to move beyond ritualized interpretations of sex (being a woman) and food (weight obsession) as the cultural culprits, and examine one's access to power as the critical social influence. Such a change in stance has implications for prevention and recovery.

DECONSTRUCTING FEMINISM IN THE TREATMENT OF
EATING DISORDERS

The actual practice of 'feminist treatment' of eating disorders engenders tension between theory and the application of this theory. Where has feminist therapy helped? Where has it failed or hampered our ability to be useful? Feminist theory, like any other heuristic, acts as a guide, a map to keep us on track. It allows us to steer a course that is meaningful for our clients. In this section we explore the path we as feminist therapists navigate, when working with clients in individual, family, and group treatment modalities. There is a balance we strive to achieve in real life, as we weigh the benefits and limits of using a feminist treatment approach (and the scales tip differently for each client, within various treatment modalities).

Individual Treatment

Terry is a 39-year-old Caucasian woman who has had superficial sexual relationships with both men and women and has been suffering from very severe anorexia nervosa for 17 years. She is the youngest of four sisters and lives with her 80-year-old mother in a middle- to low-income neighbourhood. Her father and older sister died just prior to the onset of her eating problems. Her eating disorder is so disabling that she has been unable to work for the past five years and is on permanent disability. Terry has seen many different therapists during the course of her illness. She has had numerous hospitalizations where she is 'fattened up' and released only to start the deprivation cycle once again. She has her physician baffled. Her weight often hovers between 60 and 65 pounds and she is 5 feet 3 inches tall. She defies medical wisdom in her ability to sustain her own life. How does a feminist therapist empower Terry to reclaim life and a voice that was lost so many years ago?

Many tensions exist between feminism and the institution of psychotherapy (Chesler, 1972; Greenspan, 1983). Does Terry need treatment? Should she be treated? Isn't her eating disorder a 'normal' response to a dysfunctional culture? If we treat her, are we pathologizing her and protecting the culture? Is treating her a version of blaming the victim? While these are essential questions to examine, and they keep us true to feminist guiding principles, when a dying woman is asking for help how can we turn her away? How can we privilege society over an individual? We thus come head to head with an essential tension between the theory of feminism and the actual practice of feminist therapy: that of privileging culture over the individual. Feminist therapy practice is a compromise.

Compromise One is to accept Terry as a client for individual therapy. This action defies the radical feminist position which privileges culture and cultural change above the individual. We are challenging the feminist belief that because Terry's anorexia is a symptom of a dysfunctional culture the only viable treatment is societal change. We may be participating in a patriarchal structure by choosing one-to-one individual therapy.

Nonetheless, we welcome Terry into the therapy room and attempt to engage her in a relationship in which she can articulate her experiences. She tells us of the guilt she feels over her sister's tragic death and the responsibility she feels for her father's death. She talks of needing to punish herself, to deny herself food, pleasure, nourishment, and joy. She speaks of the power she feels in her thinness and her ability to challenge medical expertise. We begin to explore other issues of power and control in her life. As Terry realizes how little power she has had in her life, both within her family as the youngest child and within our culture as a nurse in a large medical centre, she is able to feel sad; there is an absence of anger about her powerlessness, and Terry continues to lose weight. The struggle for power has now entered the therapy relationship.

Compromise Two is related to the client's right to self-determination and the negotiation of power imbalances inherent in the therapy relationship. As Terry's low weight puts her at increased medical risk and compromises her cognitive abilities, including her judgement and decision-making skills, how does a feminist therapist continue to trust Terry's self-knowledge? Is Terry's decline a signal that the material is too difficult for her? Is the grief around issues of power too much for her? Is she fearful of voicing her opinions? Is she afraid of the force of her anger? Does she have to become even more invisible to protect herself? Does she know something we don't, or are refusing to acknowledge about the contradiction between empowering women within the safety of the therapy relationship only to send them out into a world which dismantles and oppresses new-found confidence? Should the therapist assert her authority and insist on hospitalization? This is the thinking of a feminist therapist trying to understand within a social and individual context her client's decline, slow suicide, and political resistance. In order to avoid replicating destructive patterns of hierarchy and dependency, a feminist stance at this point focuses on Terry's lack of self-care and relies on her connections with others to help her begin to eat enough to survive without hospitalization. Terry cannot do this and returns to the hospital on her own initiative. As a feminist therapist, I (R. S.) breathe a sigh of relief that I did not have to assert my power over Terry to have her hospitalized against her will and I wonder about where I failed. Is this a client who cannot benefit from feminist treatment? Is feminist treatment even relevant for Terry? Are issues of gender and her role as a woman in a culture which devalues women, factors for Terry when she appears so gender-neutral? These questions challenge core beliefs of feminist therapy and may reflect some counter-transference feelings as feminist therapists begin colluding with their client's defences: the defence which denies the centrality of femaleness to the development and maintenance of anorexia nervosa. The defence which denies that the culture is a factor in the development and maintenance of any eating disorder. The defence which minimizes power as an essential component in the aetiology of eating pathology. These issues must be central to Terry's eating disorder.

Compromise Three is about the therapist exerting her expertise and authority in guiding a course of treatment. It is about using what will be helpful from traditional psychotherapy with a client suffering as a result of a toxic culture. It is also about doing it differently through the use of a real relationship, through the use of self-disclosure and joining with a client in her struggle. It is about minimizing hierarchy through the strengths and commonalities we bring to women-to-women relationships.

Terry returns to the therapy room following a four-week hospital stay during which time she 'willingly' abdicated control of her life to another. She has gained 12 pounds and is not as severely emaciated. We discuss how to prevent such a decline from happening again and Terry is adamant that this will not. But nothing has really changed in Terry's life or in the culture. Can we trust her resolve? How do we enable her to make choices in her best interest? Terry's decline in individual treatment has impacted not only on Terry, but on her therapist. Issues of trust, power and hierarchy are being questioned. A focus on the relationship between Terry and her therapist becomes central at this point in time. There are feelings of betrayal, disappointment, anger and questioning. Modelling for Terry a relationship where the dialogue comprises both anger and care provides her with a new, 'corrective' experience. The therapist shares examples of how she has been negatively impacted by the culture and how she has coped with her own feelings of powerlessness. This self-disclosure minimizes the hierarchy between Terry and her therapist, increasing trust and openness. Terry feels more able to explore her anger and fears related to issues of power and powerlessness. She is able to make connections between feeling oppressed in her life and exerting superhuman control over her appetites. Therapist and client talk about what it means to be a woman. Terry talks about how safe she feels in a gender-neutral body. How she likes not menstruating. How safe it feels not to have to negotiate relationships with men. How confused she is about her attractions to women. How sad she feels about the losses in her life and how much safer she feels knowing that loving someone is not an option for her. Terry is able to fully mourn her losses and choices to drop out of her life to protect herself from further hurt. She is able to eat just a little bit more.

What does Terry's story tell us about the tensions between feminism and psychotherapy? It teaches us about compromise and about steering a course between these tensions. When faced on a day-to-day basis with women who are behaving in severely self-destructive ways, providing a relationship in which their concerns can be articulated remains a central component of good feminist treatment. We treat clients coming to us for help, even though the dyadic relationship has the potential to reinforce patterns of oppression with therapist as expert and client in a secondary, one-down position. For if we do not treat the women who present themselves for care they may get no help at all. We make decisions on a day-to-day basis to value the individual and the priorities in her life over cultural change. At times we help clients adapt to a culture which is hurtful to them, because to do anything else would harm our clients further. Empowering eating-disordered clients is about enhancing their self-knowledge, it is about helping them express their thoughts, feelings and desires, it is about teaching them safety in connections. It is often through this process that clients on their own begin to examine the oppressive nature of our culture as well as abuses in interpersonal relationships in order to broaden their vision beyond individual dysfunction. Women helped within the context of individual therapy can then give back to the culture through better parenting, social activism, and increased professional contributions. Is not individual therapy then a form of social action?

Family Therapy

The joining of feminism and family therapy allows for the possibility of effecting social change through the process of family change (Luepnitz, 1988). Most models of family therapy help expand both the locus of the problem and, accordingly, the solution. However, systems theories have not adequately explained the genesis of eating pathology. Race- and class-specific beliefs about female socialization have privileged gender over other forms of oppression in understanding eating problems (Thompson, 1994b). What holds as true for white upper- and middle-class women may not hold true for women of colour, women from ethnically diverse backgrounds or non-heterosexual women. Eating disorders are becoming more prevalent in modernizing cultures (Dolan, 1991) where the possibilities for daughters are quite different from those for their mothers (Katzman and Leung, 1996) and where women of colour and ethnic diversity struggle for assimilation and acceptance (Katzman and Lee, 1997). Women appear to be protected from eating pathology in cultures where traditional connections within the family are valued and separation from family is not the norm (Bryan, Waugh and Lask, 1991). In recognizing eating disorders as disorders related to power, we can expand the scope of treatment to include other oppressions beyond that of gender. Family therapy is an avenue for such expansion. Integrating a much broader socio-cultural perspective into family therapy practice facilitates examination of gender roles within the family system, issues of hierarchy and hierarchical imbalances, and cultural patterns of patriarchy replicated in the family system.

Dawn is a 22-year-old heterosexual woman who has been struggling with anorexia nervosa since age 13. She comes from an intact, upper middle-class Jewish family and is the older of two daughters. Dawn's family is strongly matriarchal. Her mother, who is a twin, has three sisters, all of whom are very weight- and body-preoccupied. The connections between the women in the family are very strong. Dawn lives with one of her mother's sisters and this sister's family, including her two cousins, one of whom is an eight-year-old girl, already weight- and body-preoccupied. Dawn's sister is the most disengaged family member and does not struggle with food-related issues or body image concerns. Dawn's maternal grandmother retains a very strong but silent presence within the family. Dawn is very depressed, bored, and dissatisfied with her life. She is socially isolated, and underfunctioning in work and academic arenas. After two years of individual therapy, and a brief stay in an intensive out-patient centre, Dawn begins to make tremendous progress. She is allowing herself to eat regularly, moderating her exercise, has access to a range of emotions and is developing friendships for the first time in her life. She talks of feeling both overly involved and very disconnected from her family and fears that she is violating family norms by not restricting her food intake and learning to feel more comfortable in her body. She fears the women in her family will no longer accept her.

Families are often the vehicle for transmitting cultural messages. In fact most mothers feel tremendous pressure to impart skills for social success to their offspring so that their daughters can survive and thrive in ways in which their mothers could not or were not prepared for. Some families embrace the culture, while others defy its constraints. Either choice has an impact on all family members and has been shown to have a significant role in the aetiology of eating disorders (Root et al., 1986). Dawn's family is a family that does both. Her family has adopted without question the dominant cultural value equating slenderness with women's desirability. The fact that her family retains these norms in light of having a family member with severe anorexia speaks to the strength of this attachment. On the other hand, this is a family that defies white Protestant culture in its strong, dominant female power and presence. The women in the family appear to be vibrant, speak their minds and assert themselves within the family domain. The men in this family are attached, but their voices are absent or unheard. The men have no power over the relationships within the family or the social decisions. The women in Dawn's family seem to have settled on a compromise. They have adopted without question our dominant culture's idealization of slenderness, but defy the pressure to be passive and compliant. The family's solution is an eating-disordered solution.

The Family Gathers

Sitting round me are seven beautiful women, ranging in age from 19 to 60. Dawn sits to my right, Aunt Arlene to my left. Dawn's mother sits directly opposite Dawn. Dawn's sister sits next to her mother. Aunt Jane looks as if she doesn't quite fit in. She is taller than her sisters, wearing much less make-up. She is less adorned. Grandmother looks much younger than her 60 years. Aunt Cathy sits next to Dawn for support. Dawn appears calm, but inside she is very shaky.

The women in Dawn's family have been invited for a family ritual to welcome Dawn into the world of adult women in her family. A session that excluded men was chosen in recognition of the strong relationships between the women and the need to affirm Dawn's position with them. A later session incorporating men and women is something that remains open for the future. Each family member present has been asked to bring some advice for Dawn that they wish they had received at her age, and a gift, a token or symbol of their hopes and dreams for her. Dawn's mother opens the session with a poem speaking to the importance of family, her wish for closeness with Dawn and her pride in Dawn's recovery. Grandma cries as she recalls the years of worry and guilt related to Dawn's anorexia. We are able to do some important grief work around Dawn's eating disorder. Dawn's mother speaks of the terror she felt each night as she walked into Dawn's room to check on her breathing, always fearing the worst and feeling a mixture of relief and resentment that she was still alive. Aunt Jane challenges the family to look at the pressure they all feel to be beautiful, pretty, and to look younger than their years. There is tension and silence as Aunt Jane brings the outside culture into the family. Dawn is able to join with her, but Aunt Jane's sisters abandon her, making her feel like an outsider. This is Dawn's most awful fear. If she challenges the family (cultural) norm she will be an outsider; she will be disconnected.

This is the point at which feminist therapy and family therapy can work hand in hand to help the women in this family become aware of the costs of accepting this mandate of slenderness not only for themselves but for their daughters and granddaughters, one of whom has suffered for the family, another who is likely to do the same once Dawn has recovered. There is tremendous resistance and denial in the session. Aunt Jane retreats. I support Dawn to speak her truths about her struggle, fears of being left out, anger with her family and our culture, and her longing for connection in a way which validates her individuality and differences. Dawn feels empowered, she has found a way to speak in her family, and the women in the family are able to start acknowledging their own fears about being different and not conforming to the cultural demands placed on them. Each woman talks about feeling different from the others in the family but feeling connected around the value placed on beauty. We wonder aloud if their weight and size preoccupation keeps them feeling safe from their own power both within the family and within the culture. There is a sense of hope that they can be freer with themselves and others. We all relax.

One by one they share their gifts with Dawn. The theme of the gifts centres on self-love and self-acceptance. We all feel a little richer as a result of the process.

The combining of family and feminist therapies provides an opportunity to deconstruct culture and give meaning to eating-disorder symptoms. In the above example, the 'women only' session allowed for grief work, examination of the cultural mandate for slenderness and the value placed on external beauty, and exploration of the way in which being beautiful helped the women in this family stay connected to one another. Questioning of the mandate of slenderness began and was modelled in the gifts given to Dawn which spoke of inner beauty and the need to love and accept oneself. This session helped to empower Dawn to have a voice of difference within her family yet stay connected to them. Using family treatment as a tool for individual, family, and cultural change seems less conflictual than individual models from a feminist perspective. We are expanding the locus of the problem beyond the individual, affecting a larger social system, and the work has broader implications for the culture and future generations. Thus, there may be fewer compromises between the ideals of feminism and the practice of family psychotherapy.

Group Therapy

Feminist therapists have long advocated the use of group therapy with women clients. In fact, consciousness-raising groups supplanted traditional psychotherapy in the early phases of the second women's movement in the late 1960s. It was in groups of women that women's suffering could be acknowledged, destructive cultural norms identified, and social action projects initiated (Brody, 1987; Butler and Wintram, 1991). Thus it would appear that of all the therapy modalities, group therapy models would pose the least conflict for feminist clinicians. Feminist empowerment models of treatment support the use of group therapy and group therapy is a frequent tool used by therapists working with eating-disordered clients (Butler and Wintram, 1991).

In our analysis of the tensions between feminism and group psychotherapy related to group therapy, the theme of homogeneity versus heterogeneity emerges. Homogeneous eating-disorder therapy groups create a curative culture for women. The group serves as a counterculture for women to experiment with different ways of being in the world (Katzman, 1995a). However, there is a significant limitation in our use of homogeneous therapy groups to treat eating disorders, as these experiences may not offer women the multitude of exposures needed for transformation. In this section we address the strengths and limitations of therapy groups specifically for eating-disordered women, their homogeneity, and the resulting limits placed on opportunities for integrated experiences of diversity, analyses of real power imbalances, and exploration of issues related to role strain by choice or necessity.

Large Women/Small Voices: A Therapy Group for Large Women who Binge-Eat

We open the group with a sharing of who we are, why we are here and what we hope to get out of this group experience. One by one the women in the group speak about their experiences of being large in a culture which values small, of not being able to 'fit in' to society, literally and figuratively, of feeling like an outcast. There is anger and power as the women speak. As they join together about the culture's hatred of them as fat women, Sarah begins to cry uncontrollably. Cherie touches her gently on her arm, letting her know that she knows of her pain. Sarah speaks. She tells us of the distress she feels about the person inside that no one sees, no one acknowledges, and no one knows. She talks of her longing to be seen and how her layers of fat protect her from others knowing who she is, protect her from the unwanted sexual advances of men, and keep her connections with women safe. Mary covers herself, hiding her stomach from the group and speaks of her incest history and intense body hatred. We have gone full circle. Anger at the culture has turned into anger towards the self. Group therapy will be the mechanism for altering that cycle of self-hatred.

The greatest strength of bringing together a homogeneous group of women may be its greatest limitation. The large women/small voices therapy group is a time-limited group for women who have suffered for years with issues related to their overweight status and compulsive/binge-eating behaviours with food. The homogeneity within this group relates to size (although there is great variation here), gender, eating-disorder symptoms, ethnicity and socio-economic status, the latter two being a function of referral bias and an appreciation and acceptance of what therapy has to offer. The strength of the group is that it offers women a counterculture within which they feel safe and accepted, validated and supported. Women in the group are encouraged to experiment with new behaviours, receive nurturance and support, explore feelings about connection and competition, without the outside cultural restrictions. It is within the safety of homogeneity that women who have been disempowered as a result of their differences and nonconformity to cultural demands can begin to explore who they are, what they feel, what they think and what they believe in. In other words, it is within the safety of sameness that they can live their differences. The group provides a corrective emotional experience. Bringing together a group of disempowered women offers them a chance to try on new social roles. There is a similarity here with the work of other oppressed groups, meeting in secret to develop themselves and their plans for challenging the dominant culture. In this way a counterculture is formed to provide an alternative to a destructive dominant culture. It is perhaps a reflection of our age that this gathering takes place in a therapist's office. To be sure, 'resistance' groups can occur in varying forms throughout societies. In fact, as women gain confidence in the work the process of connecting with others and using groups to expand their sphere of influence, involvement in community and professional organizations may supplant participation in groups conducted in a 'medical' setting.

Although homogeneity may help to empower women, it does not allow for women in the group to have an integrated experience of diversity and challenge. Real power imbalances are not realized within the context of homogeneous groups. There is a notable absence of African-

American, Hispanic and Asian women from eating-disorder treatment groups. Are we creating a counterculture for white socially privileged women that is not helpful for women of colour? Are we witnessing a referral bias, in that women of colour are not being referred? Has our view of eating disorders as gender-based appearance disorders prevented women of colour from seeking help? Or has the medicalization of psychotherapy and the de-feminization of practice made us less accessible, less relevant to these groups of women (O'Hara, 1996)? Do they see therapy as another means of control rather than as an avenue for support and empowerment?

Sonya is a 19-year-old African-American woman who is seeking help for her obesity. She lives in the inner city with her mother, grandmother, brother and boyfriend. During the initial session Sonya disclosed that she is also very sad about two stillbirths she has had over the past two years. She cries as she talks about the loss of her babies, the emptiness she feels inside, and her desire to become pregnant. She knows that she has to grieve these losses. She fears that her weight is a factor in her babies not living. She fears she will go 'crazy' if another baby of hers dies. She wants to lose weight.

Will integrating Sonya into a socially privileged group of white women help her? If so, how will it help her? How will it help the group? Is Sonya's pain any different from the pain of the other women? We think not. While her circumstances are different and her culture does not so harshly judge her for being large, her grief about her losses and her need for connection with her lost babies are being channelled into self-attack, self-blame, and body hatred. The 'society' of the group will provide a corrective culture for her regardless of her ethnicity or social class. And the women in the group will be forced to live with more diversity and learn about sameness within difference. Broader issues of oppression will be explored within the group context. Someone will join with Sonya, as a woman, as a mother, as someone who has lost someone she has loved, and some of the barriers which divide us will slowly come down. We need to be careful that Sonya's needs are met and that she is not in the group to meet the needs of the other women. Supporting a multi-racial and multicultural process in group therapy will help to build bridges between women. Thus an important goal of feminist therapy is addressed.

SOCIAL ACTION AS SOCIAL CONTROL?

A hallmark of the empowerment model is the concept that the personal is political; that personal change cannot be accomplished without social change. As long as women make less money than men for equivalent jobs, occupy fewer positions of influence in politics and business, are subject to physical and sexual abuse and retain the primary responsibility for childbearing without the guarantee that they could choose abortion, women sustain a daily bombardment of messages that infiltrate and diminish their confidence. As long as science and therapy assume a chromosomal relationship between eating and sex we will characterize eating problems as a pathological response linked to gender rather than power, position or oppression.

The failure to date of prevention programmes has been our inability to alter the culture. Repeatedly research demonstrates that we can raise awareness but knowledge does not yield behavioural change (Piran, 1997). If we are to see real transformations in the delivery of mental health services or the conditions that render them necessary then we must consider the role of social change. It is often around the practice of social action, moving outside of oneself and the therapy room to make changes in the culture at large, that the goals of a feminist therapist and those of her client differ.

Not all clients will be interested in or helped by social action although a number may gain satisfaction by linking their personal conditions to larger shared issues. Again, the function of therapy may be the increased awareness of choice. As we mentioned earlier we may need to broaden our definitions of social action to embrace the importance of individual change as well as political involvement. Those women participating in the anti-diet movement, anti-diet days, eating-disorders prevention and awareness programmes, and organizing speak-outs around our country are engaging in first-line social actions. Is social action a privilege only some women can take advantage of? Can the push for social action actually disempower a women struggling to make ends meet in her life?

The financial strain of social action is a reality. Women who are economically privileged can travel, miss a day of work. Women in relationships can have partners care for their children while they attempt to make social change. Single mothers, women on welfare, cannot do this without the support of others with greater resources. Does the woman fighting for money to feed her children or for childcare in order to work dare ask for support to organize governmental rallies? Do those with more time and money work to confront the diet industry, to assure child support or work on the campaigns of female politicians?

Financial loss, distance from family and friends, increased tensions between work and family life may put undue strain on women and ultimately disempower them further. The travail of social action is unpaid work. If money gives us access to social power, are we disempowering ourselves when we work for no money? American feminists at least often reflect the norms of their culture. Individual accumulation of money and professional prestige may compete for the attentions needed to address the myriad of social imbalances. At a time in the States when funding for mental health is in jeopardy, continuing one's practice and battling with managed-care corporations for control of the therapy process may be as meaningful for rectifying cultural disequilibriums as any political or economic campaign.

Revisiting Context

The movement to reduce funding for therapy, to limit access to care and to have decisions about treatment made by administrators and not care-givers, produces a narrowed lens through which one can view social problems. Susan Wooley has argued that therapy, 'once a private undertaking in which individual patients were helped to achieve better adjustment', is now a 'route to confrontation, public exposure, social agency intervention and criminal prosecution' (Wooley, 1993: 399). Without an opportunity to put their experience into words, the struggles of distressed groups go unnamed.

To the extent that feminist therapy is linked with social action, given the fear of exclusion from preferred provider organizations, therapists who might otherwise be inclined to advocate for their clients fall silent (Wooley, 1993). That is if they had the time to do so. Energies possibly spent on challenging devaluing media images, reducing violence against women or legislating for equal rights is detoured, as providers focus their attention on increased paperwork, delays in payment and the need to enlarge case loads. The experience for therapists interfacing with managed-care systems begins to mirror what many clients experience: one feels outside of the power centre, fearful of expulsion and dependent on acceptance for one's financial existence (Katzman, 1995b).

The ways in which the therapy room interfaces with the world at large take many forms, and the question must always be asked – who will truly benefit from the choices we make? American feminism has entered its third wave, as young women begin to define feminism for themselves (Walker, 1995). Women in their 20s and early 30s have benefited greatly from the work of second-generation feminists. Many rights are now givens. Young women are struggling with how to be real yet loyal to feminist beliefs. Many are questioning feminist beliefs and principles, tired of having to be 'politically correct' and tired of feeling guilty if they are not. Those of us practising psychotherapy have confronted 'third wave' contradictions for many years. Individually, and at times in small groups, we have come to terms as best we can with contradictions about empowerment in a culture which disempowers, harnessing and adjusting feminist principles to literally save an anorexic woman's life, and forsaking political action to have the time to nurture ourselves or connect with family or friends. Echoes of guilt about not being a 'good enough' feminist are familiar. We can identify with the questioning and the individual struggle to find a comfortable definition of ourselves as professionals and relationships.

As the field of eating disorders matures, feminist views have been heard, integrated and seen for better or worse as one uniform set of principles. The next stage will be to recognize the process of differentiation within feminist therapy. We will not all make the same choices. As a predominantly female group of clinicians treating a predominantly female population we have united around commonalities and similarities. As a subordinate group within our culture and within the mental health subculture, this unification has given us strength, power in numbers, and the confidence to more openly state our beliefs, suspicions, and hunches. Feminist therapy has given us a language to use and a map to follow in our efforts to help eating-disordered clients. We must continue to honour this perspective as we begin to acknowledge differences among us, variations in our beliefs, the unique individual needs of our clients, and the many variations of actual clinical practice. The challenge is to learn to tolerate and embrace differences between therapists all practising with a 'feminist' orientation and to stay connected. After all, isn't this the lesson we have been trying to teach our eating-disordered clients?

NOTES

Robin would like to thank Melanie Katzman for inviting her to co-author this chapter.
    Melanie would like to thank her children Wyndam and Harper who, as they discovered the joys of their own writing, allowed me 'just one more minute' to finish mine.

REFERENCES

Brody, C. M. (1987) *Women's Therapy Groups: Paradigms of Feminist Treatment.* New York: Springer Publishing Co.

Brown, L. S. (1994) *Subversive Dialogues.* New York: Basic Books.

Bryan Waugh, R. and Lask, B. (1991) 'Anorexia nervosa in a group of Asian children living in Britain', *British Journal of Psychiatry,* 158: 229–33.

Butler, M. (1985) 'Guidelines for feminist therapy', in L. B. Rosewater and L. E. A. Walker (eds), *Handbook of Feminist Therapy.* New York: Springer. pp. 32–8.

Butler, S. and Wintram, C. (1991) *Feminist Group Work.* London: Sage.

Chernin, K. (1981) *The Obsession: Reflections on the Tyranny of Slenderness.* New York: Harper & Row.

Chesler, P. (1972) *Women and Madness.* Garden City, NY: Doubleday.

Dolan, B. (1991) 'Cross cultural aspects of anorexia nervosa and bulimia: a review', *International Journal of Eating Disorders,* 10: 67–79.

Evans, J. (1995) *Feminist Theory Today.* London: Sage.

Fallon, P., Katzman, M. A. and Wooley, S. (1994) *Feminist Perspectives in Eating Disorders.* New York: Guilford Press.

Gilbert, L. A. (1980) 'Feminist therapy', in A. M. Brodsky and R. T. Hare-Mustin (eds), *Women and Psychotherapy.* New York: Guilford Press. pp. 245–65.

Gilligan, C. (1982) *In a Different Voice.* Cambridge, MA: Harvard University Press.

Greenspan, M. (1983) *A New Approach to Women and Therapy.* New York: McGraw-Hill.

Hare-Mustin, R. T. and Marecek, J. (1988) 'The meaning of difference: gender theory, postmodernism and psychology', *American Psychologist,* 43: 455–64.

Katzman, M. A. (1995a) 'Women and their peers: experiments in taking up space'. Paper presented at the Annual Convention of the American Psychological Association, New York, NY, August.

Katzman, M. A. (1995b) 'Managed care: a feminist appraisal', *The Review Perspective,* 1 (1).

Katzman, M. A. and Lee, S. (1997) 'Beyond body image: the integration of feminist and transcultural theories in the understanding of self-starvation', *International Journal of Eating Disorders*, 22 (4).

Katzman, M. A. and Leung, F. (1996) 'When East meets West does disordered eating follow?' Paper presented at the Society for Psychotherapy Research, Lake Como, Italy.

Kearney-Cooke, A (1991) 'The role of the therapist in the treatment of eating disorders: a feminist psychodynamic approach', in C. Johnson (ed.), *Psychodynamic Treatment of Anorexia Nervosa and Bulimia*. New York: Guilford Press. pp. 295–320.

Lerman, H. (1986) 'Women in context: contributions of feminist therapy'. Workshop presented at the 84th Annual convention of the American Psychological Association, Washington, DC, August.

Luepnitz, D. A. (1988) *The Family Interpreted: Feminist Theory in Clinical Practice*. New York: Basic Books.

O'Hara, M. (1996) 'Divided we stand', *The Family Therapy Networker*, September/October: 46–53.

Orbach, S. (1986) *Hunger Strike*. London: W. W. Norton & Co.

Piran, N. (1997) 'The reduction of preoccupation with body weight and shape in schools: a feminist approach', *Eating Disorders Journal of Treatment and Prevention*.

Rawlings, E. I. and Carter, D. K. (eds) (1977) *Psychotherapy for Women: Treatment Towards Equality*. Springfield, IL: Charles C. Thomas.

Root, M. P. P., Fallon, P. and Friedrich, W. (1986) *Bulimia: A Systems Approach to Treatment*. New York: Norton.

Sommers, C. H. (1994) *Who Stole Feminism?* New York: Simon & Schuster.

Steiner-Adair, C. (1986) 'The body politic: normal female adolescent development and the development of eating disorders', *Journal of the American Academy of Psychoanalysis*, 14: 95–114.

Steiner-Adair, C. (1991) 'New maps of development, new models of therapy: the psychology of women and the treatment of eating disorders', in C. Johnson (ed.), *Psychodynamic Treatment of Anorexia Nervosa and Bulimia*. New York: Guilford Press. pp. 225–44.

Steiner-Adair, C. (1992) 'When the body speaks: girls, eating disorders, and psychotherapy', in C. Gilligan, A. Rogers and D. Tolman (eds), *Women, Girls and Psychotherapy: Reframing Resistance*. New York: Haworth Press. pp. 253–66.

Striegel-Moore, R. H. (1995) 'A feminist perspective on the etiology of eating disorders', in K. D. Brownell and C. G. Fairburn (eds), *Eating Disorders and Obesity*. New York: Guilford Press. pp. 224–9.

Surrey, J. L. (1991) 'Eating patterns as a reflection of women's development', in J. V. Jordan, A. G. Kaplan, J. B. Miller, I. P. Stiver and J. L. Surrey (eds), *Women's Growth in Connection: Writings From the Stone Center*. New York: Guilford Press. pp. 237–49.

Thompson, B. (1994a). 'Food, bodies, and growing up female: childhood lessons about culture, race, and class', in P. Fallon, M. A. Katzman and S. C. Wooley (eds), *Feminist Perspectives on Eating Disorders*. New York: Guilford Press. pp. 355–80.

Thompson, B. (1994b) *A Hunger So Wide and So Deep*. Minneapolis, MN: University of Minnesota Press.

Travis, C. B. (1988) *Women and Health Psychology: Mental Health Issues*. Hillsdale, NJ: Lawrence Erlbaum Associates Inc.

Walker, R. (1995) *To Be Real*. New York: Anchor Books.

Wooley, S. (1993) 'Managed care and mental health: the silence of a profession', *International Journal of Eating Disorders*, 14 (4): 387–401.

Worell, J. and Remer, P. (1992) *Feminist Perspectives in Therapy: An Empowerment Model for Women*. New York: John Wiley and Sons.

6

Feminist Object Relations Theory and Therapy

M. Colleen Heenan

The theory and practice of psychoanalytic object relations therapy constitutes a major part of the developing field of feminist psychotherapies. The feminist deconstructions of British object relations theory, provided by Nancy Chodorow (1978, 1989) and Jessica Benjamin (1988), along with Luise Eichenbaum and Susie Orbach (1982, 1983), also continue to have an enormous, albeit controversial, impact on feminist theories. By grappling with the complex inter-relationship between women's internal experiences of selves and their outer social world, these authors sought to move debates within feminism, beyond the theme of 'oppressor-victim', through raising feminist consciousness about the tenacity of the gendered dynamics of unconscious processes. This has opened up the possibilities for contemporary feminist theorists and psychotherapists to make use of psychoanalysis, for women. However, despite their contributions to understanding the complexities of why some women continue to participate in and reproduce their own oppression, and thus resistance to change, there are a number of tensions within the feminist object relations frameworks which need consideration.

In this chapter, I consider some of these issues. Indeed, the very use of intrapsychic theory continues to be regarded by many feminist therapists as completely oppositional to the political commitment of feminist therapy (Brown, 1994; Burstow, 1992; Worell and Remer, 1992). On a different level, authors such as Spelman (1988) argue that Chodorow fails to provide a culturally and socially specific theory of gendered development, while O'Connor and Ryan (1993) point out that feminist object relations theory positions heterosexuality as normative. These challenges highlight some of the ways in which, by privileging gender above and beyond other social inequalities, feminist object relations theorists reproduce universalistic notions of 'woman'. This belies their tendency uncritically to adopt feminist positions which focus on differences between men and women, as well as their tendency to reify women (Enns, 1993; Evans, 1995; Squire, 1989). In turn, these critiques have implications for the practice of feminist therapies (McLeod, 1994).

My consideration of feminist object relations theory takes as its framework some of the questions posed by the editors of this book to the authors; that is, what is your therapeutic model, and how is its theory, and your practice, informed by your feminist beliefs? Moreover, in what way is the notion of 'woman' thus understood? In using this outline, I offer a strategic selection of some of the major tenets of feminist object relations theory and clinical practice. I will also confine my critiques to summarizing those points which are most relevant to this text (see Heenan, 1995, 1996a and 1996b, for more extensive discussions).

I start with the question 'Why psychoanalysis?'. The rationale for some feminists to turn *towards* aspects of this theory was their wish to understand, and change, the entrenched dynamics of gendered relationships. Next, I ask 'Why object relations theory?', clarifying the overall aims of feminist object relations theorists, and briefly outlining their particular concerns. Through explicating some of the critiques of their analyses of the differences in men's and women's gendered developments, and the centrality of the mother–daughter relationship, I indicate the ways in which they engaged with the issues raised within this text; that is, how do feminist therapeutic theories construct, challenge and reproduce notions of 'woman'? I contrast some aspects of Benjamin's approach with that of Chodorow's, making clear that feminist object relations theory does not offer a unitary approach to these issues. The chapter then finishes with a brief summary and discussion of the model of feminist psychodynamic therapy offered by Eichenbaum and Orbach. Their gender-conscious exploration of issues central to psychoanalytic practice, such as transference, counter-transference, and interpretation, highlight ways in which the intrapsychic and the social can be actively brought together in clinical practice.

WHY PSYCHOANALYSIS?

Given Kate Millett's description of Freud as 'the strongest individual counterrevolutionary force in the ideology of sexual politics' (1969: 178), what made some feminists turn to psychoanalytic theory? Introducing the conference *Psychoanalysis and Feminism: 20 Years On* (1995), Juliet Mitchell's reflections on her own motivation, highlighted the need to understand issues of change. She argued that for her, it was the lack within Marxist class theory of an analysis of women as a marginal group, as well as the failure of left-wing political theory and action throughout the 1960s, in both Britain and the United States, to deal with the entrenchment of patriarchy, which prompted her to look beyond a purely *political* feminist analysis. This entrenchment suggested that 'there seemed to be some *absolute* difference that was socially or culturally constructed between men and women' (1995: 75). It was psychoanalysis which appeared to provide not just answers to the origins of this embeddedness, but also the means whereby interventions could be made. Mitchell turned to Freudian psychoanalysis, arguing that feminists had on their minds, 'the same question that Freud as a male hysteric was asking: what is a woman, what is the difference between the sexes?' (1995: 77).

In Mitchell's strategic feminist reading of Freudian theory (1974), she argued that Freud's biological determinism reflected its historical and cultural specificity, emphasizing that it was this very specificity of Freud's account which was crucial to feminism. As Appignanesi and Forrester put it, '[a]s long as psychoanalysis is an account of the *becoming* of a woman, not of her being – her essence, her substance – it offers feminism what it needs' (1992: 461) (my emphasis). Mitchell re-interpreted Freud's theory of women's penis envy as an insightful reading of the cultural power that is symbolically encapsulated by the penis, which is thus both envied and desired by women because of its *cultural*, as opposed to corporeal, significance.

Chodorow argued that social learning theory, popular with many feminist psychologists (Dutton-Douglas and Walker, 1988; Enns, 1993; Worell and Remer, 1992), could not explicate the psychosocial processes involved in the construction, maintenance and *reproduction* of gender identities. Instead, she argued that:

> [p]sychoalysis shows how the unconscious inner world, or worlds, developed during childhood affect the external experiences of adulthood, and how different aspects of psychic life enter into conflict. These inner worlds and intrapsychic conflicts are imposed upon and give meaning to external situations. They affect the kinds of situations in which people put themselves, and their behavior and feelings within them. Adults unconsciously look to recreate, and are often unable to avoid recreating, aspects of their early relationships, especially to the extent that these relationships were unresolved, ambivalent, and repressed. All people are partly preoccupied with internal experience and mental life, partly live their past in the present. This preoccupation, moreover, can either enrich interpersonal relations (and work), or can distort and even destroy them. (1978: 51)

However, these feminists' reading of psychoanalytic theory is not uncritical. As Benjamin noted, while 'psychoanalysis offers a most promising point of entry for analyzing that structure . . . [it] harbors the best rationalization of authority. As a result, we find in psychoanalysis an *illustration* of our problem as well as a guide to it' (1988: 8) (my emphasis). Chodorow highlighted that it was in relation to thinking about issues of mothering, gender development and heterosexuality that major epistemological discrepancies in psychoanalytical theory began to occur; instead of maintaining the tradition within psychoanalytic theory of deriving hypotheses from clinical material, appeals are made to a biological determinism which reveal uncritical beliefs in the normality of heterosexuality and exclusive mothering, and differences in development of gender identity for the two sexes. In contrast, Chodorow proposed that by *maintaining* Freud's initial theory that heterosexuality was inherently problematic for both sexes, and by exploring development intersubjectively, within a socially situated framework, feminists could make use of psychoanalytic theory, in order to explore gendered dynamics.

Feminist Interpretations of Object Relations Theory

Like those of Mitchell, the concerns of the feminist object relations theorists, Nancy Chodorow, Jessica Benjamin, plus Luise Eichenbaum and Susie Orbach, were to 'account for the tenacity of self-definition, self-concept, and psychological need to maintain aspects of traditional roles which continue *even in the face* of ideological shifts, counterinstruction, and the lessening of masculine coercion which the women's movement has produced' (Chodorow, 1978: 33–4) (my emphasis). However, Mitchell's Freudian drive/conflict theory was rejected in favour of British object relations theory. This was seen as having more depth and coherence, and thus relevance to feminism. The interest in intersubjective theory lay in the hope that it could offer an analysis of how various elements of *social* structures are internalized, not as a *direct* translation of external inter-personal relations, but as a process, 'mediated by fantasy and by conflict' (Chodorow, 1978: 50). Moreover, one of the appeals of British object relations theory to feminists is its attention to the pre-Oedipal, mother–infant relationship, as being of the same importance as, if not greater than, the Oedipal phase of development. This has led feminists to concentrate on at least two particular aspects of gendered development, albeit in differing ways. One is the polarized dynamics of heterosexual differences between men and women, while the other is the connected dynamics of the mother–daughter relationship.

Chodorow's particular interest was in understanding how heterosexual gender differentiation and gender roles were reproduced, and her text, *The Reproduction of Mothering* (1978), provided the lynchpin for the later writings of Eichenbaum and Orbach (1982) and Benjamin (1988). Chodorow's psychosocial argument was twofold. First, she highlighted how the gendered division of labour in current heterosexual parenting arrangements, occurring within the separation of the domestic-private and productive-public locations in contemporary Western society, rendered mothering an exclusively female task. She stated that 'women's mothering as an organization of parenting is embedded in and fundamental to the social organization of gender. In any historical period, women's mothering and the sexual division of labor are also structurally linked to other institutions and other aspects of social organization' (1978: 34). Second, she argued that this 'sexual and familial division of labor in which women mother and are more involved in interpersonal, affective relationships than men produces in daughters and sons *a division of psychological capacities* which leads them to *reproduce* this sexual and familial division of labor' (1978: 7) (my emphasis); that is, 'object-relations grow out of contemporary family structure and are mutually created by parents and children' (1978: 114).

Like Chodorow, Eichenbaum and Orbach 'rejected a view of a "self" conceived outside culture and began to see how individual reality and personality is shaped by the material world. We see the unconscious as the intra-psychic reflection of our present child-rearing and gender relations' (1982: 15). One of these authors' aims, like that of Chodorow, was to make use of psychoanalytic theory as a means to offer a socially situated account of unconscious processes, which could not only facilitate under-standing of gendered subjectivities, but bring about changes which would affect gendered relationships. Chodorow made it clear that change would come about only through 'the elimination of the present organization of parenting in favor of a system of parenting in which both men and women are responsible' (Eichenbaum and Orbach, 1982: 219). While Eichenbaum and Orbach agreed that widespread social change could come about only through 'equal' parenting, they also argued for the facilitative capacities of therapeutic intervention through feminist psychodynamic psychotherapy, a topic which I explore in the next section of this chapter.

In *Outside In, Inside Out* (1982), Eichenbaum and Orbach continued to develop themes from Chodorow's work around the question 'Why are women second class citizens?' In addressing this question, like Chodorow, they also theorized women's attempts to negotiate a heterosexual devel-opment as essentially problematic. Their thesis, that men are not raised to nurture but instead to be nurtured, derived from Chodorow's initial feminist object relations theory. They argued that, as a result of this, women cannot turn to men for emotional sustenance, but must remain ambivalently attached to them, in order to confirm their heterosexual subjectivity. They state that in contemporary (that is, post-World War Two) patriarchal society, women's role is to defer to men, to follow their lead and to articulate themselves in relation to others. As such, they must be connected to others; in particular, shaping their lives according to their male partners. In order to do this, women must develop 'emotional antennae' (1982: 29) which enable them to anticipate and thus duly meet others' needs. A psychological requirement in performing this nurturing and caretaking role is for woman to 'put her own needs second' (1982: 30). Eichenbaum and Orbach described the psychological demands of women's heterosexual subjectivities as resulting in a psychological 'cycle of deprivation' within women.

Chodorow was concerned to explore the tensions which she regarded as inherent to male psychosocial development, in order to understand the other 'polarity' within heterosexual dynamics. So, it is not just that '[w]omen come to mother because they have been mothered by women. By contrast, that men are mothered by women *reduces* their parenting capacities' (1978: 211) (my emphasis). As she put it, 'object-relations grow out of contemporary family structure and are mutually created by parents and children' (1978: 114). Chodorow argued that boys need to *turn away from* their female primary love object of the pre-Oedipal mother, in order to develop and maintain their masculinity. Thus a boy's heterosexual gender identification is fundamentally constructed around a *repudiation* of mother, of femininity. Although boys can subsequently symbolically possess and merge with a 'symbolic mother' via heterosexual sexual penetration, when they grow into heterosexual men, for Chodorow, their *already problematic* masculine sense of self becomes *further exacerbated* by their fear of women.

As I stated in the introduction, I am making a selective use of particular aspects of feminist object relations theory in order to address issues relevant to the themes raised by the book as a whole. In doing this, I now want to turn to some of the *critiques* of this field of theory, both to highlight some of these points and also to introduce some further nuances. One of the major criticisms of feminist object relations theory is that feminist object relations theory privileges gender above and beyond other social oppressions. Chodorow's emphasis on the differences in the way gendered subjectivities come to be acquired has led to her ideas being equated with essentialism (Enns, 1993). Moreover, she leans far too heavily on the side of biological determinism for Squire's liking (1989: 91). These kinds of critiques come partially from the ways in which Chodorow attempted to redress the negativity associated with the psychoanalytic theory depiction of women as 'lacking' differentiation.

In theorizing the development of heterosexual subjectivities, one of the presuppositions on which Chodorow's thesis operates is the psycho-analytic notion on which theories of the Oedipal complex are based, that infants and mothers are psychologically merged with each other at the time of birth. Thus, despite ongoing evidence to the contrary (Stern, 1985), psychoanalysis posits as innate, a mutual wish between mother and infant to return to this merging, a wish that needs to be destroyed by the father. The desire for autonomy, is in turn, reinforced by contemporary Western culture, which does not value nurturing but which instead idealizes independence. Chodorow agreed with psychoanalysts that girls have a longer, more intense and ambivalent pre-Oedipal relationship with their mothers than boys have (see Greenberg and Mitchell, 1983, for a fuller account of developmental stages). The implication within a psychoanalytic framework is that girls, while becoming prepared for the relational requirements of adult mothering, may not become differentiated enough:

> Because of their mothering by women, girls come to experience themselves as less separate than boys, as having more permeable ego boundaries. Girls come to define themselves more in relation to others. Their internalized object-relational structure becomes more complex, with more ongoing issues. These personality features are reflected in superego development. (Chodorow, 1978: 93)

However, while this is usually regarded as the result of same-sex identi-fication, in contrast Chodorow emphasized how this process is exacerbated by exclusive mothering. Moreover, girls have less of an investment in changing their love objects through investing in and developing a *hetero-sexual* orientation. Chodorow pointed out the political implications of this, which she suggested results in women's sexuality being positioned as requiring constraint.

Further, in contrast to depicting the pre-Oedipal mother–daughter relationship as *incapacitating* women, Chodorow instead highlighted what she regarded as women's *capacity to relate*. In doing this, she was continuing a trend endorsed in Jean Baker Miller's 1976 *Towards a New Psychology of Women*. Both Chodorow and Baker Miller were writing within the context of ego psychology's reification of autonomy as conflated with masculinity and thus maturity. The trend to exonerate and emphasize the notion of women's 'relationalism' has been taken up by both Carol Gilligan (1982) and feminist practitioners at the Stone Center (Jordan et al., 1991). Indeed, the conflation of feminist therapy with this theme is so strong that in my recent experience of teaching British counselling trainees about feminist therapy, I was met by incredulity that feminist therapy could consist of anything else but this.

However, authors such as Flax (1990) and Burack (1994) wonder what has happened to 'the passions' in the feminist object relations framework, pointing out the lack of attention to the nastier sides of women's emotional expression. In relation to criticisms of her work reifying women's relational capacities, Chodorow (1989) argued that a feminist object relations perspective does lead to theorizing women's *problems*, as well as redressing gender-biased pathologizing. She reminds us that feminist object relations theorists are equally concerned with *men's* psychologies (1989). In this, Chodorow cites Benjamin's work on sado-masochistic heterosexual relationships. Although Benjamin also promotes the centrality of relationalism, or 'mutual recognition' (1988: 16), she is careful to point out that her interests in the mother–infant relationship differ from Chodorow's (1988: 69). In *The Bonds of Love* (1988), she focused on understanding the tenacity and dualism of the dynamics of domination and submission in heterosexual relationships. Her concern was with the way in which power structures reproduce relations of domination. While Benjamin suggested that a psychoanalytic explanation, linking adult eroticism with early infantile awareness of the difference between mothers and fathers, had the potential to offer a satisfactory analysis of these aspects of adult heterosexuality, she also contended that psychoanalytic theory *contributes* to the notion that heterosexual male domination is natural.

In refuting this belief in the inevitability of asymmetry and conflict, Benjamin proposed that the appeal of erotic heterosexual domination is its offer to break the encasement of an isolated sense of self. She saw this sense of isolation as arising out of a false differentiation between self and other, encouraged through the current cultural and psychoanalytic idealization of masculinity as conflated with autonomy. Further, Benjamin argued that what lies underneath the sensationalization of power and powerlessness, for *both* men and women, is a longing for a recognition which is not possible in a subjectivity developed in the context of refuting dependence (1988: 53). It is the basic tension of forces *within* subjectivities – the tension of mutual recognition, which becomes acted out *between* male and female – in the context of cultural ideals (1988: 62). Like Chodorow, Benjamin linked the separation of the private and public with the split between the father of autonomy and the mother of dependency, positing women as bridging the two, enabling the 'fiction of independence to be preserved' (1988: 197).

Benjamin suggested that some of the conflation and idealization of masculinity with autonomy arises from within the contradictions in the way in which Freud and Kleinian drive/conflict models theorize the Oedipal complex. First, they privilege the Oedipal complex as the most crucial stage of development, because it involves moving out of the dyadic mother–infant relationship into a triadic relationship including father. Second, since psychoanalytic theory posits the crucial dynamic of the Oedipal phase as being the father's capacity to offer the child the means to *flee an engulfing mother*, this means that autonomy has come to mean an equation of the (male) father with 'an escape from dependency' (1988: 221) on the (female) *mother*.

In contrast to Benjamin's feminist critique of the failure of psychoanalysis to privilege women, except in this undermining way, one objection to feminist object relations theory is that it privileges the *mother–daughter relationship* in a problematic way, positioning it as responsible for all women's ills. Enns points out that focusing on this relationship simply adds to the tendency to blame mothers (1993: 29). Parker (1995) extends this argument, suggesting that Chodorow, as well as Eichenbaum and Orbach, reproduce the tendency in psychoanalytic theory to privilege the *infant's* perspective, to the neglect of the mother. This then functions to position the mother as inevitably *in the wrong*. This highlights another difficulty, which is that focusing on mothers and daughters locates problems *within* the relationship, as opposed to focusing on the external social factors in which families exist. This is evident, for instance, in Eichenbaum and Orbach's notion of women's cycle of emotional deprivation.

The authors suggested that the conflation of women mothering within heterosexual relationships, in which women cannot have their emotional needs met by their male partners, compounded by the lack of external social support for and denigration of mothering, results in mothers *turning to their daughters to meet their own needs*: 'The daughter becomes involved in a cycle that is part of each woman's experience, attempting to care for mother. As the daughter learns her role as nurturer, *her first child is her mother*' (1982: 39). Further, the authors suggest that mothers, because of same-sex identification with their daughters, are likely to be *unconsciously acting out their own ambivalent gendered psychodynamics* in relating to them. They argue that this is also because mothers are themselves always daughters – daughters who will have been socialized by women who will have also been emotionally undernourished. Moreover, Eichenbaum and Orbach suggested that mothers are caught in a paradox in raising daughters. Not only are they required to meet their infantile dependency needs whilst being emotionally undernourished themselves, they must also socialize their daughters in terms of learning about and taking up a position in heterosexual society. Thus, daughters must be taught from birth to *curb their needs*.

Benjamin also contended that, again with regard to the Oedipal complex, psychoanalysis fails to recognize the centrality of the mother within this process. She pointed out that this neglect belies a central contradiction in this theory. While the Oedipal complex is meant to be a phase of consolidating *differentiation* between self and others, within existing psychoanalytic frameworks, this process occurs *without* recognizing the mother, except as the one who is in control of the other (father), who is then taken as an ideal (1988: 165). As such, in contrast to Mitchell's theory of phallic monism (1988: 88), Benjamin states that the penis as a psychic and cultural symbol of revolt does not stem from women's *lack* of maternal power, but from the fantasy that it *rescues* the infant from this power (1988: 94). She thus places the girl's desire for the penis as the same as the boy's, as a desire for identification with his agency, as well as for the outside world. Benjamin regarded heterosexual male domination as an attempt to deny dependency, with the female's desire for submission representing a desire for recognition *through* the male's power. Therefore, it is women's self-abnegation which secures their access to the power and glory of the male other.

Regardless of the ways in which feminist object relations theorists problematized heterosexuality, nevertheless, they are regarded as reifying this. Contributors to an international conference on 'mothering and daughtering' (van Mens-Verhulst et al., 1993) question the heterosexual basis of the feminist object relations mother–daughter relationship (Flaake 1993; de Kanter, 1993) and thus the lack of attention to eroticism or to lesbian mothering; its eurocentric and thus cultural and racial specificity (Leira and Krips, 1993; Groen, 1993) and finally, the virginal status of the mother which renders the mother asexual (Flax, 1993). While Benjamin (1988) puts the daughter's sexuality back into the picture, her problematizing of *lesbianism* also situates sexuality as firmly heterosexual. O'Connor and Ryan (1993) further challenge the feminist object relations theorists' critiques of the Oedipus complex, regarding the positions they have taken on this matter as indicating an unquestioning acceptance of it as a universalistic concept.

Like Chodorow, Eichenbaum and Orbach argued that changes in the gendered division of parenting represent a major solution to the reproduction of psychological divisions in heterosexual relationships. They also drew on Dorothy Dinnerstein's (1976) feminist Kleinian text, *The Rocking of the Cradle and the Ruling of the World*, in order to explicate some of the reasons why changes in parenting arrangements are so slow to occur.

Apart from the obvious benefits which accrue to men in heterosexual relationships, on both an individual and social level, they utilized Dinnerstein's (and Chodorow's) argument that mothers have an *investment* in retaining their exclusive parenting position. Chodorow understood this as indicative that 'women's heterosexuality is triangular and requires a third person – a child – for its structural and emotional completion' (1978: 207). In contrast, Dinnerstein argued that this is because women derive a sense of power from the exclusivity of their maternal caretaking role and that the experience of maternity can vicariously fulfil the innate wish for merging which all infants experience. In this instance, women can symbolically merge with their initial mother, as well as prolong a sense of omnipotence, by becoming mothers themselves and exercising a life and death power over their infants.

In response to the idea that rearranging heterosexual parenting practices would redress the reproduction of mothering and thus the participation of women in their oppression, Tong highlighted three feminist reactions. One is that this elevates men to the position of *saviours*; the second is that it presupposes that 'men pick up all of the wondrous feminine qualities previously denied to them; and third, women do not pick up any of the horrendous male qualities previously spared them' (1989: 158–9). Flax points out that heterosexual parenting relationships don't explain the *cause* of 'asymmetric gender relations' (1990: 167), only the consequences.

However, there are further issues to be taken into consideration in terms of which model of *woman* feminist object relations theory has drawn upon. Little attention, if any, has been given to how 'woman' is unproblematically posited as white, eurocentric, heterosexual and middle class, resulting in a tendency, when discussing black women, for instance, towards what Espìn describes as 'add women of color and stir' (cf. Brown, 1994: 64). Thus, universalistic notions of 'woman' are not only privileged but continually reproduced. In spite of Chodorow's thesis of gendered psychological development and parenting as historically and culturally *specific*, perhaps she has succeeded in a way she had not anticipated; that is, she has instead offered an account of a thoroughly historical and culturally specific *eurocentric middle-class family*. She argued that '[a]s factors of race, class, culture, or history enter either into a labeled (conscious or unconscious) identity, or as they shape particular early object-relational and family patterns and forms of subjectivity, psychoanalytic tools *should* be able to analyze these' (1989: 4) (my emphasis). However, authors such as Spelman (1988) and Mama (1995), amongst others, point out that Chodorow's analysis consistently fails to offer this. The result is that her universalistic *psychological* claims about women's subjectivity lack *material* substance.

While I have already indicated some of the ways in which aspects of Benjamin's feminist interpretation of object relations theory differs from Chodorow's, here I want to clarify two final points. Benjamin's interest in adult heterosexual relationships differs from that of Chodorow. First, she does not posit heterosexuality as problematic *per se*, but instead is concerned about the eroticized dynamics of sado-masochism, in which desire, dependency, and agency are intertwined and interdependent. Benjamin's feminist interpretation of the gendered development of subjectivity positions the acquisition of a sense of agency as central to the child's move from experiencing herself as an 'acted upon' object, to an 'acting on' subject. Desire becomes the property of the self. However, for daughters, identifying with mothers – as they are positioned theoretically, economically, domestically and morally – means they have no *sexual* agency. Attainment of a sense of agency comes only through a repudiation of these un-agentic aspects of mother, and by means of an identification with father.

For Benjamin, heterosexuality is the only choice, and it is one fraught with continual tensions underlying intersubjective development, tensions which occur in 'the paradoxical balance between . . . sameness and difference' (1988: 49) which have implications for the development of sado-masochistic dynamics within adult heterosexual relationships. While mutual recognition enables differentiation, it also sets the scene for mutual dependency as the central dynamic of relatedness; that is, one is inevitably dependent on, and yet not in control of, an other or others, in the formation of and recognition of 'self'. This sets the stage for a definition of self occurring out of a move *away from* the other, as well as setting the stage for relations of domination. 'When the conflict between dependence and independence becomes too intense, the psyche gives up the paradox in favor of an opposition. Polarity, the conflict of opposites, replaces the balance within the self' (1988: 50).

Finally, while Benjamin applauds Chodorow's call for changes in parenting arrangements, she doubts that changes in individual families will have any major or long-lasting impact on the culture at large. Her focus on 'what happens in the field of self and other' (1988: 20), while offering some complex insights into aspects of the dynamics of adult heterosexual relationships, also marked a shift away from ego psychology's view of the self as a discrete unit. She extended her analysis of gender polarity to explore how this splitting affects intellectual and social life (1988: 184). This requires a gendered deconstruction of how notions of neutrality, rationality and autonomy have come to be regarded as 'natural' when in fact they mask a masculine ideal. As such, she regards change as needing to occur at an epistemological, as well as a social, level. At the same time, she points out that it is the same underlying fears which shore up dualistic thought, fears about 'sameness and difference', on which heterosexual domination and submission are based (1988: 49).

FEMINIST OBJECT RELATIONS PSYCHOTHERAPY

In contrast to Chodorow and Benjamin, Eichenbaum and Orbach's contribution to feminist object relations theory derives in the main from their practice as clinicians. *Outside In, Inside Out* (1982) also contained the therapeutic foundations of their feminist psychoanalytic practice. These are initially to work with the cycle of deprivation which women experience; that is, '[w]omen clients find it extremely painful to acknowledge their feelings of deprivation and consequent neediness. But the cornerstone of feminist therapy is to bring this conflict into the open, for as it is gradually exposed, the woman will come to understand more about what it is she searches for in her relationships. These dependency needs are central to the therapy relationship' (1982: 57). However, in a later collection of writings from the London Women's Therapy Centre, *Living with the Sphinx* (Ernst and Maguire, 1987), Eichenbaum and Orbach also proposed that a *feminist* psychoanalytic perspective enables the therapist to >ffer her client '[a]n interpretation that speaks to the full meaning of an ndividual woman's experience, reflects an understanding of the ways in which the material world creates individual personality, symptomatology, defence structures and so on' (1987b: 50). They argued that the therapist needs to explore not only how the client's inner world is permeated by social representations of self and other, but also how the client projects her inner world on to the outer. The authors suggested that the type of interpretations offered within a feminist psychoanalytic therapy are produced in such a way that '[o]ut of this it becomes clear that nothing short of a restructuring of social arrangements is required if the conditions that give rise to women's psychological position are to change fundamentally' (1987b: 50).

Eichenbaum and Orbach drew on Fairbairn's intrapsychic analysis of the process of withdrawing parts of self in response to environmental disappointments (see Greenberg and Mitchell, 1983, for a fuller account), in their account of the social dynamics in which women not only come to feel unsure of their emotional needs, but also come to blame *themselves* when these needs are not met. In order to preserve the relationship with the other, on whom the infant is dependent, Fairbairn proposed that the infant employs the 'moral' defence mechanism, which involves blaming the self as opposed to the other. In 'normal' withdrawal, denial of parts of the ego leaves a person not just with feelings of futility and hopelessness (about having them met) but also with a sensation wherein parts of the self seem hidden from others. Eichenbaum and Orbach call these hidden parts of the self the 'little-girl' (1982: 35). The anxiety aroused by these disappointments can lead to denial of the unmet need.

In terms of therapeutic work, their focus was not only on the internal 'needy little girls' their clients hide from others, but also on the 'needy little girls' these clients hide from themselves, *and their therapists*. Moreover, because of the splitting which occurs, these 'needy little girls' are not in conscious contact with parts of self or others and therefore are not available to receive whatever nurturance is offered to them. Thus, while the client will be *emotionally* hungry, seeking nurturance, she will also be terrified that the extent of her neediness will be experienced by the therapist as unjustifiable greed. In addition to this, having her needs named and being offered something by the therapist can, the authors argued, stir up aware-ness of these unconscious feelings, making the client feel uncomfortable, perhaps even making them want to deny the extent or depth of their feelings. Eichenbaum and Orbach described the various consequences which occur when the therapist is not tuned into these dynamics; for instance, the client may suddenly 'recover' and end therapy prematurely, or perhaps want to look after what they assume to be the *therapist's* needs.

The authors also discussed how what they describe as the 'push-pull' dynamics of the mother–daughter relationship feeds into the therapeutic relationship (1982: 58). As stated, the client may experience her thera-peutic relationship with the female therapist as both a relief and frighten-ing, because of her gendered hopes and fears. Not only is the client terrified of her dependency needs, these feelings resonate within the very powerful relationship between the client and therapist which can come to feel, within the psychoanalytic transference relationship, like a replication of the early infantile relationship between mother and daughter. There are also very obvious power differences between client and therapist which exacerbate these feelings. Like the mother, the therapist is osten-sibly 'not needy', attending to the child-client's needs as the primary focus, drawing on her more obvious and expected resources in order to meet these. In contrast, the client is, like the infant, needy, unable to cope, wanting, feeling a lack of resources, and asking for help.

The authors suggest that, while at an intellectual level the client regards the therapist as capable, confident, non-judgemental and encouraging, at an emotional level she may expect a replay of her ambivalent 'cycle of deprivation' relationship with her mother. As such, she may expect the 'mother-therapist' to withdraw from the client's needs, or perhaps keep her as the 'daughter-client' too near, possibly projecting her needs and wishes as the 'mother-therapist' on to the 'daughter-client', or envying and disapproving of the client's growing independence. Indeed, they suggest that the 'daughter-client' may feel that to leave therapy would be to abandon and reject the 'therapist-mother', and thus to incur her wrath. Moreover, the client may come to feel she has to reassure the therapist that she *is* needed, even if this means denying her own capabilities or desires to end the relationship. Even before this point, Eichenbaum and Orbach argue that the client may *not* experience the therapist as separate to her.

Eichenbaum and Orbach (1982) also make clear the emotional toll and responsibility which comes not just with being a *feminist* therapist attempting to attend to the impact of gender on self and client, but also with the onus on remaining available to clients *after* therapy. While this is a reflection of the long-term nature of their therapeutic framework, I would also argue that it may be an unconscious replication of the social expectations of mothers – or in this case, 'mother-therapists' – always being mothers in a very particular kind of way.

While the dynamics of the transference relationship will be primarily focused on the client's past relationship with her mother, the authors point out that there is also a *here-and-now* relationship between the two women in the therapy room who may share similar psychosocial histories and everyday experiences of gender oppression. My own experience of working in a therapy centre for women – an experience shared by my colleagues – is that, while the female client will approach a female therapist with the hope that she may be able to offer her something (Williams, 1993), she will also be approaching from an ambivalent position, as the result of her familial and possibly heterosexual experiences. Thus, she may believe that a male therapist would disappoint, and expect that she and the therapist will ally, as Eichenbaum and Orbach suggested mothers and daughters did, in seeing men as the disappointing figures, thereby keeping unhappy feelings about the *female* therapeutic relationship split off and located outside the room. Certainly, in women-only therapy groups, some women clients sometimes do this as a way of avoiding painful feelings *within* the group of women. Indeed, having been accused by male therapists of offering women clients a cosy 'healing' relationship, and thus seen as 'overgiving', Orbach and Eichenbaum later emphasized yet again just how reluctant their female clients were to 'take' (1995: 92).

The belief that a feminist therapist would be 'nice' only to her female clients and would collude in positing men as 'the enemy', safely outside the clinic room, has certainly been made evident in many discussions I and my colleagues have had over the years, in presenting our therapeutic work (for instance, at the Leeds Women's Therapy Service Conference 1987). I would suggest that the fact that the comment about 'niceness' usually comes from male therapists may say something not only about their fears of being devalued, but also about their guilty consciences. Moreover, it also indicates something about the ways in which their gendered and heterosexual stereotypes of masculinity and feminity – and thus fathering and mothering – preclude them from regarding female therapists as able to challenge clients and deal with their anger and ambivalence (Conlon, 1991). While a female client may have an undermining attitude towards a female therapist, given her experiences of being a 'second-class citizen', she may well also feel that she will be getting 'second best' from the therapist, who is after all, like her, 'only a woman'.

These feelings may also be even more complicated in situations where a black or lesbian woman seeks out a black or lesbian psychotherapist. At a conscious level, the client's hope is of not being pathologized because of 'difference', but at an unconscious level, perhaps because of internalized oppression, the client may feel that really, she *has* got 'second best' (personal communication, Judy Peltier). This notion could be extended to encompass situations when the physical appearance of a therapist, perhaps particularly in relation to body weight or disability, may be experienced as inferior or having 'failed' (see Bloom et al., 1994, for a discussion of 'cultural counter-transference in terms of body size').

Further, it has been argued that the 'feminization' of psychotherapy (Philipson, 1993), in which the numbers of female practitioners (in the United States) have risen sharply, also functions, by virtue of availability, not only to lower their 'value', but also to position those 'less available', psychotherapy-fathers, as having more value.

Critiques of feminist object relations *therapy*, many of which come from other feminist therapists, argue that a feminist therapy based on psycho-analytic theory and technique is inherently *anti*-feminist, due to its primary focus on early childhood relations and its emphasis on transference (Brown, 1994; Burstow, 1992; Worell and Remer, 1992). Not only is attention to unconscious processes considered to mystify the therapy process, the intensive power difference this constructs between client and therapist is regarded as antithetical to a feminist practice (Dutton-Douglas and Walker, 1988; Brown, 1994). In addition, psychoanalytic therapy is usually long term and offered in a private, fee-paying context and thus has not been accessible except to a limited number of economically privileged women.

Eichenbaum and Orbach do not regard these issues as contrary to a feminist approach. Instead, they suggest initially clarifying the process of therapy, as opposed to simply making interpretations about clients' possible confusion or curiosity. They see the exploration of the relationship between client and therapist as enabling clients to work through early issues involving mothers and daughters with a 'mother-therapist' who has some respect for women as well as a political framework for understanding the impact of inequality on the role of mothering. Thus, they see their work as reparative, giving clients space to separate out their *real* mothers from the way they are positioned within psychological discourses as continually failing to meet an idealized notion of a socially constructed 'mother'.

Moreover, they argue that it is useful to work with the power dynamic in therapy in order that clients be able to have 'real' as well as transference confrontations with a woman. This offers a different relational model from that to which many women are accustomed, in that displays of anger are not actively repressed, and assertion of need is encouraged. At an intersubjective level, clients are able to be enraged with their wished-for but inevitably disappointing omnipotent mother and see both of them survive this, intact (Conlon, 1991). Some needs *will* be met but not all. At an intrapsychic level, clients are able to explore their own internal mother and their wishes for and expectations of themselves. In relation to the criticism about elitism and inaccessibility, many feminist analytic therapists in Britain have a sliding scale for private clients, or offer their services through voluntary organizations, and women's therapy services, enabling women who wouldn't usually be offered analytic therapy to receive this.

Other critiques of feminist object relations therapy refer to the shortcomings of its feminist theory. For instance, McLeod (1994) takes up the tendency towards reifying women. She suggests that this, embedded as it is within a privileging of gender, leads to the inability of some feminist *practitioners* to deal adequately with women's oppression of men and children. Further, regardless of Eichenbaum and Orbach's problematizing of the constraints on sexual orientation, resulting in 'overwhelming cultural pressures towards heterosexuality' (1982: 43), O'Connor and Ryan (1993) also noted the way in which feminist psychodynamic therapists fail to consider issues of eroticism in their transference and counter-transference relationships with their female clients. This led them to question the ways in which they are both steeped in positing heterosexuality as the norm, while perhaps also indicating some anxiety about these feelings (1993: 184).

Despite the shortcomings of the feminist object relations theory framework, some of which I have briefly outlined, it has nevertheless presented feminist psychotherapy with some of the richest theoretical considerations in the field. Similarly it has also challenged the dearth of critically informed theories of gender theory within classical psychoanalysis, although these insights are rarely acknowledged (Maguire, 1995; Philipson, 1993). Although Chodorow (1989) later rethinks her initial position of focusing on differences between women and men, she is unapologetic about the universalistic concepts which inform her psychoanalytic framework. She says, '[p]sychoanalysis uses universal theoretical categories . . . but it need not (though it may in some versions) prescribe the content of unconscious fantasy, the inevitable invocation of particular defenses, or particular developmental or self stories' (1989: 4). In contrast, in spite of the shift in feminist writings away from universalistic notions of 'woman', the many formal critiques of their writings (O'Connor and Ryan, 1993) and the many informal challenges which I have heard put to them at conferences, Eichenbaum and Orbach never redress this in their later works, even in their book which is specifically about 'differences between women' (1987a). This must be some testimony to a tension in their thinking about the historical and cultural specificity of clinical material, and their privileging of gender oppression. Although they do keep stating that they work with women from very different backgrounds, we are left wondering if 'the little girl inside' is an ahistorical constant.

Many of the critiques of feminist object relations theory which I have cited are critiques which have also been targeted at feminist theories generally; that is, feminism does not afford a privileged position outside the boundary of its cultural, historical and heterosexual embeddedness. As I have argued elsewhere (Heenan, 1995, 1996a, 1996b), this has implications for the practice of feminist psychodynamic therapy, in that it is no longer enough to take part in the kinds of 'gender-conscious' feminist clinical supervisions which Eichenbaum and Orbach (1982) suggest, in order to develop and maintain a feminist 'vigilance' in therapeutic practice. Instead, feminist object relations therapy needs to critically reflect on the ways in which it functions both to regulate and to reproduce normality, constructing notions of 'woman'. This occurs in both the ways outlined above, as well as through extrapolating from the clinical material of the limited population it serves, and constructing universalistic theories of women's psychological 'troubles'. While I would argue that this kind of feminist therapy can offer women a resistive tool, as a practitioner I must also acknowledge that I am part of the system.

NOTE

Thanks to my co-editor Bruna Seu, the members of my feminist academic writing group, Miriam Zukas, Ann Hobbiss, Carol Sherrard and Madeline Holloway, as well as to Erica Burman, for their patient reading of, and helpful feedback on, the multiple versions of this chapter I have presented to them.

REFERENCES

Appignanesi, L. and Forrester, J. (1992) *Freud's Women*. London: Virago Press.

Baker Miller, J. (1976) *Towards a New Psychology of Women*. Harmondsworth, Middlesex: Pelican Books.

Benjamin, J. (1988) *The Bonds of Love: Psychoanalysis, Feminism, and the Problem of Domination*. London: Virago Books.

Bloom, C., Gitter, A., Gutwill, S., Kogel, L. and Zaphiropoulos, L. (1994) *Eating Problems: A Feminist Psychoanalytic Treatment Model*. New York: Basic Books.

Brown, L. (1994) *Subversive Dialogue: Theory in Feminist Therapy*. New York: Basic Books.

Burack, C. (1994) *The Problem of the Passions: Feminism, Psychoanalysis, and Social Theory*. New York: New York University Press.

Burstow, B. (1992) *Radical Feminist Therapy*. New York: Sage.

Chodorow, N. (1978) *The Reproduction of Mothering: Psychoanalysis and the Sociology of Gender*. Berkeley, CA: University of California Press.

Chodorow, N. (1989) *Feminism and Psychoanalytic Theory*. New Haven, CT: Yale University Press.

Conlon, I. (1991) 'The effect of gender on the role of the female group conductor', *Group Analysis*, 24: 187–200.

de Kanter, R. (1993) 'Becoming a situated daughter', in J. van Mens-Verhulst, K. Schreurs and L. Woertman (eds) *Daughtering and Mothering: Female Subjectivity Reanalysed*. London: Routledge. pp. 26–34.

Dinnerstein, D. (1976) *The Rocking of the Cradle and the Ruling of the World*. London: Women's Press.

Dutton-Douglas, M. A. and Walker, L. E. (eds) (1988) *Feminist Psychotherapies: Integration of Therapeutic and Feminist Systems*. Norwood, NJ: Ablex Publishing Corporation.

Eichenbaum, L. and Orbach, S. (1982) *Outside In, Inside Out: Women's Psychology – A Feminist Psychoanalytic Approach*. Harmondsworth, Middlesex: Pelican Books.

Eichenbaum, L. and Orbach, S. (1983) *What do Women Want?* London: Fontana Books.

Eichenbaum, L. and Orbach, S. (1987a) *Bittersweet*. London: Century Press.

Eichenbaum, L. and Orbach, S. (1987b) 'Separation and intimacy: crucial practice issues in working with women in therapy', in S. Ernst and M. Maguire (eds), *Living with the Sphinx: Papers from the Women's Therapy Centre*. London: Women's Press. pp. 49–67.

Enns, C. Zerbe (1993) 'Twenty years of feminist counseling and therapy: from naming biases to implementing multifaceted practice', *The Counseling Psychologist*, 21 (1): 3–87.

Ernst, S. and Maguire, M. (eds) (1987) *Living with the Sphinx: Papers from the Women's Therapy Centre*. London: Women's Press.

Evans, J. (1995) *Feminist Theory Today: An Introduction to Second-Wave Feminism*. London: Sage.

Flaake, K. (1993) 'A body of one's own: sexual development and the female body in the mother–daughter relationship', in J. van Mens-Verhulst, K. Schreurs and L. Woertman (eds), *Daughtering and Mothering: Female Subjectivity Reanalysed*. London: Routledge. pp. 7–14.

Flax, J. (1990) *Thinking Fragments: Psychoanalysis, Feminism, and Postmodernism in the Contemporary West*. Berkeley, CA: University of California Press.

Flax, J. (1993) 'Mothers and daughters revisited', in J. van Mens-Verhulst, K. Schreurs and L. Woertman (eds), *Daughtering and Mothering: Female Subjectivity Reanalysed*. London: Routledge. pp. 145–56.

Gilligan, C. (1982) *In a Different Voice*. Cambridge, MA: Harvard University Press.

Greenberg, J. R. and Mitchell, S. A. (1983) *Object Relations in Psychoanalytic Theory*. Cambridge, MA: Harvard University Press.

Groen, M. (1993) 'Mother-daughter, the 'black continent': is a multi-cultural future possible?', in J. van Mens-Verhulst, K. Schreurs and L. Woertman (eds), *Daughtering and Mothering: Female Subjectivity Reanalysed*. London: Routledge. pp. 97–105.

Heenan, M. C. (1995) 'Feminist psychotherapy: a contradiction in terms?', *Feminism and Psychology*, 5 (1): 112–17.

Heenan, M. C. (1996a) 'Women, food and fat: too many cooks in the kitchen?', in E. Burman et al. (eds), *Challenging Women: Psychology's Exclusions, Feminist Possibilities*. Buckingham: Open University Press. pp. 19–35.

Heenan, M. C. (1996b) 'Feminist therapy and its discontents', in E. Burman et al. (eds), *Psychology, Discourse, Practice: From Regulation to Resistance*. London: Taylor Francis. pp. 55–71.

Jordan, J. V., Kaplan, A. G., Baker Miller, J., Stiver, I. P. and Surrey, J. L. (1991) *Women's Growth in Connection: Writings from the Stone Center*. New York: Guilford Press.

Lawrence, M. (ed.) (1987) *Fed Up and Hungry: Women, Oppression and Food*. London: Women's Press.

Leira, H. and Krips, M. (1993) 'Revealing cultural myths on motherhood', in J. van Mens-Verhulst, K. Schreurs and L. Woertman (eds), *Daughtering and Mothering: Female Subjectivity Reanalysed*. London: Routledge. pp. 83–96.

Maguire, M. (1995) *Men, Women, Passion and Power: Gender Issues in Psychotherapy*. London: Routledge.

Mama, A. (1995) *Beyond the Masks: Race, Gender and Subjectivity*. London: Routledge.

McLeod, E. (1994) *Women's Experiences of Feminist Therapy and Counselling*. Buckingham: Open University Press.

Millett, K. (1969) *Sexual Politics*. London: Sphere Books Ltd.

Mitchell, J. (1974) *Psychoanalysis and Feminism*. Harmondsworth, Middlesex: Pelican Books.

Mitchell, J. (1995) 'Introduction to Psychoanalysis and Feminism: 20 Years On. Conference proceedings', *British Journal of Psychotherapy*, 12 (1).

O'Connor, N. and Ryan, J. (1993) *Wild Desires and Mistaken Identities: Lesbianism and Psychoanalysis*. London: Virago Books.

Orbach, S. and Eichenbaum, L. (1995) 'From objects to subjects, in Psychoanalysis and Feminism: 20 Years On. Conference proceedings', *British Journal of Psychotherapy*, 12 (1): 89–97.

Parker, R. (1995) *Torn in Two: The Experience of Maternal Ambivalence*. London: Virago Press.

Philipson, I. J. (1993) *On The Shoulders of Women: The Feminization of Psychotherapy*. New York: Guilford Press.

Spelman, E. V. (1988) *Inessential Woman: Problems of Exclusion in Feminist Thought*. London: Women's Press.

Squire, C. (1989) *Significant Differences: Feminism in Psychology*. London: Sage.

Stern, D. (1985) *The Interpersonal World of the Infant*. New York: Basic Books.

Tong, R. (1989) *Feminist Thought: A Comprehensive Introduction*. London: Routledge.

van Mens-Verhulst, J., Schreurs, K. and Woertman, L. (eds) (1993) *Daughtering and Mothering: Female Subjectivity Reanalysed*. London: Routledge.

Williams, S. (1993) 'Women in search of women: clinical issues that underlie a woman's search for a female therapist', *British Journal of Psychotherapy*, 9 (3): 291–300.

Worell, J. and Remer, P. (1992) *Feminist Perspectives in Therapy: An Empowerment Model for Women*. New York: John Wiley & Sons.

7

Psychotherapy and Working-Class Women

Pamela Trevithick

I often think of psychotherapy as a meal – an opportunity to be nourished. What this meal is made of will depend, to a large extent, on what is wanted, affordable and available – financially and emotionally – and whether we have the time, space and stomach to consume and digest all that is there. The final choice of eating house may be influenced by many factors – what is already known about the choice and range of food available, whether it has been recommended and by whom, its location and how easy it is to get there, how the food will be served, whether the menu is written in a language we can understand and will be adapted to meet individual taste, whether there is room for us and, most importantly, what the bill will be and whether we can afford it. Having money buys choice and the chance to be served quickly. It also buys the expectation that the money spent will purchase food of a particular quality.

Those who cannot 'pay their way' must seek out other alternatives. For this group, what food there is may involve long queues, be limited to one menu, and be served in a way that makes it unpalatable or even virtually uneatable. As a result, whilst having the appearance of being a nourishing and satisfying meal, it may provide neither: too often, it is a handout and that fact is not disguised. The picture that comes to mind is of one group heading for an expensive restaurant of their choice while another much more hungry group shuffles to the single-menu soup kitchens of the NHS, craving for something, anything, to 'fill the hole' as quickly as possible. If there is no food available, or it is placed tantalizingly beyond their reach or too rich for an empty stomach to digest, then they must, for lack of choice, do without.

Doing without is not new to working-class people – it is almost a class characteristic. And so, in the absence of any real alternative, other ways of addressing these needs are sought in the hope that this will take away the pain – the emptiness, the fury and the unbearable desire for more. Some turn to cigarettes, alcohol, gambling, drugs, chocolate, sugar and other addictions in the hope that these will help them cope and make life more bearable or pleasurable. Too often, these substances fail to live up to their promise and more of the same is sought – as if hope can be purchased in a packet of cigarettes or lasting comfort found in a bottle of booze. Inevitably, health and outlook begin to suffer and other more helpful options become less attractive or less possible.

Freud understood this pull towards ultimately unhelpful solutions among people weighed down by the burden of their suffering and hoped that one day psychoanalysis would be able to adapt its technique to meet the needs of what he called 'the poor man':

> Then clinics and consultation departments will be built, to which analytically trained physicians will be appointed so that the men who would otherwise give way to drink, the women who have nearly succumbed under their burden of privations, the children for whom there is no choice but running wild or neurosis, may be made by analysis able to resist and able to do something in the world. This treatment will be free. It may take a long time before the State regards this as an urgent duty . . . however, it must come. (Freud, 1924: 401)

But addictions are dangerous in other ways. People who turn to these substances for comfort run the risk of being barred from access to certain kinds of help, such as counselling or treatment programmes, if they are not 'dry' or are found to be still 'using' drugs. In some organizations, the level of motivation required for people to access these services and resources is very high and effectively acts as a selection process, excluding those whose lives are too chaotic or whose motivation wavers. Too often, little or no account is taken of the factors within an individual's life that militate against being able to meet the expectations of help-giving agencies. For example, I know of several family therapy centres, funded within the National Health Service, where lateness or absenteeism is understood only in terms of low motivation. This often results in families being denied the help they need. Whilst it is important to acknowledge the frustration and difficulties experienced when clients or patients are absent or late, I would argue that this behaviour needs to be understood in its widest context and requires a more sophisticated and compassionate professional response than denying access to services.

This chapter raises a complex and controversial issue within psychotherapy which is to explore what changes need to occur for psychotherapy to be able to speak to the experiences of people who come from poor, deprived and disadvantaged sectors of the population. What part can psychotherapy properly play when an individual's emotional energy is being consumed in the everyday struggle for survival? My perspective is that psychotherapy is worryingly out of touch with the needs, the strengths and struggles of working-class people. Guntrip answered this concern in relation to psychoanalysis when he wrote:

> psychoanalysis will hold the attention of the public only insofar as it speaks truly to the human condition . . . able to help others with their struggles to be real persons living meaningful lives. (Guntrip, 1971: 44)

It is unclear how well psychoanalysis is doing in speaking 'to the human condition'. Nor is there any indication that psychoanalysis or psychotherapy has become any more accessible to people from poorer sections of the working class than when Barbara Lerner wrote *Therapy in the Ghetto* 25 years ago:

> Therapists disagree . . . and disagree sharply, as to the how, why, what, when and where of treatment . . . but with regard to the who, there is a striking degree of consistency over time, across professions and between orientations . . . mildly or moderately disturbed middle or upper class people are good clients; severely disturbed and/or lower class people are poor ones, rejected by and rejecting of professional therapy and therapists. (Lerner, 1972: 3–4)

This chapter takes as its starting point the view that too little is known within psychotherapy circles about the plight of working-class people living in poverty. It attempts both to bridge this gap, by illuminating some key issues in relation to the growing inequalities between rich and poor within our society, and to identify the implications for psychotherapy. Drawing on the work of Freud, Donald Winnicott and Barbara Dockar-Drysdale[1], it goes on to explore how psychotherapy can be made more accessible and helpful in relation to people from poorer sections of the working class. In order to illustrate these ideas in practice, a final section looks at how these theoretical influences informed the work of Womankind, a women and mental health project based in Bristol.

It is important to state at this point that when I first drafted an outline for this chapter, it was my intention to focus solely on the therapeutic needs of working-class women. However, as the work progressed I found myself being increasingly drawn toward a particular sub-group of the working class, namely the experiences of people living in poverty – people whose lives are overshadowed by the presence of deprivation and disadvantage. And as I returned to my own childhood experiences and tentatively re-entered the world of poor people, I found myself caught up in the hardship and suffering of working-class men as well as working-class women. Once there, it felt heartless and wrong to ignore the suffering of men where this closely mirrored the experiences of women. I felt divided in my loyalties in a way often described by working-class and black women. This chapter reflects this tension and my need to relate my feminist perspective not only to women but to the whole of humanity – to men and women, boys and girls.

It may be helpful at this point to define some of the terms and words used. I use the word *psychoanalysis* both as a theory of human behaviour and as a method of treatment, based on a recognition of the importance of the unconscious, transference and resistance:

> Any line of investigation, no matter what its direction, which recognises transference and resistance, and takes them as the starting point of its work may call itself psychoanalysis, though it arrives at results other than my own. (Freud, 1914: 3)

The term *psychoanalytic psychotherapy* is used to denote the use of psycho-analytic concepts in ways which fall within a general Freudian theoretical framework but do not strictly adhere to the more traditional and established Freudian schools of thought, particularly those attributed to the Institute of Psycho-Analysis. *Psychotherapy* is used quite broadly to indicate any form of 'talking cure'. It has been estimated that there may be as many as 400 different psychotherapies.

In order to understand the experience of working-class people, it is important to identify which group of people are included within this category. Similarly, it is important to define what is meant by terms such as *deprivation, disadvantage* and *poverty* – and how these relate to one another. However before doing so, a word of caution is needed. Whilst generalizations are valuable in providing an overall picture about the lives and experiences of working-class and poor women and men, such generalizations can never properly capture all that is complex and unique about any one individual or group. For example, it is difficult to talk about the specific experiences of working-class women because what can be said of the thoughts and feelings of this group can also be claimed by those who are not working class or female. Very different experiences can bring about similar feelings, and similar experiences can produce very different reactions and emotions. So much hinges on what has gone before and the meaning attributed to those events and experiences.

WHO ARE THE WORKING CLASS?

A great deal of confusion still exists about what we mean when we use the term *social class* and who it includes – 'Sociologists are not agreed. Some define class as status or prestige, others as power, or income, or wealth and property, or say that class is what people think their class is' (Argyle, 1994: 3). Some of this confusion can be a denial of the stark realities of class inequalities. On the other hand, some confusion is understandable given the changes that have occurred since the war, both in the overall improvement in living standards for working-class people and also in the emergence of an educated group of people whose cultural heritage is working class but whose lifestyle has all the appearances of being middle class. I fall within this category.

Interestingly, more subjective definitions create less confusion. For example, one survey revealed that roughly 95 per cent of those researched thought there was a class system in this country and could identify which class they belong to (Argyle, 1994: 3). Although statistics vary, it is estimated that 46 per cent of British people describe themselves as working class, plus an additional group (1.5 per cent) who see themselves as 'upper working class', sometimes called the 'labour aristocracy'. This roughly corresponds with the Registrar General's six categories of social class which are based on occupation. These statistics showed that 52 per cent of people fall between social classes IIINM (skilled non-manual) and V (unskilled manual).[2] Women's class has traditionally been identified in terms of a woman's husband's occupation and class. This creates enormous difficulties when attempting to identify the specific characteristics of working-class women, and feminists have argued convincingly for the need to give women a separate 'class position that adequately reflects their total class situation' (Abbott and Sapsford, 1987: 30). However, to date this confusion remains.

The working class is a class of great diversity in terms of race and ethnicity and other social and cultural differences and although not all working-class people are poor, the vulnerability of this group of people to deprivation and disadvantage is very marked. Notions of deprivation and disadvantage help to identify those sections of the working class most vulnerable to poverty and its short- and long-term impact. This vulnerability affects women disproportionately, which is a point to which I return later.

Deprivation, Disadvantage and Poverty

The term *deprivation* involves a sense of loss — the loss of something good, desired or worthwhile. Deprivations are a part of life. Some losses are inevitable whilst others are deeply class-bound. For example, in relation to bereavement in the 1970s, men and women in occupational class V (unskilled manual) had a two-and-a-half times greater chance of dying before they reached retirement age than men and women in occupational class I (professional) (Townsend and Davidson, 1992: 43). Or again, the rates of sickness — that is, loss of a sense of health or well-being — showed great inequalities: 'the gradient is the steeper for limiting long-standing illness, where the rates in the unskilled manual group are more than double those of the professional group for both men and women' (ibid., 223). These are but two examples: many more could be added.

In the case of multiple deprivations and social disadvantage the causes extend beyond the experience of loss into situations where individuals are effectively excluded from gaining access to certain rights, opportunities, experiences or resources:

> Deprivations of all kinds — material, physical, social or emotional — may happen to anyone in any social group. But the disadvantaged are those who are consistently exposed to the highest risks of being deprived. Put crudely, the disadvantaged are those whose deprivations occur not because they are foolish or unlucky but simply because they belong to a particular social group. (Brown, 1983: 5)

For example, the loss of a job could be considered a deprivation because it involves a loss of income, status, social contact and so forth. This deprivation becomes *disadvantage* when being unemployed means being denied access to decent housing, education or health service provision as a result of poverty. Peter Townsend uses a different terminology to describe the same problems, preferring the term 'relatively deprived' to describe people who are excluded from participating in society – 'If they lack or are denied resources to obtain access to these conditions of life and so fulfil membership of society they may be said to be in poverty' (Townsend, 1993: 36). The social group most vulnerable to deprivation and disadvantage is working-class people of all races. Whilst certain family patterns can limit or restrict an individual's opportunity to move forward, more often it is the inequitable way that society is structured, rather than individual fecklessness or irresponsibility that results in deprivation and disadvantage.

One of the most worrying changes in recent years relates to the growing gap between rich and poor in this and in other countries. For example, by the late 1980s it was estimated that over a third of the population were living in or on the margins of poverty support. Unemployment creates poverty. According to the Unemployment Unit, the true picture in relation to unemployment is much worse than official statistics suggest and in August 1995 it was estimated that the unemployment figure stood at 3,400,500 people (Oppenheim and Harker, 1996: 48). Poverty affects different groups unevenly, and frequently affects the most vulnerable sectors of society such as older people, children, disabled people and women.

Women and Poverty

Poverty is marked among women. Women in employment tend to be low paid and for those who are unemployed or not employed, welfare benefits are very low. Where couples are on the margins of poverty, it is mainly women who have responsibility for the household budget and, as a consequence, carry the stresses and strains inherent in trying to make ends meet on the little money they have. Women's unique relationship to the burden of poverty has been described as the 'feminization of poverty' (Pearce, 1978) – a fact that is reflected in the UK statistics on poverty.

For example, it is estimated that in 1992 approximately 5.4 million women in Britain were living in poverty. Of these, in 1992 nine out of ten lone parents were women, which means that there were well over one million lone mothers. In terms of British women's employment, in 1994 nearly six and a half million women were low paid – that is, women comprised 65 per cent of the total number of people on low wages. Of the 4.8 million women working part-time, 77 per cent of them were low paid. In terms of earnings, in 1994, women's average gross hourly earnings including overtime came to only 72 per cent of men's earnings and, in the same year, over two million women fell below the threshold for making national insurance contributions and, therefore, forfeited their right to national insurance benefits (Oppenheim and

Harker, 1996: 96). In relation to older women, of the ten and a half million elderly people in Britain in 1990, women were the majority, numbering around two-thirds. Of these, in 1991 there were over three times as many women pensioners as men dependent on income support.

Women's unemployment is thought to fall somewhere between 34 per cent and 43 per cent of those unemployed (Oppenheim and Harker, 1996: 94). With regard to black women, as with their male counterparts the unemployment rates have always been higher, sometimes two or three times higher than the average for white people, although the gap is narrowing (Argyle, 1994: 100). The conclusion that must be drawn from these figures is that 'for many women neither employment nor social security can keep them out of poverty' (Oppenheim, 1993: 100). More generally, the statistics reveal that working-class people experience more 'unfavourable events of a variety of kinds' (Argyle, 1994: 275) such as loss of income, unemployment, difficult conditions of employment, bad housing, debts, etc. These are termed 'environmental stresses' by Brown and Harris (1978) or indicators of disadvantage by Brown (1983).

The Emotional Consequences of Poverty and Disadvantage

Over the years there has been an attempt to link certain types of mental disorders to social class, and particularly to the impact of poverty. The most influential research in this field relates to the work of Brown and Harris, who found that working-class women in their study were two to three times more likely to become depressed than a comparable group of middle-class women (Brown and Harris, 1978). Other research shows that working-class people are roughly five times more likely to be diagnosed as schizophrenic (Argyle, 1994: 273) and that alcoholism and drug addiction are also more common among the working class (McLeod and Kessler, 1990). In addition to the impact of poverty, the class-related nature of some mental illnesses may come about because working-class people often have fewer resources to fall back on, both externally in terms of social support and internally in terms of emotional resources.

I have explored the relationship between class, deprivation, disadvantage and poverty in order to highlight the range and depth of the hardship experienced by people living in poverty, particularly women, and the vulnerability of all working-class people to these hardships should they ever 'fall on bad times' that is, should they ever reach a point where they have nothing to fall back on but their wits and their determination to survive. It is a fear that working-class people live with and defend against on a daily basis with far-reaching consequences in terms of their capacity to seek and accept help, assuming that this help is available and of the right kind. The hard lives that poor people live was something Freud understood:

> we shall probably discover that the poor are even less ready to part with neuroses than the rich, because the hard life that awaits them when they

recover has no attraction, and illness in them gives them more claim to the
help of others. (Freud, 1924: 402)

If this is the case, then it follows that any psychotherapy offered to 'poor
people' will need to take account firstly of their 'hard life' and secondly, of
the difficulties that working-class people may experience in letting go
of their suffering, particularly when doing so risks being abandoned and
neglected in terms of access to health care and welfare services. Hence the
importance of universal services and benefits such as the social wage. It is
to the relationship between poverty and psychotherapy that this chapter
now turns.

THE THERAPEUTIC NEEDS OF WORKING-CLASS PEOPLE
LIVING IN POVERTY

In his paper 'Turnings in the way of psycho-analytic therapy'[3] published
in 1924, Freud addresses the accessibility of psychoanalysis in relation to
people from poorer sections of the population. This paper is important
because it provides a foundation from which to explore how the central
concepts of psychoanalysis – transference and resistance – can be related
in detail to the experiences of working-class and poor people and to an
analysis of the emotional impact of urban decay and neglect, discrimination and disadvantage.

Freud begins his paper by acknowledging the 'incompleteness of our
understanding' and goes on to look more closely at the importance of
working with resistances. He then turns his attention to what Ferenczi
described as the 'activity' on the part of the analyst/therapist, stating that
whilst working with 'unconscious and repressed material and uncovering
resistances' (p. 395) may be considered activity enough, for some patients/
clients this may not be sufficient to create the 'situation most favourable to
solution'. He notes that what can be achieved may be mediated by
'external circumstances' and suggests that in such circumstances it may be
appropriate and justifiable for analysts/therapists to be more active and to
intervene to lessen the impact of external influences. However, when
introducing adaptations in technique the purpose and aim of psychoanalysis must always be kept in view. This is 'not to make everything as
pleasant as possible for the patient' but to make 'him [sic] stronger for life
and more capable of carrying out the actual tasks of his life' (p. 398). The
ultimate aim is 'the patient's restoration to health' (p. 396). For people
who are 'helpless and incapable', this might involve combining the analytic
technique with the role of educator, teacher and mentor but these changes
'must always be done with great caution' (p. 399).

Freud goes on to remind us of the changes that psychoanalysis has
undergone. For example, the treatment of new diseases (hysteria, phobia)
necessitated different techniques that 'went beyond former limits'. However, he notes that the therapeutic effects benefited 'but an handful of

people' from the 'well-to-do classes' and did little to address the 'vast amount of misery in the world' (p. 401). Yet for Freud 'the poor man has just as much right to help for his mind as he now has for the surgeon's means of saving life' but he acknowledges that for psychoanalysis to reach this group will require 'us to adapt our technique to the new conditions'. This includes finding 'the simplest and most natural expressions for our theoretical doctrines'. In a final paragraph, Freud returns to the theme of analysts/therapists addressing the influence of external factors and states that 'we may often only be able to achieve something if we combine aid for the mind with some material support'. He concludes that 'it is very probable, too, that the application of our therapy to numbers will compel us to alloy the pure gold of analysis plentifully with the copper of direct suggestion' (Freud, 1924: 402).

On the whole, there has been very little attempt within psychoanalysis to explore and to relate Freud's adaptations in technique to the needs of working-class and poor people. The following section, therefore, describes how Freud's ideas could be used in practice.

WOMANKIND

Womankind was set up in January 1986 as one of 16 pilot projects scattered throughout England whose purpose was to explore what role self-help could play in meeting people's health and welfare needs. For Womankind, this initially involved setting up a range of different self-help groups for women suffering from depression, tranquillizer addiction, agoraphobia, eating disorders, a mental health system survivors group and a self-harm group. In time, it also included setting up assertiveness training and confidence-building groups and counselling skills courses for Afro-Caribbean and Asian women. Although we set up many self-help groups, we found that most collapsed once the development worker ceased to be involved. As a result, when our major funding ended in 1989 we decided to focus our limited funds on working with depressed women.

When Womankind began, we thought that feminism would answer all our questions. We hoped that, by giving women a 'good experience' and by being committed and supportive to women suffering from 'mental health' problems, life would come together for them. However, after many years of optimistic endeavour it became increasingly clear that the feminist approach we were adopting was failing to address a whole range of needs that women were expressing. We were not being successful in our efforts to help and this was beginning to affect our confidence and sense of hope. This was partly because from the beginning Womankind tended to attract a very distressed group of women. This tendency was compounded with the closure of the large psychiatric hospitals and the introduction of Care in the Community legislation.

As the years rolled past, it became increasingly clear that we did not have the knowledge or skills to work effectively with the women who came to Womankind for help. This placed us at a cross-roads. Either we had to effectively exclude women suffering from 'severe' and 'enduring' depression so that we could redirect our services towards women who were not so distressed, or we had to develop a new approach and body of knowledge. We decided on the latter. Our quest began by returning to feminist writing on women's mental health and psychotherapy and also psychoanalytic theory, because it was here that we found feminists addressing issues of concern to us about the importance of early childhood experiences in relation to women's emotional development and ongoing experiences of oppression and injustice. These authors included Jessica Benjamin (1990, 1995), Teresa Brennan (1989), Cynthia Burack (1994), Nancy Chodorow (1978, 1989, 1994), Dorothy Dinnerstein (1978), Lesley Doyal (1995), Luise Eichenbaum and Susie Orbach (1982), Sheila Ernst and Marie Maguire (1987), Jane Flax (1981, 1991, 1993), Carol Gilligan (1982), Caroline Glendinning and Jane Millar (1992), Hilary Graham (1993), Judith Jordan et al. (1991), Jean Baker Miller (1973, 1976), Juliet Mitchell (1974, 1984), Janet Sayer (1991) and Elizabeth Wright (1992).

These writings gave us an important theoretical framework but they did not help us as groupworkers and counsellors to understand how to respond in practice to the suffering that women were describing in their internal and external lives, particularly when their distress was being triggered by ongoing experiences of hardship and poverty – of deprivation (loss) and disadvantage (exclusion). What we needed was a theory and practice that could help us to understand what was happening to women and what we could say or do to make a difference. This we found in the writings of Winnicott and Dockar-Drysdale. For two years, Barbara Dockar-Drysdale acted as a consultant to Womankind and it was from these regular weekly meetings that I and other groupworkers learned a great deal about how to listen to women's conscious and unconscious communications. Time and again Mrs Dockar-Drysdale would say, 'But you're not listening to what is being said', and she was, of course, correct. Once we learned the art of listening, our work at Womankind began to change in unexpected ways.

The exploration I am about to describe ran from 1992 to 1995. During this period, Womankind ran three weekly closed depression groups each made up of nine women. Attendance at our three groups was unusually high. In addition, we also provided individual counselling for a small number of women. Towards the end of the period described, we ran several groups every month for women on our waiting-list. Finally, several times a year we ran day workshops for social workers, community psychiatric nurses and other practitioners working with depressed men and women.

It may be valuable to give a snapshot of the women we worked with: greater detail is described elsewhere (Trevithick, 1995). Towards the middle of the period described, we had regular contact on a weekly basis with about 30 women, of whom almost a quarter came from black (Afro-Caribbean) and other ethnic minority groups. Their age range spanned many years – from 22 to 65 years – out of which over half were under 30. Most of the women we worked with were mothers. Of these children, 14 were under ten years old, of whom two were babies.

Almost all the women we worked with were on benefit, which included a large cross-section on disability benefit of one kind or another. As indicated in the section on poverty, the lack of money and social exclusion it produced left women feeling intensely lonely and isolated. As a result, the sense of despair and defeat that women carried was very marked and troubling. Over half had attempted suicide at some time in their lives and two women had close family members who actually committed suicide. Their psychiatric diagnoses varied greatly. Most fell within the category of 'severe' and 'enduring' mental illness based on their long histories of depression. Most women used the word *depression* to describe themselves, and this was true of women with some history of psychotic illness, who constituted about a third of the total numbers attending our groups.

Although the majority of our initial referrals came from family doctors, social workers and other health worker professionals, our selection process was based primarily on self-referral. This involved women ringing the Womankind helpline which was open every morning. After this initial contact, a range of different pamphlets would be sent out explaining our work and how our groups were organized. Although we would have liked to offer more individual counselling,[4] we made it clear in our literature that we were only able to offer groupwork. For women who wanted one-to-one work, we provided information about where they could go for help. The names of women interested in attending a group were then placed on a waiting-list. One survey we undertook showed that early on in our work, the time involved from the point of self-referral to women attending a group was on average two weeks. However, as the names on the waiting-list grew this swift response proved increasingly difficult to maintain. For example, at one time there were 80 names on our waiting-list, which created an enormous dilemma because we did not have the resources to meet this need. Women who had been on the waiting-list the longest were usually the first to be invited to join one of the groups when a place become vacant. However, on occasion we offered places to meet specific needs – for example, to balance the racial composition of a particular group. It is important to stress that our selection procedure evolved because of our limited resources and was far from ideal. The emphasis we placed on self-referral had its limitations as well as its strengths.

Each depression group we ran had three groupworkers: two group leaders and a co-ordinator. The primary role of the group co-ordinator was to ensure that Womankind provided a setting that was 'good enough' for women to explore their thoughts and feelings. It was the task of the group leaders not to provide insights or interpretations, except as a way of caring, but to help women to find their own understandings and solutions based on the premiss that it is 'the patient and only the patient who has the answers' (Winnicott, 1987: 114).

The same concept of care, nurturance and holding described later in relation to women in our groups was also extended to ourselves as workers. This meant that we gave a high priority to using our theoretical framework as a basis from which to understand ourselves and our transference and counter-transference reactions. The emphasis we gave to peer support and supervision, which we attended once or twice a week, proved essential in helping us to understand and to work with women's anxieties, to avoid merging and to maintain boundaries. As practitioners, we had no formal qualifications in groupwork or counselling. Gaps in our knowledge were bridged by supervision and through attending counselling and groupwork training courses. Again, this had disadvantages but also the advantage of leaving us free to explore new ideas and ways of working because we had no allegiance to a particular approach.

CHANGE, GROWTH AND EMOTIONAL DEVELOPMENT

The starting point for our work came from Freud, Winnicott, Dockar-Drysdale and other writers who acknowledge the importance of early childhood experiences in the emotional development of the individual, the capacity of individuals to grow and to change throughout their lives, and the existence of conscious, pre-conscious and unconscious states and motives that influence actions. We also acknowledged the part played by the defence mechanism in mediating an individual's experience of themselves and others, the importance of transference as a process by which people displace or transfer feelings derived from the past on to others, and of the primary search and drive for relatedness within human beings.

From Winnicott, we also took as our starting point the notion that at the beginning of life, for emotional development and maturation to occur involves creating a *facilitating environment*, capable of being 'good enough' at adapting itself to meet the infant's changing needs. At first, this adaptation must be almost 100 per cent but is then gradually reduced once the baby moves towards independence. Successful adaptation means that the individual continues to develop 'an unbroken line of living growth' (Winnicott, 1987: 291). Where the infant does not experience sufficient adaptation, this constitutes an *impingement* which, if ongoing and left unrepaired, could lead to a *failure situation* where emotional development has become stuck or 'frozen'. An individual may continue to grow physically but not emotionally. Instead, emotional growth becomes 'delayed and perhaps distorted' (Winnicott, 1965: 228) and the energy or forces which would have been directed towards growth and emotional development have to be redirected to deal with or react to the impingement and the hold-up it produces. This can set in motion a range of reactions as the individual protects his or her sense of self through establishing a false self, which has the task of protecting the true self from further violations. However, whilst this strategic separation from the true self ensures survival, it comes at a cost. It harbours a sense of futility and feeling that life is not worth living, and carries a painful aloneness and grief at having to live life separated off from important parts of the self.

When working with deprived and disadvantaged sectors of the population, these 'failure situations' may be being constantly revived in the present, catapulting people into the past. This can make it very difficult to differentiate between past and present since both are operating. This may be one important reason why psychotherapists find it so difficult to work with working-class and poor people. For example, people who have been neglected and uncared for in childhood may find these memories being revived when living in an environment of urban decay and neglect where their needs are constantly being ignored. This makes it important for practitioners and therapists to acknowledge and work with the impact of painful events located in the present as well as the impact of suffering experienced in the past. The pull among human beings to return to earlier 'points of failure' is profound. However, this can easily be confused and seen as people bringing suffering on themselves. The lines are difficult to draw between masochism, addictive behaviour and returning to earlier painful experiences in order to bring about repair and recovery. But whatever drives this return to the past, it may provide an important opportunity for recovery. However, this possibility may be severely limited or inhibited by the impact of negative external, environmental factors over which people may have little control.

The successful return to earlier *failure situations* cannot be achieved unless we can create *favourable conditions*. The purpose of this return or *regression* is not to bring about change on a one-off basis although this is important. Nor is it to create an unhealthy and disempowering dependency for its own sake. Its purpose is to bring about ongoing and lasting change through 'unfreezing' or freeing-up the developmental process that has become frozen or stuck, in order to revive the innate capacity within human beings towards recovery, reparation, growth and development. Just as exposing a minor wound to the air can produce a spontaneous capacity in the body to heal itself, this theory states that emotional wounds can be healed in a similar way, but only if the body's natural emotional healing process has the capacity and energy to take on the task. The effectiveness of our work can be seen in people feeling able and driven to take on new challenges and to make changes in their lives, motivated by a desire from within themselves, rather than in response to a demand from others.

People whose thoughts and feelings are bound up in the struggle for survival – who feel vulnerable to threats within their external and/or internal world – often do not have the emotional reserves or energy needed to bring about change, no matter how much this is desired and needed. What is needed is an injection of resources from outside, in the form of care and other nurturing experiences, in order to remedy this sense of depletion so that psychic energy can gather strength and become self-generating. To see people's inability to move forward solely in terms of poor or low motivation is a gross simplification. The risks involved in change are many. It exposes people and situations in ways that can feel threatening, frightening and overwhelming. This makes it important to attend to those external factors that inhibit change and people's capacity to move forward – as well as addressing internal forces that inhibit change and development.

Creating 'Favourable Conditions'

Thus, unfreezing the developmental process so that people have the capacity to change their lives involves creating *favourable conditions*. Depending on the organization and the work being undertaken, different *favourable conditions* may be identified. For Womankind these included:

1 creating a *secure setting* – a *holding* or *facilitating environment* (Winnicott)
2 demonstrating a capacity to care and to be reliable, consistent and concerned
3 allowing regression to dependence
4 providing adaptation to need
5 using transitional phenomena
6 attending to external, environmental factors.

It is not possible to describe these concepts in detail beyond illustrating how each factor played a part in creating an environment which enabled 'the tendencies that are at work within the individual' to lead to emotional growth (Winnicott, 1965: 228).

A 'setting that gives confidence' is the context within which some repairing and recovery can take place so that change, growth and emotional development become a possibility. In the case of Womankind, this took the form of re-organizing the layout of the building so that it met women's collective and individual needs. For example, we encouraged women to decorate the project with objects that meant something to them. Some brought in photographs, paintings, figures, cushions, mugs, special teas, whilst others re-arranged the furniture in ways that 'felt right' for them. Our purpose was not to give a good experience by being indulgent or to make Womankind more homely, but to set up a situation where our reliability, consistency and concern enabled women to feel safe and to be less guarded.

The importance of reliability and consistency cannot be overstated, particularly when working with people who have been failed or 'let down' a great deal in the past. In relation to our work at Womankind, this involved regularly analysing the quality of experience that the project provided. For example, we thought a great deal about the kind of welcome women received, ensuring that drinks and the correct biscuits were bought, that the kitchen was tidy and cleared of papers, that the groupwork room had the same favourite cushions and other comforting objects and that the same sense of care, concern, permanence and consistency existed for the coffee period after their group. As groupworkers, our task was to provide a 'setting that gives confidence' in order to ensure that we created a *holding* environment where 'adaptation, concern and reliability, . . . cure in the sense of care' (Winnicott, 1986: 116) could play their part in 'creating the drive towards cure, and towards self-cure if no help is available' (Winnicott, 1965: 222). Our perspective was that unless the group members could begin to relax and to feel secure and safe, their defences would remain 'on guard', ready to react to anything that came their way. This meant that the energy needed for recovery and to bring about change was taken up in this defensive stance. It was for this reason that the setting had to be protected in the ways described.

In terms of attending to external, environmental factors, this often involved trying to ease some of the financial pressure that women were experiencing. Examples include Womankind paying for a telephone to be installed for a young mother we worked with who was severely isolated at home with her baby. In another situation where a mother was living in extreme poverty we regularly negotiated for essential services not to be cut off, and whenever we could, we paid bills in order to ease the financial pressure she was forced to bear. Again, the primary purpose of this work was to provide an adaptation to need as part of a planned therapeutic strategy based on the notion that 'cure at its root means care' (Winnicott, 1986: 112).

Regression

The concept of regression was central to our work at Womankind because it was through this process that change became possible. Indeed, it was our belief that change, growth and development could only become possible through women feeling safe enough to allow themselves to become dependent on us, if only in a limited way. From this perspective, the current trend within health and welfare services to inhibit or to redirect people's dependency needs towards independence can be completely counter-productive and helps to explain why so many patients, clients and service users fail to make progress and to move forward. It is important that this anti-dependency trend is reviewed but not in a way that creates an unhealthy dependency, divorced from any planned therapeutic strategy and approach. As stated earlier, dependency should not be encouraged for its own sake because this could have the effect of immobilizing the individual even further, thereby creating a whole range of additional difficulties.

For Winnicott, a regression or 'organized return to early dependence' becomes possible where there is reliability in the therapeutic setting (Winnicott, 1987: 286). This provides the individual with the opportunity to return to success and failure situations without having to organize the defences to protect the self from further violations. It is worth quoting Winnicott in full in relation to what he saw happening in the regression because of the clear way he describes the progression occurring:

In practice there is a sequence of events:

1   The provision of a setting that gives confidence.
2   Regression of the patient to dependence, with due sense of the risk involved.
3   The patient feeling a new sense of self, and the self hitherto hidden becoming surrendered to the total ego. A new progression of the individual processes which had stopped.
4   An unfreezing of an environmental failure situation.
5   From the new position of ego strength, anger related to the early environmental failure, felt in the present and expressed.
6   Return from regression to dependence, in orderly progress towards independence.
7   Instinctual needs and wishes becoming realizable with genuine vitality and vigour. All this repeated again and again. (Winnicott, 1987: 287)

What I find valuable about this description is that it acknowledges the importance of anger as a part of the recovery process. Several times at Womankind I experienced women shifting from feelings of devastation and defeat at being 'let down' to feelings of absolute rage and fury some time later. They felt very alive in their fury and upon reflection, enjoyed the sense of surprise and spontaneity that they experienced. When thinking about the hardship endured by people from poorer sections of the working class, anger at their predicament seems a wholly appropriate response and one that can be far more fruitful than adding further defeats and failures to the ever-growing list of hurtful experiences and disappointments. However, I know too that most working-class people cannot 'find their anger' because it is not always safe to do so – the *favourable conditions* are not yet in place. This is particularly true for those people living in areas of severe urban decay and neglect, where the odds against their making any progress are enormous, despite the well-intentioned efforts of professionals working in these settings. Some of this difficulty is due to the fact that just as our services are fragmented, so too are our responses. As a result, in recent years there has been little attempt among professionals to attend to the sources of suffering, hardship, deprivation, disadvantage and poverty. Lerner describes this difficulty as 'treating malaria victims in a mosquito-infested swamp. Treating those afflicted is a humane, even a heroic endeavour, but a rather futile one unless there is a simultaneous effort to drain the swamp to prevent new infections' (Lerner, 1972: 6). This criticism is even more damning for those psychotherapists who have positioned themselves in settings where they cannot see the swamp and are too removed even to know of its existence. Where this is the case, Lerner's description of psychotherapy as 'failing to meet their social responsibilities' carries weight (Lerner, 1972: 5). However, this need not be the case.

CONCLUSION

The history of psychotherapy and psychoanalysis is one of change. In relation to the latter, this largely occurred in response to psychoanalysis opening its doors to new and different groups of people. Its reward was to gain new knowledge. For example, Freud originally thought that psycho-analytic treatment could only be effective with hysteria in adults, but his work with phobic patients forced him to revise his views and to 'go beyond former limits' (Freud, 1924: 399). So too did the work of analysts such as Klein and Winnicott in their work with psychotic patients, children and adolescents. With the introduction of each new patient group, psychoanalysis has grown and changed. I want to argue, as Freud did, that the capacity to adapt psychoanalytic techniques to 'new conditions' – 'to alloy the pure gold of analysis plentifully with the copper of direct suggestion' – will be its strength. Psychoanalysis will, as Guntrip noted, become indispensable if its theory and practice continue to evolve to a point where it can 'speak to the human condition . . . able to help others with their struggles to be real persons living meaningful lives' (Guntrip, 1971: 44). For this reason, I see enormous benefits to be gained if, when poor people come knocking on the door, psychoanalysis has the capacity and heart to let them in.

NOTES

I am deeply grateful for the encouragement I have had from my friends, particularly Judy Carver, Robert French and Sue Pollock whose comments and corrections have been invaluable. I would also like to thank Hilary Land, David Quinton, the Child Poverty Action Group for their guidance, and Colleen Heenan and Bruna Seu for their patience in steering this chapter towards publication.

1 The late Donald Winnicott was a paediatrician, psychoanalyst and twice President of the British Psycho-Analytic Society. Barbara Dockar-Drysdale is a psychotherapist and the founder of the Mulberry Bush School for children needing residential psychotherapeutic care. She was for many years a Consultant Psychotherapist to the Cotswold Community for disturbed and deprived adolescent boys and consultant at Womankind.

2 It may be helpful to identify the Registrar General's six socio-economic classes because these are used a great deal in official statistics, particularly health statistics and to highlight the inequalities between rich and poor. They are also useful in illuminating which group of people psychotherapists are most and least likely to work with.

The Registrar General's Classification of Occupation

	Social class	Examples of occupation
I	Professional	Accountant, clergyman, doctor
II	Intermediate	Teacher, farmer, nurse
IIINM	Skilled non-manual	Secretary, shop assistant, sales representative
IIIM	Skilled manual	Bus driver, electrician, miner (underground), cook
IV	Semi-skilled manual	Agricultural worker, assembly worker, postman
V	Unskilled manual	Laundry worker, office cleaner, labourer

Source: Graham (1993)

3 This paper stands in marked contrast to Freud's better-known paper on this subject entitled 'The question of lay analysis' published in 1926.

4 We would have liked to have been able to offer a more comprehensive range of services and to assess, monitor and evaluate the effectiveness of our approach. Both became a possibility in 1995 with the securing of new funding, which included an emphasis on research in order to analyse the effectiveness of our approach over time. However, this opportunity was lost due to severe disagreements with the Womankind Management Committee which resulted in the abrupt dismantling of the groupwork and counselling we were providing. Although the stance that I and others adopted was later vindicated prior to an Industrial Tribunal hearing, and an apology given and a financial settlement agreed, neither I nor any of the groupworkers involved in the exploration described in this chapter were ever allowed to return to work at Womankind again.

REFERENCES

Abbott, P. and Sapsford, R. (1987) *Women and Social Class*. London: Tavistock.

Argyle, M. (1994) *The Psychology of Social Class*. London: Routledge.

Benjamin, J. (1990) *The Bonds of Love*. London: Virago.

Benjamin, J. (1995) *Like Subjects. Like Objects*. London: Yale University Press.

Brennan, T. (ed.) (1989) *Between Feminism and Psychoanalysis*. London: Routledge.

Brown, G. W. and Harris, T. (1978) *Social Origins of Depression*. London: Tavistock.

Brown, M. (ed.) (1983) *The Structure of Disadvantage*. London: Heinemann.

Burack, C. (1994) *The Problem of the Passions: Feminism, Psychoanalysis and Social Theory*. London: New York University Press.

Chodorow, N. J. (1978) *The Reproduction of Mothering: Psychoanalysis and the Sociology of Gender*. Berkeley, CA: University of California Press.

Chodorow, N. J. (1989) *Feminism and Psychoanalytic Theory*. London: Yale University Press.

Chodorow, N. J. (1994) *Femininities Masculinities Sexualities: Freud and Beyond*. London: Free Association.

Dinnerstein, D. (1978) *The Rocking of the Cradle*. London: Souvenir Press.

Dockar-Drysdale, B. (1990) *The Provision of Primary Experience: Winnicottian Work with Children*. London: Free Association.

Doyal, L. (1995) *What Makes Women Sick: Gender and Political Economy of Health*. Basingstoke: Macmillan.

Eichenbaum, L. and Orbach, S. (1982) *Outside in: Inside Out*. Harmondsworth: Penguin.

Ernst, S. and Maguire, M. (eds) (1987) *Living With the Sphinx: Papers from the London Women's Therapy Centre*. London: Women's Press.

Flax, J. (1981) 'The conflict between nurturance and autonomy in mother–daughter relationships and within feminism', in Elizabeth Howell and Marjorie Bayes (eds), *Women and Mental Health*. New York: Basic Books.

Flax, J. (1991) *Thinking Fragments: Psychoanalysis, Feminism and Postmodernism in the Contemporary West.* Berkeley, CA: University of California Press.

Flax, J. (1993) *Disputed Subjects: Essays on Psychoanalysis, Politics and Philosophy.* London: Routledge.

Freud, S. (1914) 'On the history of the psycho-analytic movement', Penguin Freud Library, vol. 15. Harmondsworth: Penguin.

Freud, S. (1924) *Collected Papers* (vol. 11). London: Hogarth Press.

Freud, S. (1926) 'The question of lay analysis', Penguin Freud Library, vol. 15. Harmondsworth: Penguin.

Gilligan, C. (1982) *In a Different Voice: Psychological Theory and Women's Development.* Cambridge MA: Harvard University Press.

Glendinning, C. and Millar, J. (1992) *Women and Poverty in Britain in the 1990s.* Hemel Hempstead: Harvester Wheatsheaf.

Graham, H. (1993) *Hardship and Health in Women's Lives.* London: Harvester Wheatsheaf.

Guntrip, H. (1971) 'The promise of psychoanalysis', in Bernard Landis and Edward S. Tanber (eds), *In the Name of Life: Essays in Honour of Erich Fromm.* London: Holt, Rinehart & Winston.

Jordan, J. V., Kaplan, A. G., Miller, J. B., Shiver, I. P. and Surrey, J. L. (1991) *Women's Growth and Connection: Writings from the Stone Center.* New York: Guilford Press.

Lerner, B. (1972) *Therapy in the Ghetto.* London: Johns Hopkins University Press.

McLeod, J. D. and Kessler, R. C. (1990) 'Socioeconomic status differences in vulnerability to undesirable life events', *Journal of Health and Social Behaviour,* 31: 162–72.

Miller, J. B. (ed.) (1973) *Psychoanalysis and Women.* Harmondsworth: Penguin.

Miller, J. B. (1976) *Towards a New Psychology of Women.* Harmondsworth: Penguin.

Mitchell, J. (1974) *Psychoanalysis and Feminism.* Harmondsworth: Penguin.

Mitchell, J. (1984) *Women: the Longest Revolution: Essays in Feminism, Literature and Psychoanalysis.* London: Virago.

Office of Population Censuses and Surveys (1985) *General Household Survey.* London: HMSO.

Oppenheim, C. (1993) *Poverty: the Facts.* London: Child Poverty Action Group.

Oppenheim, C. and Harker, L. (1996) *Poverty: the Facts,* 3rd edn. London: Child Poverty Action Group.

Pearce, D. (1978) 'The feminization of poverty: women, work and welfare', *Urban and Social Change Review,* February.

Sayer, J. (1991) *Mothering Psychoanalysis.* London: Hamish Hamilton.

Townsend, P. (1993) *The International Analysis of Poverty.* Hemel Hempstead: Harvester Wheatsheaf.

Townsend, P. and Davidson, N. (1992) *Inequalities in Health: the Black Report.* Harmondsworth: Penguin.

Trevithick, P. (1988) 'Unconsciousness raising with working class women', in Sue Krzowski and Pat Land (eds), *In Our Experience: Workshops at the Women's Therapy Centre.* London: Women's Press.

Trevithick, P. (1993) 'Surviving childhood sexual and physical abuse: the experience of two women of mixed Irish-English parentage', in Harry Ferguson, Robbie Gilligan and Ruth Torode (eds), *Surviving Childhood Adversity: Issues for Policy and Practice.* Dublin: Social Studies Press.

Trevithick, P. (1995) '"Cycling over Everest": Groupwork with Depressed Women', *Groupwork,* 8 (1), Summer.

Winnicott, D. W. (1965) *The Maturational Process and the Facilitating Environment: Studies in the Theory of Emotional Development.* London: Hogarth Press/The Institute of Psycho-Analysis (reprinted 1990, London: Karnac Books).

Winnicott, D. W. (1971) *Playing and Reality.* London: Routledge.

Winnicott, D. W. (1984) *Deprivation and Delinquency.* London: Tavistock/Routledge.

Winnicott, D. W. (1986) *Home is Where We Start From.* Harmondsworth: Penguin.

Winnicott, D. W. (1987) *Through Paediatrics to Psycho-Analysis.* London: Hogarth Press and

The Institute of Psycho-Analysis (first published in 1958 as *Collected Papers: Through Paediatrics to Psycho-Analysis*, London: Tavistock; reprinted 1992, London: Karnac Books).

Wright, E. (ed.) (1992) *Feminism and Psychoanalysis: a Critical Dictionary*. Oxford: Blackwell.

8

The Rhythm Model

Jocelyn Chaplin

In this chapter I explore the rhythm model (Chaplin, 1988); I argue that the usefulness of the rhythm model for feminist psychotherapy is that it provides an alternative to dualistic and hierarchical models of relating and thinking. In this way the rhythm model shares some of the fundamental ideas of postmodernism and post-structuralism such as the equal valuing of difference and an awareness that there are no single absolute truths or even therapy theories that explain everything. Meanings are fluid and not fixed in stone. But perhaps there *is* a subtle order in constant rhythmic change. This order can be seen as a striving to balance, to equalize. The striving towards equality at all levels is an ongoing activity, not a rigid structure to be idealized as a new grand narrative, totalizing explanation or religion. But by valuing this striving we do not mean that anything goes or any behaviour is acceptable. Such extreme relativism is often associated with some postmodernisms.

This chapter itself uses the rhythm model of seeing opposites as interconnected. It is both practical and theoretical, both critical and accepting, seeing both liberational equalizing factors and oppressive hierarchical ones in the feminisms, psychotherapies and postmodernisms that we look at.

ROOTS OF THE RHYTHM MODEL

Life is rhythm. From the long slow rhythms of the seasons and the even longer rise and fall of empires, to the faster rhythms of the heartbeat and even speedier vibrations of light waves, everything is rhythmic. Growing up in West Africa I was surrounded by the sounds of drumming and the sense of a closer connection between lifestyles and the rhythms of nature than we had in the West. Perhaps it was because I couldn't dance that I became fascinated by the intellectual concept of rhythm from an early age. My journey of exploration took me through Jungian ideas of the self-regulation of the psyche in which the various opposites within, such as 'masculine' and 'feminine', strive to balance and integrate. It took me to philosophers from Heraclitus (Kahn, 1979) to Hegel, to revolutionaries such as Marx and Engels and even Mao. Then there were the spiritual traditions of Taoism with its idea of continual change in nature and in

Figure 8.1   *Medusa* © *Jocelyn Chaplin 1988*

human relations, from high to low and back again. I explored all the related scientific studies that I could find and the new ways of thinking in modern physics described by Capra and others. Nature is full of rhythms. Everything is vibrating and changing. Yet our models of thinking have been so rigid, linear and hierarchical.

Often it has seemed as though only the poets and artists have kept rhythm thinking alive in male Western culture. But women everywhere have also continued to 'live the rhythms' through our menstrual cycles and closeness to birth and child rearing which requires such fluidity of response. Yet as women have been denigrated, so has rhythmical thinking and being. So my journey took me not only into political feminism but also into goddess spirituality, and an increased reverence for the rhythms of nature as well as those in our bodies. I discovered Starhawk (1982), Stone (1976), Gimbutas (1974), etc., who all write about the long-lost traditions of symbolic systems of spiritual meanings *not* based on the phallus/patriarchal male hierarchy. These range from pre-Christian African religions practised today throughout the diaspora, to the second millennium BC spirituality of Minoan Crete. Many women are reclaiming such symbols as the double axe and the goddess, snake or spiral and using them in art and ritual today.

Figure 8.2   *Sulis* © *Jocelyn Chaplin 1989*

Some feminists have seen this approach as leading to 'essentialism', which is the assumption that objects or people (e.g. women) as a category have an essential, inherent nature which can be discovered. They fear that we are implying that women are somehow naturally closer to nature or that nature is somehow essentially 'feminine'. These fears have understandably been present in the feminist therapy world in which goddess spirituality has been viewed with suspicion. After all, we as therapists are especially aware of the deep intrusion of patriarchal religious symbolism into women's unconscious, disempowering us and adding to the inequalities we suffer politically and economically.

For many feminists the response has been a total rejection of any kind of religion or spirituality. But others of us have felt that creating our own more liberational symbolic systems to replace the patriarchal ones is as important as deconstructing and transgressing/rebelling against them. Images of goddesses are not used in the same way as the old grand narratives or stories about a dominant father God giving out perfect truth. Goddess spirituality is rarely treated as a set of absolute truths and even its images are not seen as representations of reality but as having constantly shifting meanings. Its underlying model/form is rhythmic, fluid, ever-changing, rather than the rigid hierarchies of patriarchal religions. It also fits more comfortably into a postmodern world which has rejected grand narratives.

However there was a tendency in this phase of my thinking, and in my books *The Mass Psychology of Thatcherism* (Chaplin, 1985), *Feminist Counselling in Action* (Chaplin, 1989) and *Love in an Age of Uncertainty* (Chaplin, 1993b), to equate the rhythm model with female/feminine aspects of life. And hierarchical models got simplistically associated with the male/masculine, thereby keeping a gender dualism that could limit the usefulness of the ideas. In the past few years I have become increasingly aware of the complexity and multi-layered ways in which underlying structures such as hierarchies are expressed and transgressed or rebelled against. I no longer see everything female as superior and even question the very concept of male/female except in a purely biological sense. 'Queer' politics is now talking about a third gender, and indeed why not multiple and fluid gender identities? And yet there are still the realities of historical and present structures of oppression, and unconscious stereotyping still runs very deep.

Feminist insights and strategies are still vital for redressing massive imbalances of power between the genders. But on another level feminism also has a role in questioning *all* rigid hierarchies in thought as well as in action, whether these are connected to gender or not. This anti-hierarchical aspect of feminism led me to look at its links and similarities with postmodernist, post-structuralist and deconstructionist thinking as explored largely by academics in France and America, and by activists on the ground questioning white middle-class ideas of feminism and other forms of radical politics. This search has also led me to questions about my practice as a feminist psychotherapist.

THE RHYTHM MODEL AND POSTMODERNISM

I began exploring writers such as Irigaray and Spivak, Lacan and Derrida, who don't immediately appear to have much connection with the rhythm model. However the whole deconstruction project involves analysing 'systems of binary oppositions' in texts. This means looking at the ways in which one opposite (e.g. male) is implied to be superior to, or dominating, the other (e.g. female). The opposites that they are most concerned with are those in a hierarchical relationship, for example the use of 'he' to stand in for all human beings, thus implying the inferior status of 'she'.

A text can be anything which can be read for meaning, from written material to pictorial images and cultures in general. While most academics have looked at written texts, the conversations (verbal and non-verbal) of psychotherapy can also be seen as texts. So we can think of deconstructing the therapeutic text. Indeed, psychotherapy itself can be about

Figure 8.3   *Yemaya in Glastonbury* © *Jocelyn Chaplin 1988*

helping clients deconstruct unhelpful personal and socially conditioned texts, patterns of thinking or attitudes. Perhaps there may also be a therapeutic aim to loosen up inner hierarchies and have a more fluid and accepting approach to life as described in *Feminist Counselling in Action* (Chaplin, 1988). So it seems that some feminisms, some psychotherapies, some postmodernisms, just like the rhythm project, are basically concerned with dissolving hierarchical thinking and relating, and putting more fluid, equalizing forms in their place.

This process may start with turning upside down the existing hierarchies, like putting 'she' before 'he' as in s/he or even, as a first stage, asserting some notion of female superiority. But this is all part of a longer-term, wider balancing process, the rhythms of equalization.

I began to ask myself about my own inner hierarchies and how my assertion of the superiority of 'female ways' was a kind of overcompensation for feeling inferior. It was largely reactive. Was I still rebelling against Daddy? A time may have come for feminist psychotherapists like myself to question the feeling that we are always in positions of permanent transgression, rebellion. For example, Irigaray and others have been involved in such projects as struggling to turn Lacan's construct of the female signifier (central symbol) as lack (emptiness, gap, void) into a positive. Instead I prefer to adopt an ever-changing space both between and inclusive of opposites in which the value of the rhythmic way is taken for granted. It can be expected to become central, not peripheral, to mainstream life and thought. The rhythm model would not only be experienced in opposition to the 'masculine' symbolic system with its primary signifier as the phallus.

PRIESTESSES OF LOVE

I am now going to focus on a particularly important text for feminist psychotherapists. It is the speech that Plato puts into the mouth of Socrates during the famous symposium (trans., 1989). Socrates is quoting his teacher, the priestess/philosopher Diotima. Despite the distortions by Plato's own hierarchical thinking and those of scholars after him I believe that this speech is one of the few surviving indicators of an ancient 'female-inspired' philosophical and psychological tradition going back at least to Minoan Crete and probably much earlier. It is a tradition based on actual bodily human experience such as sexual love and giving birth, grounded in the rhythms of nature and rhythmic thinking. Diotima laughingly criticizes the dualistic divisions the male philosophers make at the symposium between, for example, ugly and beautiful. But it also places central importance on the place of love in human development. This is a love that widens from a narrow obsession with one beautiful body to the ability to love everyone, and to both experience and create beautiful things, including ideas, all the time. This is an aim similar to those in the mystical traditions of most religions, yet this 'enlightenment' is achieved through the body and nature, not by getting away from them. Irigaray (1989b) focuses on the early part of Diotima's speech and her laughter at the idea of love as an eternal, great God. Rather she sees love as the mediator of everything, 'never completed, always evolving' (Irigaray, 1989b). Love is the energy that constantly flows between poles/opposites always in motion, in becoming and never totally unifying or transcending them. Irigaray (1989b) is also positive about Diotima's teaching about learning to connect with this love as it starts with physical feelings, but sees her becoming hierarchical to fit in with Plato. Nye (1989) sees it differently and describes Diotima's process of psycho/spiritual growth as a widening of the love to more and more people and to the order of nature itself and as reflected in just human laws too. She thinks that Diotima is also talking about living in Beauty as constant creativity, rather than as a final attainment of some perfect form of Beauty as Plato saw it. Nye (1989) believed that Irigaray misread the speech because she saw Diotima as marginalized as herself and having to fit in with male philosophers. It was an ahistorical reading of the text. Nye (1989) recognized that there was a long tradition of female philosopher/

priestesses going back to Minoan Crete at least who would still have been respected in Plato's time. Yet what Plato and others did was to take this 'wisdom' and turn it into a hierarchy of values with the body and sensations at the bottom and abstract ideas at the top. Western civilization has been built on this hierarchy ever since. This text stands at a turning point in Western history.

> The candidate for this initiation cannot . . . begin too early to devote himself to the beauties of the body. First of all he will fall in love with the beauty of one individual body so that his passion will give rise to noble discourse. Next he must consider how nearly related the beauty of any one body is to the beauty of any other . . . he must set himself to be the lover of every lovely body . . . Next he must grasp that the beauties of the body are nothing as to the beauties of the soul, so that whenever he meets with spiritual loveliness, even in the husk of an unlovely body, he will find it beautiful to fall in love with and cherish. (Plato, 1989: 210a)

Is this not very much what we as psychotherapists do? We learn to expand and direct our love in the moment to whatever client we are with. I have often said to students that therapy can be like being in love for 50 minutes at a time with no expectations. Bell (1992) goes even further in what she calls her carnivalesque reading of the text from the position of the philosophic clitoris (Spivak, 1988). She argues that it implies that spirituality is in and through the body. Bell (1992) sees the idea of the sacred prostitute representing and actually embodying this wisdom. It is through bodily heart feelings that we can come to the wisdom of loving everything, being in a state of lovingness. Before the profession of prostitution became degraded it is likely that it was the holiest of activities which only spiritually developed people could practise. Love and even sexual energy would have been used to heal. It is unlikely that such developed women would have simply been the playthings of men's desires. The ability to love at will is probably one of the most fully human but also most difficult of spiritual achievements. Ways of achieving this were probably built into the initiation processes of many ancient female-valuing cultures. Today feminist psychotherapists are reviving these ancient ways of thinking and being that were once so central to human life before the patriarchal hierarchies took over.

HIDDEN HIERARCHIES

Even as I sit down to write this chapter I find myself strangely full of fear, the kind of fear that hierarchies create, the fear of a superior authority. But in this case I am afraid of academic feminists who are supposed to be my sisters. Do I think they might attack me for being too essentialist, too humanist, or even just not feminist enough, as if there was just one

Figure 8.4   *Aphrodite © Jocelyn Chaplin 1990*

superior kind of feminism??? As a practising psychotherapist, am I part of the hierarchical split between mind and body, thought and action, the practitioner and the academic? Do I fear that the academic thinker will look down on me, as a mere practitioner? Of course I don't consciously believe that academics are in any way superior to other kinds of workers, but something of the old patriarchal split must still be lodged in my unconscious. The word 'patriarchy' literally means 'rule of the fathers' and there are few places so clearly dedicated to this rule as academia.

But the hidden hierarchies in feminisms are nothing compared to those I've experienced in the world of psychotherapy. For example, psychodynamic therapy based largely on Freudian theory is still generally seen as superior to humanistic therapy mainly based on Eastern philosophies and 1950s and 1960s liberalism. Freud is seen as superior to Jung, materialism superior to spirituality, psychotherapy superior to counselling and long-term therapy superior to short-term. Postmodern and pluralistic ideas of different but equally valid perspectives do not seem to have reached far into this world. Many therapy techniques or theories are still being proclaimed as *the truth*, the grand narrative or story that explains it all.

However, in practice many therapists and counsellors actually do weave in and out of the different approaches depending on what is appropriate for particular clients. In their everyday therapy work they probably unconsciously use the rhythm model more often than the hierarchical one.

Yet we are all deeply affected by hierarchical dualistic models of thought, and even in this chapter I am aware of feeling tripped up time after time by unintended dualisms. They are embedded in our very language. Sometimes it seems that the harder we try to get away from them, the more intense the tension between ideals and realities (another dualism) becomes. But like most of us I live day to day with that creative and exciting tension which is inevitably present too in my therapy practice.

PERSONAL PRACTICE

As society is changing so fast we all need to learn to live in uncertainty, in a state of flux. But it is not easy. Our psychologies were developed over thousands of years of much slower social change. Perhaps the teachers and therapists of the future are going to be those who have been forced to live on the boundaries, on the margins, outside mainstream society, people in exile, people between two cultures, outsiders. I probably found the rhythm model useful because it gave a form to my own feelings of being always 'in between' – African and European, middle class and working class, etc. In the same way that the rhythm model is always fluctuating across and around borders, neither in nor out, but also both in and out, in flux, undecided, so my own life has felt like living on the edges of things.

I have been neither in nor out of academia, but both at different times and in different ways. Agreeing to write this chapter and other books in male languages is being in. But trying to create my own female languages, symbols and myths is being *out*. Yet even while being involved in this creation I am aware that I am still unconsciously invaded by the deeply entrenched male symbolic order.

I have been neither totally in nor totally out of the patriarchy, but both. I never married legally but have been passionately heterosexual, often giving lovers far too much power. I never belonged to a man but never chose to live completely apart from them either. I have always felt a bit like Lilith, Adam's first wife, who was banished to the desert for refusing to lie beneath her husband. Instead she consorts with daemons on the shores of the Red Sea and is blamed for men's wet dreams. Yet I can honestly say that I prefer the loneliness of the desert to belonging to the male-symbolic city.

However, of course I do also long to belong. So I search for and sometimes find oases in the desert. One of these was humanistic psychology.

Figure 8.5   *Yearning for the Moon* © *Jocelyn Chaplin 1985*

CLINICAL PRACTICE

Humanistic Connections and Contradictions

Humanistic psychology grew out of the ideas of the Enlightenment and the more recent postwar optimism of the USA. Its values are largely based on Western liberalism with all its contradictions, now being questioned by postmodernists and neo-conservatives. Some of this questioning is really important for humanistic psychotherapists and counsellors to explore. However, there may also be some values of the Enlightenment, such as freedom and equality, justice and dignity, that need to be retained. But such values can be looked at afresh within a more complex and changeable framework for thinking and acting. Some postmodernists seem to be in danger of making the same totalizing, grand gestures that they criticize by throwing out absolutely everything about the Enlightenment. Even their talk of the end of history is a despairing, nihilistic approach to life. Perhaps it largely developed in deliberate (dualistic) opposition to the over-optimistic humanistic tradition.

However, some aspects of humanistic psychology do deserve closer critical examination. They have probably only escaped it because of the hierarchical thinking of academia in which humanistic psychology is not even seen as worthy of such scrutiny.

Firstly, there is often a simplistic belief in a single unitary self that is self-contained, self-directed and self-motivated. These single selves may be seen as ultimately equal, as all having human worth for simply existing. But this approach tends to deny the complex relationships both within and between us, and the social, historical, economic factors affecting us all. Such denial can lead to an acceptance of hidden hierarchies and patterns of domination, for example between men and women. It could be called a kind of naive indivualism. However there have always been some humanistic psychologists, e.g. Rowan, who have been aware of structural issues, and recent interest in subpersonalities has encouraged many to appreciate more the fragmented and complex nature of these things we call our *selves*.

Secondly, humanistic psychology can also be deeply hierarchical through its belief in individual self-directedness from a lower place to a higher one. There are often clear goals such as self-actualization which are then generalized to be the aim of *all* human beings. There may be an implicit or explicit hierarchy of human needs or values: for example, Maslow's, that puts physical needs, even love, *lower* than the very individualistic needs for self-esteem and self-actualization. If people are encouraged to feel fully responsible for not achieving these goals it could result in self-blame, low self-esteem, inadequacy, the very things that many clients come into therapy for. The needs and values of this generalized human are usually based on those of the white, middle-class males who are still mainly the movement's leaders. Because of the lack of structural awareness mentioned above, there is also often insufficient appreciation of the far-reaching effects of gender, class, race and other differences on individuals' ability to self-actualize. That is, assuming self-actualization as a common goal.

These dangers, especially in relation to gender blindness, are well described by Waterhouse (1993). She wrote an important article questioning the role of person–centred humanistic principles in the context of rape crisis counselling. Her conclusions were that the humanistic tradition has 'failed to address the specific problems that women face in their search for personhood and agency'. Although I agree that gender needs addressing far more within humanistic psychology, I find the above statement too totalizing and general. Far too many women *have* been helped to 'personhood' by humanistic practitioners for her conclusions to be valid. It is important to distinguish between humanistic theory and its practical implications in humanistic psychotherapy.

In many ways the theory of humanistic psychology fits in better with postmodernist thinking than other therapy traditions such as object relations or behaviourism. One important feature of postmodernism is that it is pluralistic, or accepts different approaches as equally valid. We have already described how most humanistic psychology practitioners today actually do use a pluralist method of working. Not only does this include a wide range of traditional therapy skills but they may also use meditation or guided fantasies that are more associated with 'the New Age'. Generally, approaches are geared to the particular client at a particular time in their life. For some this might mean strengthening their sense of a centred self and for others it might mean letting it go and becoming more a part of the flow. Like Diotima's description of love, it can be a constant process of co-creation, always in between. When the creative therapy moment requires it, there may need to be a concept of the autonomous centred self to help a person feel powerful enough to make even a minor decision in their life. It could be seen as a useful and appropriate myth. The therapist does not need to believe in the unitary, permanent self as a theory, simply as a strategy in the practice of co-creation.

Another of Waterhouse's criticisms was that humanistic psychology always has 'an essentially harmonic view of social interaction' (1993). Yet gestalt psychotherapy and psychodrama, as just two examples, focus very much on difference and conflict both within and between people. There may be a mixing up of levels here. Some therapists, especially those involved in the more spiritual end of humanistic psychology, may have a theory of the universe being essentially harmonic, with humans striving towards being a part of that. But in practice most of us are working with the realities of conflict.

In practice also, a high proportion of those very person-centred therapists and counsellors that Waterhouse (1993) suggests might not be politically aware, actually work in the public sector, often for very low salaries. They are found throughout the health sector, in the education service, in bereavement counselling, etc. I have personally found more political awareness of the structures of injustice among those practitioners than among psychoanalysts, for example. Often the very reason that counsellors and psychotherapists work in the public sector is that they want to change society towards greater equality, albeit sometimes from an unconsciously patronizing position. The person-centred approach is essentially to focus attention on the clients to encourage them to speak, open up and feel valued, often so that they can deal more effectively with those very social problems that Waterhouse (1993) fears they don't care about.

Rescuing clients by offering too much advice too soon and/or making too many interpretations could detract from their self-esteem. Counsellors are often especially aware that women are devalued and constantly being advised and interpreted by men, and try not to replay that role. But there are few rigid rules. A genuine respect for the person helps keep a balance between total emphasis on the client's responsibility and autonomy *and* a recognition of the social and political factors affecting her. If those social and political factors are over-emphasized she can start to feel like a hopeless victim. Once again it is not one approach *or* the other but *both* in creative co-creation.

Humanistic psychology, like the closely connected New Age and self-help approaches, is full of contradictions. As we have seen, they all have both liberatory and dominatory aspects, social radicalism and neo-conservatism, beliefs in equality and in hierarchies. Many writers in these fields are socially concerned but within a context of naive liberalism. Few have engaged fully with either feminism or black studies, Marxism or socialism. And yet there are, perhaps surprisingly, commonalities with, as well as differences from, feminism.

As Waterhouse (1993) points out, humanistic psychology stresses the uniqueness of each individual while feminism emphasizes women's commonality. Yet these approaches do not need to be seen as hierarchical binary opposites and can *both* be important for a client. So it is always more complex than such simple oppositions would suggest. In the same way, changing oneself and changing society are not in either/or opposition. There is an ever-flowing rhythm between them at many levels and layers. However, Waterhouse (1993) does go on to recognize that the person-centred approach and the feminist one do have much in common. They both stress equality between therapist and client, value emotion as much as intellect, and are concerned 'to eradicate dualistic thinking'.

To relate these ideas to practice I am going to introduce a particular client who is both fictional and true, made up of many people that I have worked with. We will call her Laura. She is white, 29, and comes from a working-class background in the north of England. She came to London in her early 20s to work as a secretary, then worked her way up to a senior position as a successful buyer for a large retail manufacturer. Laura is very interested in alternative medicine and it was her acupuncturist who suggested that she might try psychotherapy. She presents herself elegantly in a dark, well-cut suit, smiling nervously. She explains that she has come because of anxiety attacks, but it is soon clear that she has been taking on far too much responsibility from an early age and now at work and at home. Laura does not get enough nurturing for herself and her self-esteem is low, although she appears confident on the surface. I see that there are going to be many different levels to work on and a range of techniques and theories which will be of potential use to her. These vary from teaching her to manage anxiety through meditation and relaxation methods, to regression and a lot of initial holding work with her very unsafe-feeling inner baby.

But at first it seems most appropriate to focus on her in a broadly person-centred style with a few directives to encourage her to talk about herself rather than others and to say precisely how she felt or feels in the present. Laura has little sense of her own core, but does have a well-developed false self which she imagines is her 'real self'. The more that she learns to focus on what she is actually feeling in the here and now, the stronger becomes her sense of existing and mattering. She needs this sense of existing before she even begins to explore the conflicting frag-ments of her unconscious and the mother transference which happens in the sessions. For Laura, a feeling of being a unitary, centred self who can have direction over her own life is a neccessary strategic in her complex process of becoming. This is not becoming a pre-defined particular or universal human being, through having set goals. Nor is it about finding some pre-existing 'real self' just waiting to be discovered. No, the kind of becoming I work with in therapy is open-ended, continuously co-creative, with no fixed end or goal. But Laura was not ready to fully engage in this process until she had at least some sense of herself as an existing, valued subject. This need to feel as if one were a unitary self-directed subject is often a necessary stage, especially for women.

On the surface Laura had benefited greatly from feminism, and was independent and financially successful beyond the wildest dreams of her grandmother. But she was still essentially identifying herself as an object of others' subjectivities, desires and goals. She was actually passively fitting in with the demands of the phallocentric, achievement-crazy 1990s patriarchy. To begin with, at least, I decided not to use a psychoanalytic approach that would not help with these factors. It was her first experience of therapy. It was therefore appropriate to talk to her initially in a warm and friendly way rather than to simply sit and wait for the transference to arise. I believe that it is important to allow the outside world into the sessions and to value events outside the room. But in all kinds of therapy, respectful, equalizing human contact seems to be the key to growth and transformation.

However, after several months of working humanistically, I did begin to point out to her that ways in which she was reacting to me might remind her of her relationship with her mother. Laura had always wanted to protect her alcoholic mother and couldn't trust her to be strong and available for her as a child. So of course she tried to protect me and took a long time to trust me and know that I wouldn't abandon her. I started to see her twice a week eventually and this intense and often painful relationship became the main focus of our work. However, this new focus did not stop me from frequently referring to both gender and class issues in relation to her problems. I also used such gestalt techniques as talking to a chair when she began to get angry with her real mother. I do find using the transference an extremely useful approach, but see it as one skill among many, not enough to base my whole practice on. Yet I also have to watch my own tendency to slip into the hierarchical binary oppositions of humanistic versus psychodynamic psychotherapies. As with perhaps the majority of practitioners today, the split is not there in my actual practice but rears its ugly head in theoretical discussions or supervisory situations.

The Myth of the Universal Human

We have already noted the dangers of this concept in its denial of inequalities and other differences. Yet perhaps it can sometimes be a useful *strategic* concept for political change in the same way that the concept of a unitary self can be useful in psychotherapy at a certain stage. Elam (1994) and Spivak (1988) talk about this way of seeing, especially in relation to the 'dangerous' concept of the universal woman. Without a concept of women in general being oppressed within patriarchal structures, many of us might find it difficult to act. The complexity of the oppressive situation could easily paralyse us. Yet we can still act politically from what Elam (1994) calls 'groundless solidarity' in spite of differences between women and a more uncertain set of beliefs. The ideals of human rights as well as women's rights can play strategic roles in equalizing societies and redressing social injustice. But we do not have to believe that universal Western middle-class males stand in for everyone else. However, the Enlightenment concept of the universal man created by those Western males did bring us the end of slavery, and votes for women. And it is still needed in many different contexts throughout the world. We still need to use concepts such as justice, respect and dignity and I believe equality too. These ideas have been labelled as constructs of the Enlightenment by some postmodernist writers and thrown out with everything else. Yet I see that the striving for equality through deconstucting hierarchical binary opposites actually underlies many of the postmodernist projects. That little word *equality* has however been criticized for its political simplicity and the way that so many associate it with the idea of 'sameness'. It is true that for some women becoming equal has in many respects been seen as becoming like men. Yet when we talk of the constant struggle of equalizing and dissolving binary oppositions in the very fabric of our thought, we are in some sense continuing the Enlightenment project. We are showing how deeply inequality lurks in our language and thought. But today we are both theoretically analysing inequalities and practising equalizing in far more complex and politically and psychologically sophisticated ways than the theorists of the French Revolution could have imagined.

In psychotherapy too it is vital to see all clients as equally valuable human beings. This deep respect for their souls, if not always for their actions, is essential for building the framework within which the fluid rhythmic interplay of co-creation can take place most effectively. The concept of 'soul' can also be seen as a strategic idea. In the same way the thought that everyone is on their (equally valid) soul's journey is useful. We need to create these new, and very ancient, stories to tell ourselves. Another such story is that of the essentially *ungendered* soul existing in a different space/time dimension, taking on different physical and cultural forms at different times. Each lifetime can then be thought of as giving the soul particular tasks to achieve, perhaps to do with such general human themes as power or love. This kind of story helps give our own and our client's lives meaning now that the grand narratives of religions and political ideologies often no longer do.

After we have deconstructed all those grand narratives such as Marxism or Christianity, what have we left? Some say romance. Others say joy or

Figure 8.6   *Ariadne* © *Jocelyn Chaplin 1989*

sexual ecstasy. But for most of us there also has to be meaning, meaning for each person in interconnection with others, meaning in relation to the environment. These meanings need not be fixed. They are fluid and changeable, strategic and useful, appropriate to the moment and not fixed in stone. Even just properly listening to another person telling their story is giving it and them meaning, value and significance. Making sense out of apparently random life events gives them meaning.

It can also be useful to create or re-use old myths and stories so long as we know that they are basically mythical. We can even live 'as if' they were true. However, we have to be careful with this process. I believe that some myths are more useful than others for helping rather than hindering the equalizing processes in individuals and in society.

I have personally found many of the myths around goddess-orientated cultures of the past like Minoan Crete especially useful. In these cultures, as Lucy Goodison (1990) has pointed out, it seems that nature's cycles and rhythms gave enough meaning to life in themselves. This resonates with many people today who reject religion but feel deep affinities with nature. The Goddess and God forms can be seen just as vehicles for the energies to come through. I have written about the love goddesses in particular in *Enter the Wild Woman* (Chaplin 1993a) and *Love in an Age of Uncertainty* (Chaplin, 1993b). But it is always important to remember that the myths and the society in which they develop or change are very interconnected. Most of the Greek myths, for example, changed over the years as the patriarchy took over. The familiar classical ones are generally much less empowering to women than the earlier versions. Jung helped to bring the use of myth in a flexible way into the field of psychotherapy. But unfortunately some Jungians do use his archetypal images as if they were universal and ahistorical.

Yet we cannot deny that there is some physical common humanity. There are more genetic similarities in the human race than there are between races or genders. At the very least we are all born, grow and die. Most of us still spend around nine months in a mother's womb and then are dependent on adults for many years. We could go further like Rorty (1989) and say that we need to learn to see others as 'us' not 'them'. He also argues that the similarities such as our shared experience of pain and humiliation are much more important than the differences. Indeed, in workshops that I have led on issues such as race and gender, a starting point has often been to get participants to re-experience a time when they felt put down and humiliated. Even the most confident of white, middle-class males can usually access such a memory.

The Myth of the Real Self

We have already touched on this problematic concept several times, but there is a particularly good discussion on this in Jane Flax's (1990) book. She argues that, despite an appreciation of a fluid view of human nature, there is a need for a sense of a core self. She refers to Winnicott who describes this 'true self' in terms that have 'many of the characteristics of the Postmodern decentred one, but fewer of the deficiencies' (Flax, 1990). This core self is contrasted with the overly rigid intellectual controlling false self which is just the kind of self targeted by postmodernist critiques.

This core self is also the kind of self that most humanistic psychologists would be working towards. It would be a spontaneous 'being in relation', always creating itself, with the body, mind and soul interconnected and in tune with the environment. It is actually a process rather than a thing. 'Core' is a misleading image.

It is also important not to see the self as a pre-existing thing to be found or discovered, as can sometimes be the implicit understanding in psychotherapy. It is constantly in creation and in co-creation with others and the environment. It is always becoming and never ending. It is made up of ever-changing relationships in moving rhythms inside and outside and between and neither. Past and present also interweave.

This co-creation involves learning to know and accept *all* of our multiple selves, trying to exclude nothing. Yet however hard we work at making the unconscious conscious, at accepting the unacceptable, at loving the whole of ourselves, it is probably impossible not to exclude something. For example, in my work with Laura, accepting her angry side was a slow but vital process. Yet there were depths of rage at her mother that she never fully faced. The longer we worked, the more unaccepted bits of her came to light. They included the frightened child, the furious woman and the part of her that longed for children. The task was not to integrate all these into one mushy whole, but rather to have all these aspects of her out 'on the playing field'.

This self is not about the arrogant I of the Enlightenment either. It is not a controller, a boss or an isolated genius who is not a part of others. The dissolution of this kind of I or Ego is part of most mystical and New Age thinking. It includes letting go of one's pride and sense of separation and superiority/inferiority and can result in a strong feeling of connectedness and even mystical identity with others. This can be a useful state to be in as a therapist but must not be confused with a symbiotic merging born out of a need not to grow up. In therapy the ability to empathize comes from a strong core self able to connect with the client without merging. Through this empathy I 'become' the client and then return to my sense of separate self, then I 'become' her again in a rhythm, until there is only the rhythm. A new presence, a new energy, a new connection has been made. The therapy room then becomes like Winnicott's transitional space of neither subject nor object. In another discourse it would be called a sacred space.

CONCLUSIONS

To live rhythmically is to live with uncertainty, undecidedness, forever open, in process and unfinished. This would probably be too much to cope with for humans brought up on certainties and hierarchies. That is, unless firstly it is all given meaning as discussed earlier, and secondly it is fuelled by love. This love in its fullest form is incompatible with fear. No wonder some postmodernists think that the only hope is romance. But romantic love is so full of social construction, tends to be short-lived and ultimately unsatisfactory. And even the joyfulness and ecstasy described by Lacan and Irigaray tend to be occasional, reactive experiences. A far more useful approach I believe to be the learnt lovingness of Diotima's method described above. It may start with falling into the sea of love but it then develops into learning to swim in it, feeling a part of its rhythms and tides, being in love with life itself. I have written about this in *Love in an Age of Uncertainty* (Chaplin, 1993b). It also has much in common with the Buddhist Metta practice involving learning to 'send' loving-kindness and compassion to people imagined during meditation. Both approaches require considerable hard work and practice.

Learning to live in love is going to be essential for us to cope with living rhythmically and in uncertainty. In therapy the love-trained therapist helps to heal through the same kind of loving attention used in the Buddhist Metta meditation. It involves deliberately thinking loving thoughts as well as 'opening the heart'.

Perhaps women have tended in general to learn to love more easily and more continuously than men because they have usually cared for babies and young children who would die if not loved. I doubt if we are biologically better at loving. And after all, those babies wouldn't even have been born without some form of male desire. Although desire and love are not the same, they can be interconnected as when we are in love. I don't want to go into the complex differences here. But I do want to argue like Spivak and others that we need to make strategic use of those attributes stereotypically attributed to women even if we don't believe that they are biologically female. Unconditional love, compassion and tenderness are all vital for human survival. They are also essential as a kind of fuel or energy to deconstruct, dissolve and especially to construct new ways of learning to dance life. Once this process is under way, differences of gender and/or between women and men will probably seem less important.

Dancing with the Opposites

Therapy is a good example of a process in which dancing with the opposites is actually part of the healing/growth. There are the rhythms of speech and silence, for example. An intuitive and attuned therapist will flow with this rhythm appropriately, not being afraid of the long well-timed silence. This can help an important new insight to really sink in. Any binary opposition between passivity and activity is also dissolved in therapy, not only through the play between them, but also because what the therapist is often doing can be described as active listening, being active in passivity.

There are many more opposites that dissolve in therapy, but at the very heart of the process is learning to cope with the reality of ambivalence itself. It may involve seeing the therapist and then parents and others as being both good and bad, accepting and rejecting, strong and weak. In this sense we as therapists are involved in the same project as post-modernists and feminists to fully accept and even enjoy the way that everything can be both one thing and another.

For Laura it came as quite a shock that she could both love and hate her mother at the same time. She had spent so long not being able to say a bad word about her mother, that it was not until I became the less than perfect therapist that she was able to face the fact that her mother had neglected her. But even after this realization she made excuses for her mother and could not at first be really angry. She was afraid that she would become all hate and lose the love for her mother. So I suggested that she metaphorically put the love for her mother in a box to keep it safe in our room, so that it wouldn't go away while she raged. This is just one of many humanistic psychology techniques that can help with ambivalence. Laura also saw that I could make mistakes and be vulnerable. She could only accept these other sides once she had experienced enough of my strength to know that it would not go away. It has to be safe to dance.

Difference

There will always be difference. People who deny gender or race difference haven't even started in the equalizing struggle/dance. Often differences need to be acknowledged and even defined before we can begin political change. But in Western dualism, by hierarchalizing difference the 'lower' side is turned into an 'other' always defined by the 'higher' opposite. Learning how to think differently about difference is one of the major tasks of the present historical time.

A simple celebration of difference can mask a political naiveté about existing inequalities. We are not all starting this 'game' on a level playing field. The 'other' does not usually want to be the same as the 'higher' group either. However there is sometimes a stage when there is a desire for the other to copy or even identify with the dominant/higher group. Many women are today being as much like men as possible, whether it be in business or in the bedroom. Working-class people become middle class and black people sometimes act white. Even therapy clients often often go through a stage when they want to be like the therapist and may even start a therapy training. There may then be a stage of compensatory superiority such as we see in many nationalist movements where the previously 'inferior' group assert themselves as 'superior'. A client might rebel at this point. The third stage would be where difference is dehierarchalized with no superior and inferior and connections made that do not deny difference. Now we are back to Rorty's (1989) strategic use of the concept of 'us'. He sees this as moral progress without any of the grand narratives like Marxism.

There is also the problem of the many levels and complexities of difference. In some sense each one of us is different. When are classifications and commonalities useful and when are they not? Can any one human being speak for another? What is perhaps most important is that no one human being sets herself or himself up as an authority on others who may be very different. Many white middle-class feminists have talked as though they are experts on *all* women, even appearing to speak for us *all*. The range of differences between women in the world is enormous, but there can also be a danger of generalizing when talking about a specific group of women.

I am writing this chapter from the singular position of my present process of 'being in relation', not on behalf of, representing or as an

Figure 8.7 *Demeter and Persephone* © *Jocelyn Chaplin 1988*

authority on women. This includes both women in general, feminists in particular and postmodernist, feminist psychotherapists especially. My identity as a postmodernist feminist psychotherapist is only one of my many identities and it could change tomorrow. In the same way our clients have multiple and flexible identities and as they get to know them all better we learn to dance with them too.

Laura had hierarchalized her different sides so much that she only really identified with that of the career business manager. The identity associated with mothering was not even recognized at first. And even when she did recognize this side it was seen as very inferior. She also saw them as either/or choices in life, despite the social changes that had made the possibility of being both easier. Gradually Laura made friends with her mothering side and many other hidden sides that appeared. Eventually she was able to 'dance' between them without fearing that she had to stay stuck in one or the other for the rest of her life. And totally new ones are always waiting on the side lines ready to be played out. In these times of such rapid social change we all need to be able to shift identities frequently. But this is always easier if there is a core self present and an ability to trust and love.

The need for rhythmic, fluid identities can also be applied to sexuality. Gender identities are already becoming more flexible but the whole area of sexuality can be opened up away from rigid hierarchical dualisms. Undecideability, ambiguity and an awareness of the many sites of pleasure and desire is part of this new era. Yet rhythmic living works best if there is some safety and containment, especially in the early years. Sometimes therapy can help compensate for any lack in this safety early in life. But therapy can also help improve self-esteem and our capacity for loving, both of which are essential for living, thinking and enjoying life based on the rhythm model.

REFERENCES

Bell, S. (1992) 'Tomb of the sacred prostitute: the Symposium', in P. Berry and A. Wernick (eds) *Shadow of Spirit: Postmodernism and Religion*. London: Routledge.

Capra, F. (1982) *The Turning Point*. London: Wildwood House.

Chaplin, J. (1985) *The Mass Psychology of Thatcherism*. London: Socialist Society.

Chaplin, J. (1988) *Feminist Counselling in Action*. London: Sage.

Chaplin, J. (1993a) *Enter the Wild Woman*. London: Body Politic.

Chaplin, J. (1993b) *Love in an Age of Uncertainty*. London: Harper Collins.

Deleuze, G. and Guattari, F. (1988) *A Thousand Plateaus: Capitalism and Schizophrenia* (trans. B. Massumi). Minneapolis, MN: University of Minnesota Press.

Derrida, J. (1976) *Of Grammatology* (trans. G. Spivak). Baltimore, MD: Johns Hopkins University Press.

Elam, D. (1994) *Feminism and Deconstruction*. London: Routledge.

Flax, J. (1990) *Thinking Fragments: Psychoanalysis, Feminism and Postmodernism in the Contemporary West*. Berkeley, CA: University of California Press.

Gimbutas, M. (1974) *The Goddesses and Gods of Old Europe*. London: Thames and Hudson.

Goodison, L. (1990) *Moving Heaven and Earth*. London: The Women's Press.

Irigaray, L. (1989a) *Speculum of the Other Woman* (trans. G. Gill). Ithaca, NY: Cornell University Press.

Irigaray, L. (1989b) 'Sorcerer love: a reading of Plato's Symposium, Diotima's speech', *Hypatia*, 3 (3).

Kahn, C. (1979) *The Art and Thought of Heraclitus*. Cambridge: Cambridge University Press.

Lacan, J. (1977) *Ecrits: A Selection* (trans. A. Sheridan). London: Tavistock.

Nicholson, L. (ed.) (1990) *Feminism/Postmodernism*. New York: Routledge.

Nye, A. (1989) 'The hidden host: Irigaray and Diotima at Plato's Symposium', *Hypatia*, 3 (3).

Plato (1989) *The Symposium*. Translated and annotated by A. Nehames and P. Woodruff. Indiana and Cambridge, MA: Hackett Publishing Co.

Rorty, R. (1989) *Contingency, Irony and Solidarity*. Cambridge: Cambridge University Press.

Spivak, G. (1988) *In Other Worlds*. New York: Routledge.

Starhawk (1982) *Dreaming the Dark: Magic, Sex and Politics*. Boston, MA: Beacon Press.

Stone, M. (1976) *When God was a Woman*. San Diego, CA: Harvest/Harcourt Brace Jovanovich.

Waterhouse, R. (1993) '"Wild women don't have the blues": a feminist critique of person-centred counselling and therapy', *Feminism and Psychology*, 3 (1): 55–71.

Whitford, M. (1991) *Luce Irigaray: Philosophy in the Feminine*. London: Routledge.

Winnicott, D. (1975) *Through Pediatrics to Psychoanalysis*. New York: Basic Books. p. 21.

9

The Creative Feminine: Kristeva and the Maternal Body

Tessa Adams

Renowned for her debated feminist psychoanalytic stance, Julia Kristeva[1] situates the creative feminine as an unrepresentable subversive dynamic challenging paternal signification. Its manifestations (maternal jouissance – primary 'joy'), typically visible within poetry and painting, are seen to offer the promise of our repatriation with the maternal body. This is a thesis of the human subject's original loss in which the maternal realm is irrevocably eclipsed by the 'Name of the Father'.[2]

Although Kristeva demonstrates that she is influenced by Winnicott and Klein, her approach is essentially Lacanian in that she positions (for the Western economy) language as the foundation of social oppression. We are in her terms repressed by our entry into language (the *symbolic order*)[3] and, as speaking and writing subjects, are required thereafter to survive the rupture from maternal signification. And from this position we are seen to endure inordinate loss, the subversion of the feminine, which is sustained by our ensuing acculturation. This is banishment from the Garden of Eden in the fullest sense. But clearly not a dismissal from a paradise that is essentially patriarchal, rather a relentless exile from those sublime conditions of maternal communication (lallation and gesture) which furnished our earliest moments of life. Here is an image of the infant as original possessor of her/his 'mother's tongue' being called to forfeit the pleasures of the primary encounter in order to access articulated language – the symbolic realm.

What this means is that Kristeva presents psychotherapists with a dilemma. Arguably the most readily accepted concept of psychological maturity is one which privileges the features of linguistic communication, yet she points out that it is precisely this accomplishment which divorces the individual from essential relationship with the feminine principle. The question that I am raising within this chapter is: what are the implications of such a position in the context of an ambition to locate and explore the nature of feminist psychotherapeutic practice?

I tackle this question in several ways. First, my concern is to illuminate both the potential and limitations of Kristeva's theoretical framework as a revolutionary project for a feminist psychodynamic. Second, her assumptions, in respect of the semiotic disposition, are explored as pertinent comparison with Klein's and Milner's compensatory analyses of the creative impulse. Third, the works of Chodorow and Irigaray are drawn upon in order to situate, in a broader debate, Kristeva's principle that the female subject suffers the loss of 'authentic feminine' signification. Finally, I focus on semiotic activity within creative practice and Kristeva's view that it is by this means that our experience of the maternal body is made manifest. I conclude the discussion with a poignant case of a woman in severe psychosis whose creative expression alleviated her world of verbal incoherence.

Let us now consider Kristeva's positioning of the problematic of maternal signification in more detail. We find that her fundamental view is that 'language as symbolic function constitutes itself at the cost of repressing instinctual drive and continuous relation to mother'. She puts this unequivocally by stating that 'matricide is our vital necessity' in ensuring our entry into the 'social-symbolic-linguistic contract with the group' (Kristeva, 1980: 136). That is to say, it is her view that the imperative to relinquish the 'dialogue' of the original maternal encounter rests on a matter of survival, for to remain outside Language/Law (rational discourse) would be to submit to psychosis.

In brief, this is a thesis which proposes that rational discourse achieves its coherence by repudiating maternal relationship. What is given up, Kristeva claims, is a form of original communication that is both of and with the maternal body: a communication deriving from what she terms the semiotic disposition; a domain of reciprocation devoid of the conflict of gender and difference in which the infant meets (in joy) the mother's communications through pre-verbal vocalizing and somatic exchanges (Kristeva, 1980). Particular to this conception of the infant/mother dyad is the characteristic of pre-verbal signification, the features of which never can (in Language) be fully expressed. This is a proposition that owes much to the Winnicottian view of the special nature of the infant/mother union, which is in keeping with classical psychoanalytic assumptions that privilege the unconscious dynamic of early infant bonding (Winnicott, 1971).

Thus it is clear that this picture of infant development profiles the subject's unavoidable sacrifice. From Kristeva's Lacanian approach the Tree of Knowledge is situated as the Name-of-the-Father, constraining the human subject by its symbolic signification (Lacan, 1977). At root the fruits of rational discourse are therefore seen to be a bitter feast, for with maternal signification necessarily subordinated, the individual is conceived as inevitably harnessed by dissatisfaction. That is to say, as speaking/writing subjects, we are seen to remain in a state of permanent longing provoked by our continual unconscious striving to reinstate the pre-linguistic (pre-symbolic) semiotic bodily exchanges of the original maternal encounter.

Although Kristeva heralds a lament to this irrevocable banishment of primary symbiotic reverie from conscious expression, it is the case that she is equally concerned to stress that all is not finally lost. Identifying us as 'subjects in process', she establishes our disenfranchised position as continuously mitigated by 'semiotic activity'.[4] That is to say, she points to a dynamic of the maternal realm which persists as subliminally active throughout life – seeking recognition through unconscious manifestations. In other words, although the maternal element is conceived as primarily bodily in affect, it would seem that it is essentially transcendent in its function. For her claim is that, through semiotic activity, maternal signification is ever-present in its sublimations (bidding to subvert rational discourse), remaining a challenge to patriarchal coherence. This is a view that frames the feminine as unconscious agency (semiotic activity) modifying Patriarchal Law (symbolic order – with its grammatical constraints and codes).

Identifying how Kristeva comes to define her principle of semiotic activity, we find that it is primarily within poetic texts that she locates its subversive features. And significantly both classical poetry and poetic prose are cited. Termed 'productive', these texts are seen in contrast to rational discourse by the fact that meaning is left ambiguously in question. We are told that the special feature of the 'productive' text is that it remains actively creative through the interplay of the two signifying realms – the unconscious demands of the semiotic, on the one hand, and the prohibitions of the symbolic, on the other. Kristeva explains this oppositional dynamic thus:

> The semiotic activity, which introduces wandering or fuzziness into language, a fortiori, into poetic Language, is, from a synchronic point of view, a mark of the workings of drives (appropriation/rejection, orality/anality, love/hate, life/death) and, from a diachronic view, stems from the archaisms of the semiotic body . . . The unsettled and questionable subject of poetic language (for whom a word is never uniquely sign) maintains itself at the cost of reactivating this repressed instinctual, maternal element. (1980: 136)

In short, Kristeva, conceiving the human subject's oppression through symbolic signification as unavoidable, looks towards artistic endeavour to be the custodian of the maternal body – the semiotic. Situating the creative act as compensatory, she indicates that this lack, termed the 'privation of fulfilment and of totality: exclusion from a pleasing and natural sound state' (Kristeva, 1980: 136), is nevertheless productive. Which is to say that the unorganized pressures of pre-verbal desire, which originate in maternal dependency, are seen to be subliminally ever-present through creative process, dismantling formal reasoning. This process can be encapsulated in the following way.

Imagine an ordered garden with a well-kept lawn, neatly mowed, with every blade seeming to be in place. This precise cultivation can be likened to the precise cultivation of rational discourse (the symbolic order) with each word framed in distinct signification. Now consider how such a lawn might have been before the gardener's intervention with its ordered purpose. Picture the original uncultivated field with its wild flowers, briars and grasses, and this pre-cultivated state can be seen to be representative of the pre-symbolic ('natural') state referred to by Kristeva as the 'semiotic realm'. It can stand for the 'field of the Maternal' before the Word of the Father (gardener's tools) ensured its subjection to enculturation. Further, looking closely at this lawn, so prized for its quality and order, we can observe that the original field does not appear entirely to be subdued, for, springing up as daisies through the uniform grass, 'nature' is seeming to bid for its restoration, subverting the gardener's immaculate achievement. It is easy to identify these daisies, pushing through the cultivated lawn, as a metaphor for semiotic activity, pushing through the grammatical constraints of cultivated discourse. That is to say, for Kristeva, these 'daisies' of the semiotic – primary maternal communication – erupting through the cultivated 'grass' of the Symbolic – secondary paternal communication – are in fact the agency of maternal creative function, and as such are surely the essence of life.

Let us now explore Kristeva's principle of the subversive nature of the creative feminine in a broader context, keeping in mind how it might inform psychotherapeutic work. It can be argued that Kristeva offers the psychotherapist a subtle feminist perspective that is both dispiriting and heartening. We have seen that, on the one hand, she confirms the weight of patriarchy, with its project for coherence, dominating maternal discourse, while on the other hand, she indicates at least some scope for its deconstruction by framing the dynamic of the feminine as revolutionary through creative process. Since the creative feminine, as agency, is seen to operate solely through unconscious process, notwithstanding her optimistic view of subversive maternal activity, the imbalance between paternal and maternal function appears to be impossible fully to redress. In other words, Kristeva certainly brings attention to the feminine as hidden discourse, but fails to indicate how we might provide for its restoration. For if it is the case that the process of the creative feminine is essentially unconscious, it is clear that its significations cannot be harnessed through conscious deliberation.

Bearing in mind that Kristeva's principle of the subversive/passive maternal element derives in part from her experience of her own clinical work, let us now think about her thesis in relation to other psychoanalytic propositions for the creative dynamic. Although her work is criticized for privileging maternality and androgyny (Wright, 1992: 199), it is notable that she promotes what alone is the crucial factor of the multifarious conditions of communication – that is the encounter. But a maternal encounter with its significations withdrawn from direct communication with the prevailing masculinist discourse. What is at stake here is that she re-visions the implicit conditions of psychic structure, while at the same time begging the question as to whether it is possible to transcend the prohibition of linguistic determinism through creative process. And if it is the case that the maternal realm embraces an essential capacity for deconstruction, which, defeating the dominant patriarchal discourse, finds its expression through the creative project, the question becomes one of relevance to practising analysts. This raises the issue of the weight of her innovatory proposition within the context of psycho-analytic tradition.

In general terms it is not unusual for psychoanalytic thinkers to privilege the maternal realm as the site of creative functioning, and there are several ways in which the mother/infant dyadic union is heralded as it is the bed-rock of creative impulse. In fact, looking closely at the analysis of creative process, in the way that it is conceived by much of psychoanalytic theory, there certainly appears to be a case for suggesting that there is an intrinsic relationship between creative impulse and feminine consciousness. It is interesting, too, that it can be argued that mainstream psychodynamic debate, circa 1950,[5] concerned with the genesis of creativity, prefigures significant aspects of Kristevian thought. We only have to look towards certain leading post-Freudians to find that this speculation is possible to substantiate. Two cases in point would be the analyses of creativity presented by Melanie Klein and Marion Milner.

First let us consider Klein. It is clear that she equally identifies the genesis of the creative impulse as a bid for the restoration of the maternal body. Yet in her case this is not a restoration based on its *actual* denial through rational discourse (in Kristevian terms); instead it is a restoration that is essentially symbolic. Klein proposes that the damage requiring restitution is in fact the pre-genital 'damage' meted out by the infant whose paranoid/schizoid phantasized attacks on the maternal body (in the first months of life) engender a powerful drive for reparation. That is to say, Klein's view of the infant's original sacrifice is hardly that of relin-quishing the reverie of maternal jouissance; rather it is a relinquishing of the primitive aggressive impulses that characterize the infant's first experi-ences. What this means is that in leaving the 'language' of the maternal body, the infant is seen to mobilize creative process; a dynamic which at root features a reparative contract in the service of autonomy (Klein, 1977).

Klein's view is similar to Kristeva's in that she conceives the creative act as deriving its impetus from the loss of the maternal body. Yet both writers are in contrast in respect of their analyses of creative ambition. In Klein's terms the creative impulse is fundamentally reparative with the purpose of releasing the subject from pre-genital maternal preoccupation, while in Kristeva's terms this impulse is seen to be one of reinstatement, in which creative activity is concerned with repatriating the subject within the maternal realm of pre-genital communication (the semiotic disposition).[6] In other words each writer associates the genesis of the creative impulse within the maternal body, but conceives its ambition in opposing terms: in Klein's case the creative project is one of reparation and separation, while in Kristeva's case it is one of repatriation and affirmation.

It could be argued that the classical psychoanalytic explanation of creative impulse most similar to Kristeva's is that of Marion Milner. Of particular note is Milner's influential text *On Not Being Able to Paint* (1950) which features her struggle to understand the roots of her own artistic output. What is of interest here is that Milner equally privileges the infant/mother symbiotic dyad as fundamental to creative endeavour. Milner's central theme is the relationship between the infant's deification of body products and creative process, which could suggest that she anticipates Kristeva's principle of maternal jouissance as the heart of artistic potential. It is her view that the reverie of the symbiotic maternal union engages the infant in a delusion that 'he has created himself' which provides the impetus for subsequent creative acts (Milner, 1950: 153). Her claim is that, in this state of omnipotence, the infant is preoccupied with offering the mother the body products (faeces, urine, etc.) as 'love gifts' in order to secure the phantasy of her unconditional devotion (Milner, 1990: 219). This is a picture of pre-genital communication which mirrors Kristeva's mother/infant encounter of the semiotic disposition, placing equal emphasis on the ecstatic pleasures of this undifferentiated realm of maternal functioning. Milner tells us that the infant 'cannot distinguish between the body products and the ecstatic experiences of producing them', and that these manifestations of 'pre-genital orgiastic reverie' are imbued with maternal signification; notably, in her view, to become the raw material of artistic creation (Milner, 1990: 219).

Although Milner cites maternal reverie as the substance of the creative act, her thesis differs from Kristeva's in terms of the specific nature of the intrinsic relationship between these early bodily sensations and creative desire. As we have seen, there is a distinct similarity in the way that each writer pays attention to the pre-genital dynamic, yet it appears that Kristeva's position is more complex, since Kristeva profiles the reciprocal dynamic of the infant/mother exchange. It has been shown that Kristeva interprets this primary state as one of symbiotic reverie in which the infant meets the mother's communications in a common 'language' that is both of and through the body. The significant issue here is that the potential of this non-verbal interplay is situated by Kristeva as a realm of signification which transcends the corporeal. This is a development which goes beyond Milner's proposition, since Milner essentially interprets this phase of pre-genital expression without emphasizing the issue of mutual communication. While Milner admits that the infant experience is one of 'oceanic undifferentiation' (1990: 226), her thesis is based on literal pre-genital orgasmic supremacy. This bodily proposition could appear unnecessarily concrete in the light of Kristeva's emphasis on the transcendent quality of jouissance which is seen to derive from the ecstatic exchanges of the semiotic disposition.

I would claim that it is significant that these earlier influential psycho-analytic interpretations of the creative project situate its genesis within the maternal frame. As we have seen, Klein proposes innovative desire as the object of the maternal body in terms of a reparative act, which mitigates a past of phantasized attacks, while Milner focuses on maternal engagement with the idealized body products of pre-genital orgiastic indulgence as the subliminal ingredient of creative achievement. In the light of these earlier views it is not surprising that Kristeva, claiming that maternal function is of its nature harboured by an explicit signification, should make the case for a hidden maternal discourse with its subterfuge within poetic/eidetic sensate imagery.

What is of interest here is that each proposition implies an inevitable over-ruling of the maternal element in the service of psychological development. Although this relinquishing of essential maternal dialogue is conceived differently, there seems to be at least a degree of congruence that would support the prospect of a subordinated maternal discourse which furnishes creative expression. Yet should this analysis of probability lead us to accept fully the Kristevian position, there are crucial concerns which cannot be overlooked for psychotherapeutic practice.

First, since psychoanalytically the body of the mother is the female body (framed in terms of the Western economy), would it be correct to imagine that typically women's position in respect of the subordination of maternal signification is different from that of men? Second, is the wealth of feminist concern which seeks to deconstruct the socio-cultural posi-tioning of male prerogative inevitably problematized by a psychodynamic analysis that proposes language as intrinsically patriarchal? Further, bearing in mind the extensive psychoanalytic discussion on the status of women's maternal identifications, and all that is implied, is it possible to locate a discrete feminine language?

These questions bring us to the heart of feminist debate on essentialism with its extensive and complex history which cannot be explored within this context (Wright, 1992: 77–83). However, before moving on to discuss the implications of Kristeva's interpretation of creative process, it will be useful to touch upon, and compare (with her view) the work of two leading contemporary exponents of feminist psychoanalytic thought – Luce Irigaray and Nancy Chodorow; particularly since each of these writers addresses the issue of maternal signification in terms that offer a distinct challenge to classically based psychotherapeutic practice.

The work of Irigaray is closely associated with Kristeva. A proponent of the French feminist movement *Ecriture Feminine*,[7] Irigaray's attempt to give definition to the maternal feminine has been variously received. In reaching out to privilege female specificity, Irigaray has drawn considerable criticism, not least since her writing style is academically obscure, contrasting, arguably, with her utopian objectives. Significantly, though, Irigaray's publication *Speculum* in 1974, with its psychoanalytic debate outspoken in its attack on the profession's patriarchal bias, caused her to lose her position within the Department of Psychoanalysis at the Vincennes. She tells us that this challenge ensured that she was placed 'into quarantine' by the psychoanalytic institutions (Wright, 1992: 178).

Critical of Freudian/Lacanian phallocentricity, Irigaray seeks to address the problematic of the patriarchal Symbolic by instating 'the Feminine' as dynamic language (Wright, 1992: 178). This suggests that her position brings into question Kristeva's apparent passivity, since Irigaray points to an urgency that the subversion of maternal signification be deliberately re-visioned. What this means is that Irigaray situates our responsibility (as women) as semantically productive, rather than reactive, confronting us with her notion of our difference as a potentially positive alternative matrix of feminine representation. In other words, it is her view that there can be developed a strategic specifically feminine language that defies representation through rational discourse. Irigaray's contribution is complex. It is not her intention to define 'woman', nor is it to analyse what it is to speak 'as woman' (Whitford, 1991: 9), as she states: 'There is simply no way I can give you an account of "speaking (as) woman": it is spoken, but not in meta-language' (Irigaray in Whitford, 1991: 9). Yet, developing the Kristevian principle of the 'subject in process', she looks towards a deliberate re-elaboration of the feminine, through mimesis, designed to undermine the oppressive structures of Symbolic Law. Thus we find that both writers agree that language as it is constituted 'is refused to our female body' (Wright, 1992), but regard the possibility of redressing the anomalous situation in different terms. Simply put, Irigaray looks towards 'the conditions under which the status of the "female" in the Symbolic realm might be altered' (Whitford, 1991: 15), while Kristeva calls attention to the unconscious manifestations of maternal jouissance.

Of further interest is that there exists a significant difference in the way that Irigaray positions the male subject (Wright, 1992: 179–80). We find that Kristeva's interpretation of the infant's entry into language as the 'privation of fulfilment and continuous relation to mother' identifies the speaking subject as suffering permanent loss (and the desire for repatriation), whether male or female. She suggests that feminine signification, as semiotic activity, is accessible to both men and women through the experience of creative process. In Irigaray's case there is a marked difference in this respect since she implies that feminine 'language' is not fully repressed, but rather primarily historically oppressed. And, claiming that it can be deliberately accessed through deconstructive process, further contrasting with Kristeva, Irigaray situates the feminine discourse as retrievable solely by women. We could say that Irigaray inscribes men in the language that they themselves, through power and privilege, have continuously sought to sustain, and in turn, calls upon women to take up the project of articulating a new vision of 'the Feminine', which she anticipates can be potentially alternatively signified. In other words, her project is one of seeking the female 'imaginary' as the Phoenix to arise out of women's 'dereliction' brought about by the oppressive structures of the male 'imaginary'[8] of phallic Symbolic signification.

Let us now move on to consider Chodorow's analysis of maternal function in the light of Kristeva's and Irigaray's propositions for a subverted feminine signification. Notably Chodorow is distinguished for her influential critique of Freudian drive theory to include the framing of a mother/daughter psychodynamic. Her seminal text, *The Reproduction of Mothering* (1978), re-defines the mother/daughter relationship as one of complex identification, drawing attention to the fact that the history of the societal responsibility for mothering (typically women's) impacts upon the female subject's relational experiencing. Basically Chodorow's proposal points out that 'mothering begets mothering', and that this unconscious dynamic is detrimental, leaving the mother and daughter subduing desire and full relationship. We are told that 'for the girl, identification is likely to be – at best – with the mother's maternality rather than with her as an active sexual being' (Chodorow, 1994: 60).

It can be argued that Chodorow appears to both accept and dispute Kristeva's concept of a fugitive maternal function. Although she equally situates the primary-maternal relationship as canalized through the societal dominance of male signification, she directs our attention away from the concept of intrinsic lack toward a re-visioning of self-in-relationship. For Chodorow, the 'authentic' maternal discourse is essentially hidden, but nevertheless retrievable. In telling us that 'most girls seek to create in love relationships an internal emotional dialogue with the mother', she brings to mind Kristeva's view of the speaking subject's 'exclusion from a natural and sound state'. But in Chodorow's case this search is not conceived as a search for jouissance. Rather it is identified as primarily compensatory in the light of unresolved conflicts and desires deriving from infant experience, which she claims operate (for women) subliminally to impede autonomy (Chodorow, 1994: 82–3). Chodorow in fact questions the view of an original blissful symbiotic baby/mother union, implying instead an exchange charged with libidinal anxiety.

Thus, from Chodorow's object-relationist perspective, this subversive maternal dialogue is mutable (rather than fully repressed as in the case of Kristeva), since it is through the screen of complex psychological attachments that the female subject is seen to develop the capacity to acknowledge fully (and own) maternal signification (Chodorow, 1994: 82–3). The male subject, in Chodorow's terms, is also subject to the subordination of the maternal element, but in a way which appears to be less repressed. She proposes that societal privileging of masculinity, in which male superiority is applauded, engenders boyhood identifications that leave the male subject caught up in a web of denial of maternal attachment (Chodorow, 1994: 59). In short, Chodorow sees the maternal element in terms of cathexis, defensively repudiated by men and narcissistically adhered to by women (through gendered identification). Simply put, this is a contrast in affect, which places the girl as prospective nurturer in the position of subordination and the boy as autonomous adventurer in the position of comprehension. This is an analysis of the maternal which presents the subject as ego-centred internalizing social/ cultural influence and, by situating women as suffering the corruption of original dyadic dependency, the implication here is that (in keeping with Kristeva) the creative feminine will be essentially subverted.

To summarize, at root Chodorow positions female subject formation as primarily maternally based, rather than Oedipally centred, and, drawing in part upon the Winnicott/Fairbairn paradigm, she reframes classical object relations perspectives to bring into question the mother's *actual* experience (Wright, 1992: 48). Although criticized as essentialist, this is a view which has much influenced feminist psychotherapeutic practice to take as its project the prospect of interpreting the ambivalence within the mother/ daughter relationship. It can be seen that Chodorow positions the maternal dynamic as both creative and inhibitory. This is not a picture of the maternal sublime; rather the maternal body is presented as the site of risk, harnessing the female subject to the imperative to nurture. Here again, in keeping with Irigaray and Kristeva, Chodorow tells of the female subject's exclusion from 'authentic feminine' signification, but in a more concrete way. For to fail to achieve autonomy means that productive communication with the body of the mother is (for women) denied full expression.

LOCATING THE SEMIOTIC IN PRACTICE: THE CREATIVE TEXT

Let us now return again to the garden. It will be noticed that I have presented two images which frame the human subject's exile from the maternal realm. The first, the garden of prohibition dominating the Western economy, the Garden of Eden; out of which the Word of the Father becomes the legacy of generations of unbridled celebration of patriarchal signification. This is the garden in which speech becomes command: a command historically interpreted as unequivocally male, heralding the privilege of authority in logocentric terms. The second, a garden of human cultivation; its verdant lawfulness serving as a metaphor to frame our banishment from a paradise of a different order. This is the garden of enculturation which, as we have seen, in Kristevian terms, situates language acquisition as the purveyor of oppression. It is a garden in which the achievement of order eclipses creative growth, representing the speaking/writing subject's unwitting sacrifice of direct communion with the maternal element. And it cannot escape our notice that Kristeva uses the 'Word of the Father' to tell us about the unrepresentable 'Mother', which is an irony she is concerned to expose. For it is in *Tales of Love* (1987: 239–59) that she provides a text ('Stabat mater') designed to evidence maternal function. In the form of 'two voices', one staying within the boundaries of rational discourse, the other personal and subvertively disruptive, she experiments in an attempt to visibly situate the creative dynamic of the hidden maternal element *actively* eroding the 'Law'. In fact we find that throughout Kristeva's writing her style typically bids towards releasing the grip of Symbolic coherence, resulting in texts which are both challenging and poetically enigmatic. That is to say, in keeping with her vision of semiotic activity, Kristeva demands of the reader that they call into question the need to secure unequivocal meaning, thereby demonstrating *in practice* her concern that maternal signification be distinguished.

However complex Kristeva's principle of semiotic activity might seem to be, what she asks the practising therapist fully to consider is something that is commonly recognized, namely that creative intention stands apart from everyday systems of human communication. There is no doubt that a different order of meaning is associated with creative acts. Arguably, too, most clients entering psychotherapy have a vested interest in the status of their own creative potential. How often we hear the phrase 'the trouble is that I am not very imaginative' as a contributing factor to feelings of low self-esteem. Another relevant issue is that it is not unusual for artists to stay away from psychotherapeutic support, since creative activity itself is often thought to provide sufficient connection between conscious and unconscious processes.

It is interesting to see that Kristeva 'has taken up the arms' that Freud had apparently laid down when, in his confusion about the creative process, he stated, 'Before the problem of the creative artist analysis must, alas, lay down its arms' (1955: 177). We could say that, by promoting art as the 'privileged object of investigation' (Wright, 1992: 196), Kristeva has, in fact, profiled our critical need for creative expression and the interpretation of its manifestations. Yet her thesis underlines the possibility that creative process puts us at risk. For, with its project primarily disruptive (bidding to challenge the constraints of Symbolic signification), the creator is placed in the wake of primary process, that is within the trajectory of psychotic functioning. But how do we position 'psychotic art' within this framework? Can we see the excess of imagery which typifies psychosis as the evidence of maternal signification in Kristevian terms? In other words, is it possible to interpret the many paintings, poems, etc. that play a part in the sessions of borderline clients (where conventional communication has failed) as distinct attempts to privilege the body of the Mother? Certainly there would seem to be a search for the maternal symbiotic union within much of psychotic representation, as is the desire to locate the Self. Yet this is a quest which would appear to be problematic. For Kristeva claims, in contrast to the more valued neurotic manifestations of semiotic functioning, that the psychotic search can only be fraught with conflict. She bases this premise on her view that the necessary Symbolic death of the mother, in psychosis, will be continually resisted. This means that she situates those in psychosis stranded in language. Between, that is, semiotic and Symbolic functioning, with productive access to the 'Law of the Father' (the group) and the sublime of the Mother (jouissance) inevitably inhibited.

Without recommending precise conditions for semiotic signification (which can be argued)[9] I would suggest that the status of 'psychotic art' is put into question if it is framed as marginal to notions of a productive hidden maternal discourse in Kristevian terms. Interestingly, in recent years the societal positioning of this realm of work has drawn much concern, and a re-visioning of psychotic creative activity has been virtually established;[10] not simply for the richness that a therapeutic analysis of psychotic expression can offer, but rather in terms of a discourse unrecognized and uncharted. That is to say, entitled *Outsider Art* as a means by which to nominate its subversion, psychotic creative process is situated as a poignant challenge to the prevailing aesthetic. In fact, when we study Jean Dubuffet's 'acultural' positioning of this aspect of art practice, we see that 'psychotic works' stand apart to be applauded for apparent lawlessness, since Dubuffet tells us, from the 'opposite camp to the camp of knowledge', it is the 'psychotic artist' who is authentic in accessing that imagery which speaks of 'an ecstasy of intoxication [and of] complete liberty' (Dubuffet, 1976). Thus from this position we might be encouraged to believe that it is through psychosis *alone* that maternal signification primarily could be made manifest.

Finally, since it is not my intention to end this chapter with any definitive conclusions, I will draw upon the 'Outsider Voice' as a fitting image by which to complete this discussion. To this end I present to you a woman whose passion to create demonstrates as much a communication subverted as it does inordinate loss; whose extensive art works speak of that space between. Of the realm, that is, in which language appears to be 'out of process' (neither semiotic nor Symbolic), anticipating the maternal body in wait for primary signification. This is someone whom I nominate to represent all those whose creativity, in existential protest, harnesses their dislocation in which the body, disowned and muted, strives with daunting expression.

Her name is known as Aloise and, in common with other patients of her time, her family name − significantly the name of the father − is virtually forgotten. She was born in Austria in 1886 and died at 78 years old after spending most of her adult life in psychiatric institutions classified as 'an incurable'. Unable to communicate coherently, in time she began to write and draw incessantly, her vibrant images claiming a significance that her dislocated utterings had failed to achieve. The calm that this creative expression brought released her from the autistic violent outbursts which had precipitated her internment. Although initially doctors destroyed her work as irrelevant, Aloise carried on with an urgency that remained until her death. It was during her middle age that the climate of opinion in respect of psychosis began to change, leading to

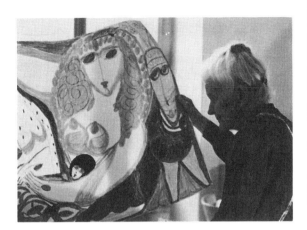

Figure 9.1   *Aloise painting in the Roseière Asylum 1963, aged 78*

a recognition of her creative needs. Only then was she appropriately resourced and with her work valued by an innovatory female doctor (Jacqueline Porret-Forel), she began to establish relationship. It was from this time on, contrasting with her fragile frame, that extraordinary images broke to the surface (see Figures 9.1 and 9.2). Working in solitude Aloise engaged with her theatre of 'legendary evocations', of which the maternal body seems paramount. Women intertwined and powerful, frequently part naked, gaze towards the viewer with an intensity that is difficult to avoid. In one picture each naked breast holds within it a child-image, while in others the child is deliberately embraced. Elegant and larger than life, her subjects call us to meet her internal dialogue of which an abundance of expression records her autistic world (Thevoz, 1976).

In the last analysis we can ask if Aloise, in her process of repudiation, situates, through her urgent expressions, the dynamic of the creative feminine striving against the constraints of the Symbolic Law? Notwithstanding her resistance to the 'contract with the group', her images portray a distinct demand to be seen. Yet, significantly, as is often the case in outsider art, Aloise believed her work to be 'divinely inspired', suggesting an absence of conscious deliberation. Arguably this imperative to 'speak' without being *symbolically* 'heard' (a state in which the creator identifies as medium for a communication disowned) gives credence to a view that a lost arena of expression continuously seeks representation. Could this be, at root, that denied maternal signification of the female body to which Kristeva, Irigaray and Chodorow, in their various ways, have seemed to refer?

Figure 9.2   *Typical work by Aloise, entitled 'Luxemburg – the Beautiful Lady Behind her Fan' 1952–4*

NOTES

1 Julia Kristeva, writer and practising psychoanalyst, has provided clinical texts on abjection, depression, desire and love.

2 Kristeva in addressing this rupture is speaking of the human subject as framed within the Western economy. Drawing from Jacques Lacan she accepts the view that Law is historically privileged as patriarchal, and language as it is constituted 'speaks' solely of the male prerogative.

3 Jacques Lacan's term for the processes (rules) of rational discourse.

4 Kristeva's term for the unconscious dynamic of the Maternal as it strives for recognition through creative process.

5 See writings on creative impulse at this time including Hannah Segal, Charles Rycroft, Donald Winnicott and Susan Isaacs.

6 Kristeva's term for the pre-genital phase of symbiotic reverie.

7 For a discussion of *Ecriture Feminine* see Wright, 1992: 74–6.

8 Lacanian term for the field of fantasies and images that are internally constituted from the 'mirror stage' in infancy. See Sarup, 1992.

9 See Adams, 1993.

10 See Navratil, 1987.

REFERENCES

Adams, Tessa (1993) 'From primal scream and primal scene', *Women's Art Magazine*, 54.

Chodorow, Nancy (1978) *The Reproduction of Mothering*. Berkeley, CA: University of California Press.

Chodorow, Nancy (1994) *Femininities, Masculinities, Sexualities: Freud and Beyond*. London: Free Association Books.

Dubuffet, Jean (1976) *L'Art Brut* (catalogue collection). Geneva: Skira Editions.

Freud, Sigmund (1955) *Complete Psychological Works. Vol. XXI.* (trans. J. Strachey). London: Hogarth Press.

Irigaray, Luce (1985) *This Sex Which Is Not One* (trans. C. Porter with C. Burke). Ithaca, NY: Cornell University Press.

Klein, Melanie (1977) *Love, Guilt and Reparation and Other Works 1921–1945*. London: Virago Press.

Kristeva, Julia (1980) *Desire in Language: A Semiotic Approach to Literature and Art* (trans. T. Gora, A. Jardine and L. S. Roudiez). Oxford: Blackwell.

Kristeva, Julia (1987) *Tales of Love* (trans. L. S. Roudiez). New York: Columbia University Press.

Lacan, Jacques (1977) *Écrits: A Selection* (trans. A. Sheridan). London: Tavistock Publications.

Milner, Marion (1950) *On Not Being Able to Paint*. London: Heinemann.

Milner, Marion (1990) *Suppressed Madness of Sane Men: Forty Years of Exploring Psychoanalysis*. London: Routledge.

Navratil, Leo (1987) 'The artist's house: outsider art in Austria', *Art Monthly*.

Sarup, Madan (1992) *Jacques Lacan*. Hemel Hempstead: Harvester Wheatsheaf.

Thevoz, Michel (1976) 'Art Brut', in Jean Dubuffet (ed.), *L'Art Brut*. Geneva: Skira Editions.

Whitford, Margaret (1991) *Luce Irigaray: Philosophy of the Feminine*. London: Routledge.

Winnicott, Donald (1971) *Playing and Reality*. London: Tavistock Publications.

Wright, Elizabeth (1992) *Feminism and Psychoanalysis: A Critical Dictionary*. Oxford: Blackwell.

10

Jung, the Transference and the Psychological Feminine

Joy Schaverien

For some readers Figure 10.1 will be instantly recognizable as denoting a Jungian approach to the transference in psychotherapy. For others the image may seem arcane and so unlikely to have anything serious to contribute to feminist psychotherapy. However I hope to show, in this chapter, that this image, and the series from which it is taken, offer a powerful metaphor for the psychotherapeutic relationship and that furthermore it is relevant within a feminist approach to clinical practice.

The picture is one of a series discovered by Jung in an ancient alchemical text, the *Rosarium Philosophorum* (Jung, 1946). Although it may at first seem esoteric, unworldly and even irrelevant to our present-day concerns, it is an image which Jungians understand as a metaphor for the unconscious meeting in the analytic relationship (Samuels, 1989b). So what does this ancient image hold for present-day therapists? And how can the mating of a heterosexual couple help in thinking about the transference/counter-transference dynamic with regard to feminism? In this chapter I will address this question and show how this series of images informs my analytic work.

THE PSYCHOLOGY OF THE TRANSFERENCE

In the *Psychology of the Transference*, illustrations from the *Rosarium* are equated by Jung with stages in the transference and counter-transference in depth psychology. In the woodcuts the alchemical (or analytic) journey is pictured through the transformations in the (psychological) relationship of the two people. These are the alchemist and his assistant, his *soror mystica*, who are symbolized by the 'imaginary figures of the king and queen' (Samuels, 1985: 181). In psychotherapy the couple are intended by Jung to be seen as the patient and analyst in the transference as well as aspects of the individual psyche. Jung describes how, in alchemy, there is a well-sealed vessel in which a chemical reaction takes place. There is an affinity (an attraction) which draws opposing elements together, causing

CONIVNCTIO SIVE
Coitus.

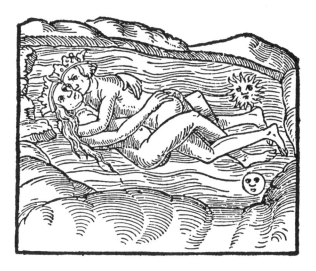

Figure 10.1 *The coniunctio*

an intense chemical mix. There is a fusion of these elements out of which is produced something new, gold, or the philosopher's stone.

The first illustration in the series is the Mercurial fountain (Figure 10.2); this is the vessel, containing the *prima materia* or the divine water, in which the elements are understood to combine. In Figure 10.3 the opposing elements are shown as the sun and the moon, on which stand the king and queen. They are also a brother–sister pair and, although they are clothed, Jung writes that the incestuous connection is revealed in the contact of their left hands. In the next illustration they are naked (Figure 10.4). Then, as the process deepens, they are shown immersed in the bath which is the Mercurial fountain (Figure. 10.5). The transformation is continued in several pictures where they are depicted in copulation, of which the picture shown here as Figure 10.1 is the first. We see the soul, in the form of a child, depart, leaving a state of stasis, the *mortifactio*, a near-death state. It returns symbolizing rebirth, and eventually the disparate parts of the self are united. They come together anew, as is shown by the androgynous figure (Figure 10.6).

This series of pictures can be seen as an illustration of the unconscious relationship in psychotherapy. The alchemical vessel is the analytic relationship sealed by the boundaries and limits of the setting. The confidentiality and the undivided attention of the analyst all contribute to making it possible for the unconscious of patient and therapist to meet. Like the chemical elements of alchemy, there may be an affinity which draws the

ROSARIVM

Figure 10.2   *The Mercurial fountain*

two people together. The analyst lowers his consciousness sufficiently to be open to the influence of the patient and, in the counter-transference, he may temporarily become infected with the patient's neurosis. (I am paraphrasing Jung and therefore using the pronoun 'he' in this context.) There is an intensity, even an attraction, when the unconscious of the patient meets the unconscious of the analyst and an incestuous atmosphere may draw the analyst, in spite of himself, into a repetition of the dynamic of the patient's family. An intense and often erotic form of relating may temporarily dominate in the transference and counter-transference. The point is that Jung's *Psychology of the Transference* (1946) indicates that within a therapeutic relationship all is not as it first appears. This central Jungian text has been discussed by a number of Jungian writers including Jacoby (1984), Schwartz-Salant (1989) and Samuels (1989b), and the full series of pictures may be found in Jung (1946).

Contrary to first impressions, there is a complex gender mixing in this text in which nothing is as it first appears. The story is told through a series of pictures of a heterosexual coupling, but to understand it in merely gender-specific terms would be to miss the complex subtlety of

PHILOSOPHORVM.

Figure 10.3   *The king and queen*

Jung's meaning. Many of Jung's texts have a rather fixed approach to gender difference, but not this one. The couple represent unconscious elements in the transference and so there is a crossing of gender boundaries; the unconscious of the woman may sometimes manifest itself in male guise and the unconscious of the man in female guise. If the pictures are viewed as symbolic of different forms of psychological intercourse they can be understood to be applicable regardless of the reality of the gender or the sexual orientation of the analytic couple. To be open to this we need to relinquish fixed ideas of gender; it may be that a form of gender uncertainty liberates us to apply this understanding to working in the transference.

The Context of Practice

Theories from many schools of psychoanalysis are applied in the clinical practice of present-day analytical psychologists. Fordham (1971, 1973) developed Jungian views of the 'self' through infant observation, applying a Kleinian and object relations framework, and his influence has been considerable in Britain. However, in the space I have here I cannot do

Figure 10.4   *The king and queen naked*

justice to the international literature in this field; instead I have included them in the bibliography at the end of this chapter and refer the interested reader to Samuels, 1985, who gives a helpful overview of the different schools. There are also various international journals on different facets of analytical psychology.

In offering the relevance of alchemy as a metaphor for analytic practice, it is necessary to be clear about the way that I actually work. The wood-cuts, and the sense Jung makes of them, are like a template, a pattern of understanding of unconscious processes, which inform my practice alongside other theoretical models and, most importantly, in response to the patient's material. In *The Revealing Image* (Schaverien, 1991) I analysed a series of pictures, made by a patient, showing how the therapeutic process related to *The Psychology of the Transference*. Although I am informed by understandings gained from many other psychoanalytic schools, particularly Winnicott, Freud and Lacan (Schaverien, 1991, 1995), I will leave aside other psychoanalytic models for the purpose of this chapter and discuss Jung in the context of feminism.

In the analytic encounter, the construction of the frame is carefully planned. In the first session I establish the boundaries of the setting, the

Speculum

Figure 10.5 *The bath*

Figure 10.6 *The androgynous figure*

limits of what is on offer, and negotiate the fee. In this first session I will answer questions regarding my qualifications but I do not generally answer personal questions. However, I have no illusion that the therapist is a blank screen; we communicate about ourselves in many subtle ways which are not always conscious. The layout of the room, clothes and body language all contribute to giving an impression of who we are as people. In my room there are two comfortable chairs, a couch and art materials; this communicates a good deal about what is on offer. Analysis is centred in the transference and counter-transference but, before we can engage with the transference, it is essential to establish a therapeutic alliance (Greenson, 1967). Only then is it possible to interpret the unconscious elements as they unfold within the therapeutic relationship.

To work with the inner world we also need to take account of the reality of the outer world. In certain ways women and men experience the world differently. This may be attributed to cultural factors rather than an essential biological difference (Brennan, 1989; Wright, 1992). A feminist approach enables me to understand that many men, as well as women, are oppressed by the cultural expectations of their social role. In therapy this cannot be ignored and, in my practice, I aim to take account of the social and cultural effects of gender role as well as the personal history. In *Desire and the Female Therapist* (1995) I give a detailed discussion of this.

The counter-transference informs my understanding of the transference. This means that if I feel an arousal, or alternatively none, in relation to a client, I will consider it as a possible unconscious communication. If, for example, I realize that I am feeling bored I might wonder if something in the material is evoking this in me. First I will check myself and question if I am resisting something in the counter-transference. However, if the same thing is repeated in the following session, I begin to suspect that my boredom may be a response to the patient's attempt to remain unconscious of some split-off aspect of the psyche. (This sort of situation has been discussed by Samuels, 1989a.) Interpretations informed by this understanding may reveal some powerful feeling, such as anger, love or a fear, such as of abandonment or psychosis, which has been split off. It is this unconscious situation, that which is unstated, unsayable or unconscious, which is depicted in the woodcuts.

JUNG AND THE PSYCHOLOGICAL FEMININE

It is common for the dominant schools of psychoanalysis to disregard Jung. Insights which Jung wrote about in the early years of psychoanalysis are often 'discovered' by psychoanalysts without due reference or the acknowledgement which any other analyst would receive. This is probably a legacy of the split which developed between Freud and Jung. It was their disagreement over the aetiology and purpose of eros in the analytic encounter which was central to the break in their relationship.

Whilst Freud considered the erotic transference to be based solely in infantile and bodily experiences, Jung understood it rather differently. For Jung eros was seen as a purposive aspect of the life force. In *Symbols of Transformation* (1956) (originally written in 1922) he elucidated this and later, in *The Psychology of the Transference* (1946), he developed it further through understandings gained from his studies of alchemy (Jung, 1953, 1967). Therefore, eros in its widest sense, or the lack of it, is considered to be a central indicator of the life within the analytic encounter.

Jung's erudite knowledge of and interest in other cultures is part of the richness of his writings, but some of the views he expressed are problematic and pose a challenge to those who find his work helpful. It is important to read Jung in order to distinguish the wealth of valuable insights from attitudes which are clearly unacceptable today. Only then is it possible to revision some of his work. One area where this is called for is his writing on gender and particularly the psychological feminine. Here I am intending to make a distinction between what may be regarded as the 'feminine' in the psyche of both men and women and 'female psychology' – i.e. the psychology of women. A number of analysts have written critiques of Jung's views of the feminine and of homosexuality in attempts to distinguish the positive aspects of his thought from his cultural bias, but before discussing them it is necessary to outline some of the concepts on which Jung's theories are constructed.

The Collective Unconscious and Archetypes

Central in Jungian terminology is the collective unconscious. This is considered to be a layer in the psyche which underlies the personal unconscious. It is sometimes likened to geological strata where, as one layer is revealed, it is discovered to be founded on another and yet another (Jacobi, 1942). The collective unconscious is the deepest and least accessible of these layers; it is the foundation of all the others. Jung writes that it can never be fully known nor depotentiated and he suggests that all we can hope for is to gain a conscious attitude in relation to it (Jung, 1959a: 3). The assumption is that all human beings are, at some fundamental level, linked to each other; not separate but related.

The collective unconscious is expressed through archetypes. These are instinctual patterns which have no form in their own right; they are not tangible nor visible but rather sense perceptions. They are the underlying pattern from which images take form in dreams, myth and art. Archetypes are often attributed human form and characterized by figures such as the 'hero' and the 'great mother'. They may manifest themselves in psychological types which centre around generational aspects of the personality such as 'senex', where someone who is very young may have an elderly outlook on life, or 'puer', the 'Peter Pan' character who does not grow up. An archetypal constellation in the transference taps into the collective unconscious and as a result may be experienced as transfixing. When this is activated in the analytic encounter the therapist may find herself under its influence and have difficulty separating from the atmosphere which is evoked. Schwartz-Salant (1989) has drawn parallels with projective identification.

The problem with theory based on archetypal states is that it can be used to argue an essentialist position so that certain characteristics may be attributed as innate in women or in certain ethnic groups. This theory appealed to the Nazis and so its dangers are evident (Samuels, 1993). This is not the topic of this paper but it is as well to acknowledge it because it is for this reason that we must maintain a critical stance in relation to such theories.

Anima and Animus

In Jung's view the psyche is made up of opposites; i.e. any conscious attitude is compensated by an unconscious one.[1] In the context of feminism this merits attention because the concept of anima and animus, which is central in Jungian theory, attributes gendered status to the opposites. Taken too literally this may foster a fixed attitude to gender and sexuality. In Jung's view opposites manifest themselves in culture as well as in the psychological development of the individual. They may be characterized by extremes such as hot and cold, light and dark, day and night. With regard to issues of race this can be problematic, as very often black and dark are attributed to the unconscious state whilst white and light are seen as conscious (Dalal, 1988). Similarly, and this is my interest in this chapter, the feminine element in the psyche is attributed to the dark unconscious state whilst the masculine is associated with light and consciousness. The problem is that, in the language of opposites, there is always an 'other' who may become the convenient and unthinking repository for unwanted projections.

In Jung's writings the feminine is equated with eros and the masculine with logos (1959b: 14). There are aspects of both in men and women which, if they are unconscious, will be projected and attached to a figure of the opposite sex. Thus the unconscious in a man may be characterized by the appearance in his 'dreams, visions or fantasies' of an idealized female or 'anima' figure who carries the archetypal feminine. Jung writes: 'I have suggested the term anima as indicating something specific for which the term soul is too general and too vague' (Jung, 1959b: 13/14). The anima in men is very often attached to the mother imago. 'Every mother and every beloved is forced to become the carrier and embodiment of this omnipresent and ageless image which corresponds to the deepest reality in a man' (Jung, 1959b: 12/13). The anima is the often (but not exclusively) idealized feminine which leads man towards individuation and to a resolution of a projected part of his personality; it is ultimately an aspect of the 'self' (Fordham, 1971; Redfearn, 1985). This accounts, in part at least, for the incestuous dynamic which may be experienced in the transference. The projection of the anima may lead to idealization or else an intense hatred propelled by fear of intimacy which may be particularly intense for a man working with a female therapist (Schaverien, 1995).

In order to find the richness in this theory it is necessary first to confront some of the excesses of androcentrism in Jung's writings with regard to the feminine. In woman, the unconscious element is associated with the animus and, although Jung speculates that this is similar to the anima in man, he is less eloquent, even perhaps a little reluctant, when discussing it. This is shown when he writes: 'if the anima is an archetype that is found in men, it is reasonable to suppose that an equivalent archetype must be present in woman. For just as the man is compensated by woman so the woman is compensated by man' (Jung, 1959b: 14). We have seen that the anima in man is often the romantic temptress whilst the form taken by the animus in woman is less clear.

Furthermore, whilst unconscious possession by either anima or animus results in behaviours which are undesirable, both seem to be attributed to negative aspects of the feminine. For example, animus possession in women produces the aggressive uncooperative mate of the man. Of women, who are unconsciously identified with the masculine element in the psyche, Jung writes: 'no matter how friendly and obliging a woman's Eros may be, no logic on earth can shake her if she is ridden by the animus. Often the man has the feeling . . . that only seduction or a beating or rape would have the necessary power of persuasion' (Jung, 1959b: 15). In cultural terms we have here the traditional justification for violence by men towards women; the woman is blamed. However it is also the feminine which is denigrated in men when he writes: 'men can argue in a very womanish way too, when they are anima-possessed and have thus been transformed into the animus of their own anima' (Jung, 1959b: 15). I present these quotes because they are among the worst of his excesses and characteristic of the problem which we have to confront when applying Jungian concepts within a feminist frame. However, within the same chapter in *Aion* (1959b), Jung makes it clear that the purpose of understanding the opposite elements within the individual psyche is to develop a conscious attitude and so recognize and integrate the projections within the personality: 'The autonomy of the collective unconscious expresses itself in the figures of anima and animus. They personify those of its contents which, when withdrawn from projection, can be integrated into consciousness' (Jung, 1959b: 20). I find this a really helpful way of understanding the psyche. This is the problem; there are so many significant insights in Jung's writing that, if we dismiss him for his misogyny, there is the danger of ejecting the alchemist's gold with the murky waters in which it is disguised.

Rigsby (1994) has pointed out that Jungians often reject feminist arguments and feminists very often ignore Jung; there is frequently avoidance from both when it comes to addressing these problematic areas.

However, if Jung's work is to continue to be useful clinically it is necessary to open these issues for debate in an attempt to revision some of the theory. Among those who have engaged with this are Wehr (1987) who is both a Jungian and a feminist. She has shown that one of the problems is that Jung often confused men's anima projections with female psychology. She writes: 'Had he located both discussions within the context of patriarchy's influence on men and women's sense of self, both would be improved' (Wehr, 1987: 104). Here it seems to me that she makes a significant differentiation between the inner world (particularly of men), and the outer world. She attributes this to the probability that: 'Jung derived his concept of anima from his own experience . . . [and she proposes that] . . . Even though in some ways he was unable to see through his own projections he did come up with a remarkable model for understanding men's feelings about women' (Wehr, 1987: 117). It seems to me that this is the crux of the problem and I concur with Wehr who concludes that there is a real difficulty in resolving a critical attitude to his sexism whilst maintaining a regard for his 'very real contribution to human self-understanding' (Wehr, 1987: 124).

Young-Eisendrath (1984) and Young-Eisendrath and Weidemann (1987) have given accounts of the ways in which these theories can be understood and applied within a feminist frame of reference. Young-Eisendrath (1984), working with heterosexual couples, directly confronts the negative image of the Hag and the apparently more positive image of the Hero, to offer an understanding of the woman who is denigrated in a relationship by her male partner. Through case examples she shows how it is the inability of the couple to communicate with each other and integrate anima/animus projections that causes both to feel resentful, misunderstood and unable to relate to each other. Transformation of the psychological state of both may occur when the projections become conscious and so are withdrawn. In working with individuals, which I am discussing, we can see similar patterns played out in the transference/counter-transference dynamic.

In a collection of papers (Schwartz-Salant and Stein, 1992), anima and animus are addressed from a number of different perspectives. Young-Eisendrath (1992) writes that she finds the concept most useful clinically when applied to Jung's theory of contra-sexuality which 'invites a psychological analysis of the other arising in one's own subjectivity. This is extremely useful in clarifying gender differences . . . providing . . . we revise our theory of gender so that it is relative and contextualised' (Young-Eisendrath, 1992: 175–6). She argues that there is no self-evident or neutral truth about gender: 'gender has no ahistorical, universal meanings' (Young-Eisendrath, 1992: 159). This is a point made in a different way by Hopcke (1991) who has analysed the contradictory attitudes to homosexuality in the writings of Jung and his followers. He argues for a less fixed attitude to sexual orientation which could be understood to be the result of a 'personal and archetypal confluence of the masculine, feminine, and androgyne' (Hopcke, 1991: 187). Significantly he proposes that sexual orientation may be fluid and changing in different phases of life. This may be a helpful way of viewing the woodcuts from *The Psychology of the Transference* (1946). It could be that they too reveal aspects of the psyche which are fluid in relation to gender and, further, offer a pattern of relating which is both interpersonal and intrapersonal.

I will give two brief examples of psychotherapy in an attempt to establish the difference between the inner world, psychological feminine, particularly in the psyche of the man, and female psychology, as lived by a woman. I am informed by counter-transference responses which I have discussed in detail in *Desire and the Female Therapist* (1995). In that book I drew on feminist and psychoanalytic theory to discuss particular issues faced by the female therapist. In the case examples which follow I take a similar position with regard to the material presented.

The first example, a vignette from therapy with a male patient, will show the way in which anima projections may be unconsciously acted out and lived. When they become activated within the transference, the analytic vessel offers a container where they may be held and eventually integrated, leading to a more conscious state. The challenge here is that the female therapist may have to overcome a certain resistance to the attitude to women expressed by the client.

Clinical Vignette – Robert

Robert was married to a woman he described as cold. On his honeymoon he had met another woman, who was on holiday with her husband, and they had had sex while their partners were asleep. The two couples had become friends and the affair between Robert and this woman had continued for 15 years. When he came to me it had recently concluded. This had been a significant relationship for him of which his wife had remained ignorant. Over the years there had also been a number of other brief sexual encounters which had had a less permanent place in his life. We might understand that his anima projections had been embodied, and so lived, in his relationships with these different women. They could all be understood to hold different facets of him and their unconscious purpose had been to enable him to avoid becoming conscious of himself. They had served the purpose of maintaining a split which had been necessary for him in keeping at bay fears, grief and insecurity which had now broken through and driven him to seek therapy.

As I learned his story I came to understand that Robert's particular form of loneliness drove him to search for his ideal feminine partner in many women. No one woman could satisfy his yearning and each seemed temporarily to offer a solution to his feelings of abandonment. Thus his anima projection took form in 'other women' as well as his wife. As time progressed I came to understand how this had come about and how it related to his need to keep sexual passion and daily living arrangements separate. To love and make love in the same place would have meant an integration for which, until now, he had not been ready. He became frightened of his lover, who was passionate, and he realized that he had unconsciously married a woman who was unresponsive to him. This reproduced his early experience of a cold boarding school and an absent but longed-for mother.

With the therapeutic relationship there were again two women in his life; this time his wife and myself. A similar split to that of the wife/ woman friend and the boarding school/mother emerged within the transference. Gradually this made it possible for him to begin to bring all the projected parts of himself together in the one place. Positive and negative elements emerged as the idealization of women gave way to his admission of his disgust and fear of them. Thus we began to understand that the 'other women' served a purpose for him by keeping at bay consciousness of both his homosexuality and his fear of women.

Such material can be regarded from many different points of view. The man is the client and yet the sympathies of the female therapist may mean that she is drawn to consider the position of the women in this story. A feminist's immediate empathy might be with the women, and yet the patient is troubled and searching for insight. It may be helpful to view the analytic setting as the stage on which the patient plays out his drama, assembling all the characters in his story. This helps to see them as elements of his own psyche. Thus it is possible to take both an outer-world, social view, which includes the reality of the effects of this drama in his life, and an inner-world, psychological view.

This example of therapy in a heterosexual pairing can be seen to fit with the alchemical process as illustrated by the woodcuts discussed by Jung. Robert's pattern of relating to women had become manifest in the transference. Much of the time we had been engaged in negotiating a process of intimacy and distance which might be understood to be the psychological parallel of the meetings in the woodcuts. Sometimes he might desire me as a mother or a woman; but at other times, associated with memories of being in the parental bed, he had been repulsed and disgusted at the thought of closeness. In the transference these could be viewed as similar to the meeting in the 'Mercurial fountain' where transformation becomes possible through the immersion. The incestuous intensity increased for a while, and then decreased and turned bad, eventually leading to a more conscious resolution. At the conclusion of our work together Robert summarized the way he had experienced the process and said that he had seen me for a while as his 'mystical' mistress. This choice of imagery, from someone who was not familiar with Jungian theory, seemed to graphically encapsulate the temporary intensity of the engagement in analysis. Perhaps this is particularly so when the patient is a man and the therapist a woman (Schaverien, 1995).

Over time the client takes different positions in relation to the therapist, and when we maintain an element of gender confusion in relation to the process, the patient may experience in the female therapist the paternal function. This is similar to the way in which the male therapist is often understood to carry the maternal transference. The therapist has to be fluid and prepared to be seen in all these roles for the client to be able to fully work through all the elements of the psyche which are evoked by the analytic process. The therapeutic alliance in this case could be understood to parallel the image of the brother/sister pair. I turn now to consider the sister/sister pair.

Clinical Vignette – Flora

The relevance of the alchemical imagery for the transference is less immediately clear for the female therapist when working with women patients. The heterosexual metaphor does not immediately seem to represent intercourse in the same gender pair and yet similar processes occur. In the second case I present, it is not the anima nor animus which was the most significant point, although similar idealized images of men sometimes emerge in the transference with women. However here it is the erotic engagement within the transference on which I will focus; there are times when this may challenge the female therapist to consider her own sexual orientation.

Flora, a married woman with three children, had recently increased her therapy sessions from once to three times a week. She was describing feeling excited today. It was her eldest child's birthday and she was pleased that, contrary to her mother's prediction, she had found that she was able to make a cake and do the other domestic chores necessary to provide for the party. Then she went on to talk about the sexual relationship with her husband, a common theme in recent sessions. She was experiencing herself as passionate and wishing to initiate sex and this had been altering the relationship between them; she felt that he preferred her to be more passive. After a while she turned to me and said, 'I feel this is not what I was wanting to talk about today. It feels as if there is something between us which I wish to talk about but I don't know what that is – I think it relates to the couch.'

In the past the couch had terrified her and, although she had tried it once, she had refused to use it since. She felt that if she were to lie on it she would fall into a black hole. Today the atmosphere was different. Mentally reviewing the material in the session so far, I noted that she had talked about her mother's lack of affirmation of her as a mother, and her husband's lack of affirmation of her initiating sexual contact. It seemed she was feeling creative but constrained and, as this was followed by her reference to the couch, I wondered if she might be experiencing me as constraining her.

After a pause, I told her that I found myself wondering if it might have something to do with sex between us. She said 'maybe', and then went on to talk at length about a transference she had had to a previous, female, counsellor. She had found herself having fantasies about the counsellor's breasts, and this had confused her and she had become concerned about her sexual orientation. She then described how, on a recent weekend visit to her mother, she had slept in her mother's bed. There were only two beds and her children were sleeping in the other one. She had asked her mother if she had ever had lesbian relationships and her mother replied that she had not. It seems that, in Flora's mind, her desire for closeness with her mother and her fear of it had become sexualized. The mother did not affirm her as a viable adult woman, but rather encouraged her dependency, as did the husband who seemed anxious about the power of her sexuality. This seemed to encapsulate the undifferentiated feelings which now began to emerge in the transference.

In the theoretical context of *The Psychology of the Transference* it seems that there was an immediate engagement which was in the process of deepening. Flora had recently committed herself to three sessions a week and was now considering using the couch. We could say that we were both increasing our investment in the process and so were in the vessel together. In the transference the couch seemed to represent getting into bed with me. The excitement, associated with her desire for bodily closeness, and the identification with therapist/mother's body was experienced as sexual. In terms of the alchemical metaphor this could again be understood as the immersion in the process. Furthermore the erotic bond, which is necessary for the individuation process, was beginning. The couch seemed to indicate the intercourse which she desired but also feared with me – an unconscious mix. In psychoanalytic terms the fantasies of breasts clearly evokes a maternal transference which could be understood from a Kleinian frame of reference, and the terror associated with the couch was probably linked to fear of regression to an abandoned baby within. However there was also the sexual passion which she discussed earlier in the session and so it would have been a mistake to understand the transference solely in terms of infantile desires. Equally it was important to acknowledge the infantile aspect of the transference. My understanding is that the sexual issues which seemed to be emerging between us came from trust of the unconscious mix. The memory of being in bed with her mother paralleled the deepening of the therapy, and the discussion of the intercourse with her partner paralleled the intercourse she both desired and feared with me. Would she be too much for me – too able a cook or too passionate? Thus I understand this as the beginning of the affinity, the attraction of opposites, which draws therapist and client into an intense form of relating.

In terms of the counter-transference, too fixed a view of gender and sexual orientation might have caused me to avoid this aspect of the transference as O'Connor and Ryan (1993) have suggested. When considering the female therapist working with a female client, the similarity in the gender experience of the couple makes for identification. This can be a positive benefit but it may also lead to repetition of possible problems with regard to separation (Chodorow, 1978, 1993). Intersubjectivity (Benjamin, 1988) is a helpful way of understanding the mutual need for separate identities which emerges between the mother and her child. However, first the desire for closeness needs to take its particular shape in any therapeutic pairing. This may sometimes challenge the therapist to question her own sexual orientation; is it fixed or can we freely experience within ourselves the variety of possibilities?

CONCLUSION

In this paper I have elaborated and developed my interest in issues of gender in analysis from the perspective of the female therapist (Schaverien, 1995, 1997). I have attempted to apply Wehr's (1987) idea that in Jungian theory a distinction must be made between the psychological feminine and the psychology of women. It seems to me that this makes it possible to apply Jungian theory in the light of feminism. *The Psychology of the Transference* shows us how eros in all its many manifestations is a guide to life in the therapeutic relationship. This is the main point of the somewhat arcane, alchemical imagery. It lends itself to an imaginative approach to the varied material which emerges in the analytic encounter. I do not consider that the story ends here but rather hope that this chapter will encourage others to explore and find their own relation to the original Jungian texts.

NOTE

1 This is similar to other psychoanalytic schools of thought, for example, Racker (1968) who writes of the talion law in this regard.

BIBLIOGRAPHY

Benjamin, J. (1988) *The Bonds of Love*. London: Virago.
Brennan, T. (ed.) (1989) *Between Feminism and Psychoanalysis*. London: Routledge.
Chodorow, N. (1978) *The Reproduction of Mothering; Psychoanalysis and the Sociology of Gender*. Berkeley, CA: University of California Press.
Chodorow, N. (1993) *Femininities, Masculinities, Sexualities: Freud and Beyond*. London: Free Association Books.
Dalal, F. (1988) 'The racism of Jung', *Race & Class*, 29 (3), Winter.
Fordham, M. (1971) *The Self and Autism*. Library of Analytical Psychology vol. 3. London: Heinemann.
Fordham, M. (1973) *Analytical Psychology: a Modern Science*. London: Heinemann.
Gordon, R. (1978) *Dying and Creating: A Search for Meaning*. London: Library of Analytical Psychology/Karnac.
Gordon, R. (1993) *Bridges: A Metaphor for Psychic Processes*. London: Karnac.

Greenson, R. (1967) *The Technique and Practice of Psycho-Analysis.* London: Hogarth.

Hillman, J. (1973) *The Myth of Analysis.* New York: Harper Torch.

Hillman, J. (1979) *The Dream and the Underworld.* New York: Harper & Row.

Hopcke, R. H. (1991) *Jung, Jungians and Homosexuality.* Boston/London: Shambala.

Hubback, J. (1988) *People Who Do Things to Each Other: Essays in Analytical Psychology.* London: Karnac.

Jacobi, Y. (1942) *The Psychology of CG Jung.* London: Routledge and Kegan Paul.

Jacoby, M. (1984) *The Analytic Encounter: Transference and Human Relationship.* Toronto: Inner City Books.

Jung, C. G. (1946) *The Psychology of the Transference,* volume 16 of *Collected Works.* Princeton, NJ: Bollingen.

Jung, C. G. (1953) *Psychology and Alchemy,* volume 12 of *Collected Works.* London: Routledge & Kegan Paul.

Jung, C. G. (1956) *Symbols of Transformation,* volume 5 of *Collected Works.* Princeton, NJ: Bollingen.

Jung, C. G. (1959a) *The Archetypes and the Collective Unconscious,* volume 9, part 1 of *Collected Works.* Princeton, NJ: Bollingen.

Jung, C. G. (1959b) *Aion,* volume 9, part 11 of *Collected Works.* Princeton, NJ: Bollingen.

Jung, C. G. (1967) *Alchemical Studies,* volume 13 of *Collected Works.* Princeton, NJ: Bollingen.

Lambert, K. (1981) *Analysis, Repair and Individuation.* London: Academic Press.

O'Connor, N. and Ryan, J. (1993) *Wild Desires and Mistaken Identities.* London: Virago.

Perry, C. (1991) *Listen to the Voice Within: A Jungian Approach to Pastoral Care.* London: SPCK.

Racker, H. (1968) *Transference and Countertransference.* London: Hogarth.

Redfearn, J. (1985) *Myself my Many Selves.* Reprinted (1994) London: Karnac.

Redfearn, J. (1992) *The Exploding Self.* London: Karnac.

Rigsby, R. K. (1994) 'Jung, archetypalists, and fear of feminism', *Continuum,* 3: 35–58.

Samuels, A. (1985) *Jung and the Post Jungians.* London and New York: Routledge and Kegan Paul.

Samuels, A. (1989a) 'Countertransference and the Mundus Imaginalis', in *The Plural Psyche: Personality, Morality and the Father.* London and New York: Routledge.

Samuels, A. (1989b) 'The alchemical metaphor', in *The Plural Psyche: Personality, Morality and the Father.* London: Routledge.

Samuels, A. (1993) *The Political Psyche.* London and New York: Routledge.

Schaverien, J. (1991) *The Revealing Image: Analytical Art Psychotherapy in Theory and Practice.* London and New York: Routledge.

Schaverien, J. (1995) *Desire and the Female Therapist: Engendered Gazes in Psychotherapy and Art Therapy.* London and New York: Routledge.

Schaverien, J. (1997) 'Men who leave too soon: reflections on the erotic transference and countertransference', *British Journal of Psychotherapy,* 14 (1).

Schwartz-Salant, N. (1989) *The Borderline Personality: Vision and Healing.* Wilmette, IL: Chiron.

Schwartz-Salant, N. and Stein, M. (eds) (1992) *Gender and Soul in Psychotherapy.* Wilmette, IL: Chiron.

Wehr, D. S. (1987) *Jung and Feminism: Liberating Archetypes.* London: Routledge.

Wright, E. (ed.) (1992) *Feminism and Psychoanalysis: A Critical Dictionary.* Oxford: Blackwell.

Young-Eisendrath, P. (1984) *Hags and Heroes: A Feminist Approach to Jungian Psychotherapy with Couples.* Toronto: Inner City Books.

Young-Eisendrath, P. (1992) 'Gender, animus and related topics', in N. Schwartz-Salant and M. Stein (eds) *Gender and Soul in Psychotherapy.* Wilmette, IL: Chiron.

Young-Eisendrath, P. and Weidemann, F. (1987) *Female Authority: Empowering Women Through Psychotherapy.* New York: Guilford Press.

11

A Feminist Systemic Therapy?

Elsa Jones

In this chapter I shall discuss aspects of systemic therapy and their relationship with feminist ideas as propounded by feminist critics from within the systemic field. This will be illustrated by, from time to time, using extracts from therapeutic work with a couple to demonstrate the applications and dilemmas of such an endeavour. I shall be exploring whether it is possible to achieve a coherent feminist systemic position, that is, a therapeutic orientation in which one can take an ethical and effective stance towards the abuse of power in relationships, from an intellectual perspective which honours the validity of many and different voices and points of view, while also holding the systemic view that recursive patterns of behaviour and constraint are co-constructed between participants in relationships. In other words, is a feminist systemic therapy possible?

INTRODUCTION

Systemic therapy is the term currently used to describe a wide range of interactional and narrative approaches to psychotherapeutic work. The term can be used to indicate one particular 'model' (Milan-systemic therapy) or can be used to embrace all the approaches which originated from Gregory Bateson's applications of Von Bertalanffy's General System Theory (Bateson, 1972; Von Bertalanffy, 1968). Even the brief sentence above could be read as controversial within the systemic therapy field, and would indicate, to a reader from within this field, that the author is writing from the standpoint of certain prejudices and preferences (Cecchin et al., 1994). The acknowledgement of the subjectivity of the observer/ describer's perceptions is central to contemporary systemic thinking, and will be discussed further below. Since this chapter does not set out to describe systemic therapy *per se*, which has been discussed at length elsewhere (Boscolo et al, 1987; Burnham, 1986; Jones, 1993), I will devote myself here to describing only certain aspects of the approach which seem to me relevant to the topic of this book, and I will throughout use the term 'systemic therapy'. I will also not refer to the many, significant, and ongoing changes in theory and practice, except insofar as they are relevant to the matter of this chapter.

Initially systemic therapists worked exclusively with families. This reflected the origins of the approach in clinical dissatisfaction with individual approaches, and in the theoretical emphasis on the significant influence, on individual action and emotion, of context, patterns of interaction over time, and the constraints exercised on the parts by the whole. Recently systemic therapists have applied their theories and techniques to working with many different relational groupings (couples, mixtures of family, friendship or work relationships) and also with individuals. This change is in part a response to a less normative and rigid view of how a system may be said to be constituted (and by whom) which derives from theory changes; however, work with different client groups has reflexively influenced the theories and techniques of systemic therapy.

Systemic therapy was slow to provide a hearing for the voice of feminism. As one of the early feminist critics of the approach, I know that, like my colleagues, I co-operated for some considerable time in a largely silent agreement that our 'political' perspectives did not belong in the therapeutic domain. We did so long after, for example, critiques of psychoanalysis had become available (e.g. Mitchell, 1974). This may have been because the field was significantly dominated by male theorists and teachers, but since this was also the case in other approaches it cannot be a full explanation. I incline to the idea that, since systemic family therapy was coming into its own during the 1970s (thus coinciding with the second wave of feminism), the members of our newish in-group may have been displaying solidarity by stifling our own subversive critiques, and pursuing our feminist development in our personal lives but not in our interactions with clients and colleagues. Instead, we pursued the (valuable) systemic goals of neutrality and even-handedness, and the attempts to understand the complementary participation in systems maintenance by all system members. (The problematic implications of these ideas are discussed later.) Systemic therapy worked hard to maintain a tight boundary around itself, as all newly formed groupings do, in order to declare itself distinct from the other therapies and in particular from psychoanalysis, which had been the training ground of most early systemic practitioners (Jones, 1993; Flaskas and Perlesz, 1996). Thus, like women in other revolutionary contexts, we put our shoulders to the wheel and buttoned our lips!

However, feminist critiques of systemic practice did eventually find a voice, and now are seen as significant, if not yet central and dominant, within the field (e.g. Burck and Daniel, 1995; Burck and Speed, 1995; Carter et al., 1984; Goldner, 1985; Hare-Mustin, 1986; Jones, 1990, 1994; Perelberg and Miller, 1990). By this I mean that feminist-informed writing, teaching and practice now pervades the field; it is agreed, by the training bodies responsible for standards of qualifying courses in family and systemic therapies in Britain and the USA, that anti-oppressive (including 'gender-sensitive') theory and practice must be integrated into the content and process of all courses. It may be that systemic therapy eventually proved responsive to feminist critiques for several reasons: the anti-oppressive validation of 'minority' and marginalized perspectives fitted with wider theoretical developments, especially during the 1990s, and allowed systemic therapists to acknowledge that their practices had served and perpetuated the dominant discourses of patriarchy, sexism, heterosexism, and racism; and, in a field where women and men work together, often in teams, with male and female clients simultaneously, it is harder, in the long run, to ignore gender inequities in relationships. Nevertheless, a recent conference (Countering Oppressive Practices – Gender and Systemic Therapy, Oxford, March/April 1996) attracted the same disproportion of women to men as all previous gender- or feminist-focused conferences have done.

I will discuss below the ways in which systemic and feminist perspectives may enhance as well as contradict each other. Feminism, constructivism, and social constructionism will be discussed under separate headings, and linked via a case example.

Feminism

My current working definition of feminism would characterize it as a position concerned, in the first place, with women's rights to equity in the personal, social and political sphere, and, in the second place, with consideration of the deformations and constraints experienced by women and men under androcratic systems. Starting in the early 1980s, feminist systemic therapists have used the lens of feminism to critique the practices of family systems therapy. This has entailed a questioning of many of the shibboleths of systemic therapy at the pragmatic as well as at the theoretical level. Two typical areas may serve to illustrate these changes.

The Fragile Guest

Family therapists in the early days worked very hard to include fathers in family therapy sessions, rather than accepting, as many traditional approaches to child-focused problems did, that seeing the mother and child, together or separately, constituted adequate work with the relevant system. Techniques were evolved for persuading fathers to join in the family sessions, and therapists were sensitive to the fact that, for many men, the terrain of therapy might constitute a new and risky world in which they felt threatened or de-skilled.

However, as feminist critics pointed out, this often meant that the father was treated like an honoured and fragile guest who could not be upset for fear that he would withdraw from the therapeutic work. Thus therapists often placed most of the onus for change, and responsibility for child or marital problems, on the woman. This emphasis was frequently not in awareness, but when challenged, therapists realized that it rested on the assumption that, no matter how blamed a woman felt for the problems of her family, she would be likely to stay in therapy, at least in part because she shared the worker's views about her own primary responsibility for the well-being of family members. Sometimes fathers of troubled children would be involved in the change process – e.g. via tasks that required the father to take over parenting roles previously fulfilled (by implication inadequately) by the mother, thus resulting in an implicit or overt disqualification of the mother's position and an allocation of blame to her, while the father became characterized as the saviour of the child. The stereotype, often backed up by observation, of the 'over-involved mother' and the 'disengaged father' served to pathologize mothering; it was feminist protest that allowed systemic therapists to consider that both positions are mandated by social role expectations (e.g. who is expected to remain in paid work after the birth of children, and who is expected to take responsibility for children's well-being), and then become part of a complementary vicious circle, where the less time a father spends with children the more involved a mother becomes with children, and the more involved – i.e. knowledgeable, close, burdened – a mother becomes, the more disengaged – i.e. inept, marginalized, unaware – a father becomes. This is a circular interaction, whose 'starting point' can be punctuated arbitrarily anywhere on the fluid, mutually reinforcing cycles of interaction over time. Systemic therapists excel at the construction of such circularities – how strange then that, for so long, this particular circle was always punctuated as starting at the woman's end.

Blaming the Victim

Perhaps the most problematic therapeutic domain, which obliged systemic therapists to change their theory and practice, is that of sexual abuse and gendered violence (Jones, 1991). Systemic theory postulated that all system members influence the patterns and relationships of their system. In practice this became a (theoretically questionable) view that all system members had equal influence. Put together with the vaunted neutrality of systemic therapists this was a recipe for victim-blaming and the therapeutic abuse of already abused women and children. Systemic therapists were (laudably) anxious not simply to act punitively towards, for example, men who behaved violently towards their female partners, but rather to search for a systemic understanding of the man's position, and for potentials for change. However, this search, via systemic 'curiosity' and the exploration of complementary patterns in the behaviour of both partners before a violent incident, very often led to the overt and covert blaming of the victim for her victimization, or at the very least to a false attribution of equivalence to different behaviours (she makes him feel inadequate *therefore* he hits her).

Feminist responses to such blatantly unsatisfactory practices have brought about significant change in the systemic field. Feminists insisted that inequities in systemic influence, deriving from inequities within familial and social constructions of role, choice, economic power, or gender ascription, had to be taken into account *as well as* the systemic recursiveness of mutually reinforcing behaviour within the couple. The absence of an adequate theoretical account of power use and abuse within systemic thinking was then connoted by feminists as a failure of the theory itself; the challenge is whether the theory can prove flexible enough to evolve in response to these demands. This position is articulated clearly by Goldner and her colleagues (1990) in the description of their approach to their pioneering work with couples where the man's violence and the woman's loyalty to him constitute an intractable therapeutic dilemma:

> The *psychoanalytic* aspect of our work involves inquiry about ideas, beliefs, and, more deeply, internal representations of self and other, which are sometimes out of awareness but, when elucidated, often seem to constitute the organising and unworkable premises underlying these couples' fierce attachments. The *social learning* dimension focuses on how these particular men and women were socialised into their gendered positions in these relationships. At the *sociopolitical* level, we include all of the external power differentials between men and women, including men's subjective sense of entitlement, privilege, and permission to rule women, and women's subjective belief that they must serve men. Finally, at the *systemic* level, we are interested in the transactional sequences, especially positive feedback loops, which are the immediate 'cause' of the escalations that lead to· violence, as well as all the double-binding processes between the couple, the extended families, and the treatment and social-service contexts that constitute the problem-maintaining system. (My emphasis, ibid., p. 346)

While there are still sections of systemic thought and practice which insist that attention to difference and inequity between women and men constitutes an abandonment of a systemic perspective, nevertheless for many of us it has opened the door to a flexible practice which can simultaneously consider the differences in relational power and role attribution between system members, and pay attention to the ways in which such system participants collaboratively co-construct interactive patterns which may be mutually constraining, or partially beneficial, or damaging to one or both.

Tracey and Gareth are a white couple in their late twenties who were referred for couple therapy by Tracey's general practitioner because of Tracey's long-standing and severe depression, for which she had been treated unsuccessfully with drugs, intermittently, since adolescence. Gareth agreed to participate in therapy because Tracey was threatening (as she had done before) to leave him unless something changed. They lived together with their daughter Emma (aged two and a half) and Marilyn (10), Tracey's daughter from a previous relationship.

Tracey's life had been characterized by many abusive relationships. She described her early childhood as happy. By this she meant that she remembered instances, before the age of six, of cuddling with both parents, and of being read stories. However, both parents were violent towards her and her younger brother. When Tracey was six her mother left the family, breaking off all contact. Her father remarried quickly, and from this time seemed to lose interest in Tracey. She construed this as an indication that anyone she loved would always prefer someone else; whenever there was a relational triangle, she expected to be the rejected one. This dynamic was crucial to her inability to break away from Gareth.

At the age of 12 Tracey was raped by a friend's cousin and became pregnant. Subsequent action by family and public agencies, including the termination of the pregnancy, all occurred without any discussion with Tracey herself. She behaved delinquently for a period after this, including traunting from school, shoplifting, and engaging in sexual promiscuity. At the age of 14 she asked to be taken into care (evidently hoping, like so many children who make this request, to be cared for) and spent two unhappy years in a children's home. At 16 she moved to London. Her first marriage, to Marilyn's father, was characterized by his violence to her. She became pregnant with Emma very soon after meeting Gareth, and he moved into her flat. She is not currently employed. She had in the past had some fleeting interactions with therapists and counsellors which she did not find helpful. Her account is that their insistence that she should leave her violent partners made her feel misunderstood and 'useless'. She feels unable to bear the relationship with Gareth and unable to leave it.

Gareth is the youngest of three children. His father drank to excess, and was routinely violent to his mother, who explicitly stayed with him 'for the sake of the children'. When Gareth turned 16 his mother left his father, inviting Gareth to accompany her. However, at this point he saw his father collapse into helplessness and grief, and decided to stay with him. For about two years he attempted to achieve some closeness with his father, but eventually left; the final straw for him was that his father gave the last food in the house to his drunken gambling cronies, leaving Gareth hungry. He describes himself in childhood as being on his mother's side, and critical of his father's violence. He works at unskilled labour. Tracey is the first serious relationship for Gareth. When she was in hospital giving birth to Emma he had had a 'one-night stand' with another woman.

Gareth has frequently been violent to Tracey, and early in the therapy they described a recent violent episode. Gareth had defaulted on a planned family outing because he had gone drinking with workmates. When he arrived home in the early hours Tracey had shouted at him and demanded to know where he had been – she was sure that he had been with another woman – and he had punched and kicked her. She had not seen the doctor for this nor called the police, though she was badly bruised.

Gareth's predominant perception of this and other violent episodes was that he couldn't help it, and that she made him do it. In contrast to his traditionally 'macho' presentation of self, via language, posture, and so on, his descriptions of events gave a striking impression to the therapist of helplessness and passivity. Thus when his workmates wanted to go on drinking he 'had' to stay with them, and when Tracey confronted him he 'had' to hit her. In the session he is startled and later intrigued by the therapist's framing of the passivity underlying his aggressiveness, and by her invitation and challenge to him to achieve some control over how he expresses distress, and over his life generally. This, and the therapist's simultaneous signalling of interest in wider systemic antecedents and influences on his and the couple's current dilemmas, enables him (although not easily) to co-operate in a 'safety contract' for therapy, which aims to ensure that he will take responsibility for refraining from violence while changes in the relationship are explored.

Tracey also finds her part of the 'safety contract' difficult, in that she is required to act so as to ensure her own safety, rather than holding Gareth responsible for it. It seems to her unfair that, for example, she should call the police or go to a refuge in the middle of the night with the children, when he is the one who is to blame. This view is understandable, but is also part of what keeps her locked in place in an escalating interaction which often ends in Gareth's assault on her. When both of them accept that, at the end of the escalating cycle leading to violence, the final trigger might be their joint sense of being trapped, they are more likely to co-operate in defusing the situation via the woman's initiation of a safety manoeuvre, and the man's backing off. A sentence like the one above is easily written, but of course the achievement of such a position is the consequence of much intense and skilled therapeutic work.

This mutual attribution of responsibility is common in situations of 'domestic' violence. It is as if the woman says, 'If he loved me he would protect me and keep me safe', and the man says, 'If she loved me she would not let me get upset'. Behind these positions lie the complexities of gender discourse which shape their expectations of femininity, masculinity, and the role of the couple relationship. The therapist invites each of them to take responsibility for that part of the interaction over which each can exert control (namely their own actions), while also being clear about the nature and impact of a violent assault which, if directed toward a stranger in public, would unquestioningly be deemed criminal, rather than being dismissed as 'domestic'. Nor does the therapist accept the pretence of equivalence between Tracey's actions, which may be seen as triggering the assault, and Gareth's, which consist of the use of physical force. Their presentation of these behaviours as equivalent rests on a long history of familial and social gender prescription which results in Gareth's belief that violence is a legitimate expression of his frustration, and in Tracey's sense that she has to put up with it.

It is not easy for a therapist in this situation to hold a 'both/and' position (Goldner, 1992), but it is systemic.

Constructivism

Systemic therapy, like many other disciplines (e.g. philosophy, literary studies), has inevitably been influenced by the postmodern ideas prevalent in the current intellectual climate of post-industrial Western societies. The systemic version of constructivism derives in particular from the work of several biologists and philosophers concerned with how we may apprehend 'reality' (e.g. Maturana and Varela, 1988; Von Foerster, 1981; Von Glaserfeld, 1984). The notion that the observer brings forth or constructs that which is observed, and that such observation is constrained by the structure (cognitive, physiological, relational, cultural, etc., etc.) of the observer, brought systemic therapists to the position where 'everything said is said by an observer, and there is no possibility of referring to objective truth or reality in order to choose between descriptions' (Jones, 1993: 24).

In practice this has meant an abandonment of normative and prescriptive views of 'healthy' family functioning, which was already implicit in earlier systems thinking, and an acceptance of the 'multiverse' (Mendez et al., 1988) of many different views constructed by many multi-faceted individuals in interaction. What we see, and the meaning we attribute to it, is constrained and constructed by the perceptual and meaning-making biases, limitations, preferences, learning, and so on, of ourselves as observers. Therefore a change in the 'lenses' (Hoffman, 1990) through which we view interaction, and a change in the meanings constructed through interaction in language, can also lead to a dissolving of problems and new openings for change (Anderson and Goolishian, 1988). The implications of such a position for feminist therapists are not simple: on the one hand it means that the voice of the marginalized must be heard as valid; on the other hand it means that the view that, for example, male violence towards women is unacceptable, is only *a* point of view. (See Krüll, 1987, for a fascinating discussion of how a constructivist therapist may hold a 'multiversal' position on relative truths *as well as* a feminist certainty on issues such as violence and inequity.)

Moreover, the therapist is part of the observing system which she attempts to observe and influence. Thus her descriptions (for example of Tracey and Gareth) are subjective, and will influence and be influenced by Gareth and Tracey's descriptions. The therapeutic endeavour becomes a co-operative and recursive attempt to construct new accounts or 'narratives' for client lives which will not coalesce around intractable problems, but will increase the range of choices for all involved (Von Foerster, 1990).

By placing herself within the observing system, the therapist makes her own (gendered) presence, her perceptions of clients and their perceptions of her, part of the therapeutic discourse. Instead of pretending to objectivity, there is an acknowledgement that the therapist's values, personal and professional history, gender and so on influence and subjectively construct that which is being observed and described about the clients in therapy. For example, in working with Gareth and Tracey, their relatively ill-educated and 'working-class' situation, compared with the therapist's well-educated and 'middle-class' presence was seen as relevant and was at times discussed as a potential obstacle to understanding, as well as a source of tension-relieving jokes – e.g. the therapist confessed her belief that husbands and wives sometimes went out together, which to the couple seemed very strange. Their and the therapist's shared white ethnicity, and the therapist's age, which placed her in a 'motherly' relation to them, were not discussed, but undoubtedly allowed the therapist some latitude in being able to challenge Gareth to a degree which, coming from a male or black colleague, might have elicited a backlash. (The subjectivities of class, age, culture, ethnicity, sexual orientation and so on of the therapist and the clients are highly relevant to a constructivist therapeutic position, and may be dealt with either within the therapist's awareness or in overt discussion with clients. They are not discussed in any detail here, for reasons of space. See, for example, Burck and Speed, 1995, or Van Lawick and Sanders, 1995).

By maintaining a multi-positional and tentative stance in relation to 'truth', the therapist is able to hear and join in a range of client positions, articulated and inchoate, and to collaborate in a search for new meanings rather than operating from a position which coerces clients into 'acceptable' and 'healthy' behaviours and roles.

In inviting Gareth and Tracey to take responsibility for their own actions in ensuring the safety required to continue with therapy, the therapist also overtly takes responsibility for her decision to require this of them. That is, she holds certain values and professional positions about, in this instance, physical violence and coercion, and needs to feel reassured that she can explore freely in the therapy sessions without having to fear, for example, that by inviting Tracey to speak out in the session she will be contributing to her getting beaten up afterwards. The therapist, in other words, is entitled to feel safe in carrying out her professional responsibilities. However, since she holds a tentative rather than an absolute position in relation to her own 'truths' as well as those of Tracey and Gareth, she is able to take a position while remaining open and available to the exploration of their respective positions.

In hearing Gareth and Tracey's different versions of their interaction the therapist's stance makes it possible for these to be framed as points of view, perceptions, constructions, and not as immutable truths. In this atmosphere it becomes possible for Gareth to explore his belief that Tracey only stays with him because his violence makes her too frightened to leave him; the fact that he believes she stays under coercion makes him despair of ever being loved by her. He thinks that his violent, neglectful and uncommunicative habitual stance towards her has destroyed anything she may have felt for him once, but cannot face losing her, and so continues to hold her by force. Tracey sees herself as worthless and unlovable, so that Gareth's actions merely confirm for her what she has learned about herself in many other relationships; because of her long history of abuse she finds it hard to give weight to Gareth's violence – even though she has suffered considerable physical damage. Any suspicion on her part that Gareth may prefer another (a woman, his father, his mates, their child) obliges Tracey to cling to the relationship, since for her it reactivates the fear that she will once again be the outsider in a triangle.

By exploring these beliefs, as well as the detailed narration of specific interactions, from a framework that asks repeatedly 'And what is *your* point of view?', 'What would happen if . . .?', 'How might it be different . . .?' 'How do you explain that you reacted like that?', and so on, the therapist offers her intense interest in Tracey and Gareth's constructions of their reality, *as well as* a framing that suggests these are points of view among many other potential points of view. As Gareth and Tracey begin to make changes in their constructions of self and relationship, this is also signalled by changes in language, and they begin to use phrases like 'Mind you, this is just my view', or 'I thought, I wonder how she sees this?'

However, as already mentioned, constructivist positions had more and less desirable consequences for systemic therapy from a feminist perspective. The idea that many various voices and truths could be seen as equally valid meant that previously silenced and marginalized discourses within the field – such as feminism, gay and lesbian perspectives, ethnic minority experiences and values – could now claim a forum in which to be heard. Therapists were freer to attend and respond to the many different perspectives within client groups, and to expand these in the mutual search for change, access to client creativity and resources, and tolerance of difference.

Categorizing all these voices as equally valid also meant, paradoxically, a potential silencing of feminist attempts to draw attention to the inequities women experienced within traditional family structures. Thus feminist attempts to discuss and respond to violence and oppression became just another point of view – the view that everything mattered led to the conclusion that nothing mattered (Brodribb, 1992). As Irigaray (1985) has observed, postmodernism may be the last ruse of patriarchy.

SOCIAL CONSTRUCTIONISM

Dissatisfaction with the relativism of radical constructivism led systemic therapists, and feminists in particular, to reach for the different relativism of social constructionism. While from a certain perspective these two positions can both be described as constructivist (i.e. different from and in opposition to an empiricist position regarding the status of truth or reality), it is their differences that are relevant here. A constructivist position emphasizes the individual construction of reality, whereas a social constructionist position emphasizes the role of culture, history and society in such a construction. In particular it is social constructionism's emphasis on the social context in which descriptions of self and other are organized that allows systemic therapists to hold feminist positions within a multi-positional systemic frame. This contextualizing stance is coherent with the practice of systemic therapy, which sees meaning as being in part determined by the context in which relationships and behaviours occur. Thus a feminist systemic position would argue that to consider, for example, an interaction in which one member of a couple hits another *only* within the recursive loops of the couple interaction, without including contextual influences such as the social discourse on male violence, on gender, on power and submission, on love and the couple bond, and so forth, would be to act unsystemically, since systemic perspectives are significantly rooted in the view that individual actions are organized and constructed within a relational context, and cannot and should not be viewed in isolation.

In exploring how the relationship between Tracey and Gareth is, and how it might change, the therapist invites them to make connections with how they learned to be as they are in the context of family history and of wider social learning, in particular about gender, love and violence. Gareth explores his childhood contempt for his father, and pity for his mother, in the light of the realization that he has turned out exactly like his father. He faces the possibility that his daughter Emma might, in another 20 years' time, talk to a therapist about him as he now talks about his father. He faces the daunting task of learning how to monitor his own emotions (having previously experienced himself as 'blank'), of becoming emotionally articulate, of being able to feel vulnerable or in the wrong without converting this into violence, and of taking the risk that Tracey might leave him if he unlocks the cage door. He realizes that he has no models for alternative ways of constructing masculinity, and begins, with the therapist's help, to search for different ways to be a self-respecting man. Tracey not only examines the messages she received from so many significant people in her early life about her value as a person and a woman, but also explores the social and cultural messages about womanhood that she has absorbed which have held her passive in the face of abuse and rejection. Her changes, in regard to self-assertion and a sense of self-worth, link recursively with the changes Gareth attempts, and these also resonate in the life of the family, where both parents find different ways of interacting with the children.

CONCLUSION

Is a feminist systemic therapy possible, or is the opposition between these two positions necessary for good practice? I would like to continue to maintain the 'necessary contradictions' (Goldner, 1992) of continuing to be aware of the differences between them. Systemic therapy has, so far, proved itself to be flexible and adaptive, rooted in theories without normative or prescriptive positions, available to explore and construct narratives which are respectful of client resources, history, culture and capabilities. Because the approach takes a collaborative, co-constructive path, it allows clients to find the space to empower themselves. Because the work involves women and men (clients and therapists, the latter often working in teams), systemic therapy has been forced to find ways of being respectful and clinically responsible to both genders, including the respect implicit in the assumption that someone is capable of change.

However, systemic therapy has historically had a tendency to reify the boundaries it places around particular systems, forgetting that its theory would describe this act of punctuation as arbitrary. For a period systemic therapy privileged the system above the individual (and thus could not think about inequity). At present the resistance to feminist ideas, and theorizing about power, rests on the tendency to privilege the hetero-sexual couple or family system above the social context (and thus to be unable to think about inequity). It may be for this same reason that systemic therapists have been able, within largely separate groupings, to address problems of gender, ethnicity, sexuality and even, tentatively, class, but have not been able to unite all these strands in a truly subversive critique of the still dominant discourse which maintains power by not theorizing power. Thus systemic thought, which proceeds via a sceptical, curious, deconstructive approach, repeatedly becomes blind to its own prejudices.

Feminism, on the other hand, easily moves into the position of privil-eging gender only, and within this category privileging women only, which contains the potential for deteriorating into fundamentalism. A focus on women's issues has been historically necessary, in order to lift women's oppression from the taken-for-granted obscurity where it could not be seen or changed. However, it has left many therapists in despair about how to reach men therapeutically, and indeed about the question of whether it is possible to work successfully with men like Gareth, as well as sometimes leading to pejorative characterization of women like Tracey who will not or cannot leave the men who abuse them.

Systemic therapists, because of their choice of domain, have chosen not to take a unilateral stance in relation to an exclusively female perspective. Thus a feminist position within the systemic model can, at its best, be characterized as 'radically' feminist, in the sense that it concerns itself with the way in which men as well as women have been damaged by patriarchal social systems (Evans, 1995).

As long as systemic feminist therapists (and that includes the author!) can continue to hold a both/and, and a yes/but, position in relation to the shortcomings of both feminist and systemic positions, and see both of these as tentative, though passionately held, subjectivities, it is likely that clients will benefit from the resulting sceptical, self-reflexive and continually adaptive psychotherapeutic stance.

REFERENCES

Anderson, Harlene and Goolishian, Harold A. (1988) 'Human systems as linguistic systems: preliminary and evolving ideas about the implications for clinical theory', *Family Process*, 27 (4): 371–93.

Bateson, Gregory (1972) *Steps to an Ecology of Mind: Collected Essays in Anthropology, Psychiatry, Evolution and Epistemology*. Chandler Publishing Company (reprinted 1973/8, St Albans: Granada).

Boscolo, Luigi, Cecchin, Gianfranco, Hoffman, Lynn and Penn, Peggy (1987) *Milan Systemic Family Therapy: Conversations in Theory and Practice*. New York: Basic Books.

Brodribb, Somer (1992) *Nothing Mat(t)ers: A Feminist Critique of Postmodernism*. North Melbourne, Australia: Spinifex Press.

Burck, Charlotte and Daniel, Gwyn (1995) *Gender and Family Therapy*. London: Karnac Books.

Burck, Charlotte and Speed, Bebe (eds) (1995) *Gender, Power, and Relationships*. London: Routledge.

Burnham, John B. (1986) *Family Therapy – First Steps towards a Systemic Approach*. London: Tavistock Publications.

Carter, Elizabeth, Papp, Peggy, Silverstein, Olga and Walters, Marianne (1984) *Mothers and Sons, Fathers and Daughters*. Washington DC: The Women's Project in Family Therapy.

Cecchin, Gianfranco, Lane, Gerry and Ray, Wendel A. (1994) *The Cybernetics of Prejudices in the Practice of Psychotherapy*. London: Karnac Books.

Evans, Judith (1995) *Feminist Theory Today: An Introduction to Second-Wave Feminism*. London: Sage Publications.

Flaskas, Carmel and Perlesz, Amaryll (eds) (1996) *The Therapeutic Relationship in Systemic Therapy: A Collection of Papers*. London: Karnac Books.

Goldner, Virginia (1985) 'Warning: family therapy may be hazardous to your health', *The Family Therapy Networker*, 9 (6): 19–23.

Goldner, Virginia (1992) 'Making room for both/and', *The Family Therapy Networker*, March/April: 55–61.

Goldner, Virginia, Penn, Peggy, Sheinberg, Marcia and Walker, Gillian (1990) 'Love and violence: gender paradoxes in volatile attachments', *Family Process*, 29 (4): 343–64.

Hare-Mustin, Rachel (1986) 'The problem of gender in family therapy theory', *Family Process*, 26: 15–27.

Hoffman, Lynn (1990) 'Constructing realities: an art of lenses', *Family Process*, 29 (1): 1–12.

Irigaray, Luce (1985) *The Sex Which is not One* (trans.). Ithaca, NY: Cornell University Press.

Jones, Elsa (1990) 'Feminism and family therapy: can mixed marriages work?', in Rosine J. Perelberg and Ann C. Miller (eds), *Gender and Power in Families*. London: Routledge.

Jones, Elsa (1991) *Working with Adult Survivors of Child Sexual Abuse*. London: Karnac Books.

Jones, Elsa (1993) *Family Systems Therapy: Developments in the Milan-systemic Therapies*. Chichester: John Wiley & Sons.

Jones, Elsa (1994) 'Gender and poverty as contexts for depression, *Human Systems: The Journal of Systemic Consultation and Management*, 5: 169–83.

Krüll, Marianne (1987) 'Systemic thinking and ethics: political implications of the systemic perspective', in Jürgen Hargens (ed.) (1990), *Systemic Therapy: A European Perspective*. Broadstairs, Kent: Borgmann.

Maturana, Humberto R. and Varela, Francisco J. (1988) *The Tree of Knowledge: The Biological Roots of Human Understanding.* Boston, MA: Shambala.

Mendez, Carmen L., Coddou, Fernando and Maturana, Humberto R. (1988) 'The bringing forth of pathology', *The Irish Journal of Psychology*, 9 (1): 144–72.

Mitchell, Juliet (1974) *Psychoanalysis and Feminism.* Harmondsworth: Penguin Books.

Perelberg, Rosine J. and Miller, Ann C. (eds) (1990) *Gender and Power in Families.* London: Routledge.

Van Lawick, Justine and Sanders, Marjet (1995) *Family, Gender and Beyond.* Heemstede, The Netherlands: LS Books.

Von Bertalanffy, Ludwig (1968) *General System Theory: Foundations, Development, Applications.* Harmondsworth: Penguin Books.

Von Foerster, Heinz (1981) *Observing Systems.* Seaside, CA: Intersystems.

Von Foerster, Heinz (1990) 'Ethics and second-order cybernetics'. Paper presented at the International Conference on Systems and Family Therapy: Ethics, Epistemology, New Methods. Paris.

Von Glasersfeld, Ernst (1984) 'An introduction to radical constructivism', in Paul Watzlawick (ed.), *The Invented Reality.* New York: W.W. Norton & Co.

12

Change and Theoretical Frameworks

I. Bruna Seu

He who despises himself still nonetheless respects himself as one who despises. (Nietzsche, 1973: 92)

One of the crucial questions in this book is: what is feminist therapy? Many of the contributors have explored the constraints, contradictions and limitations imposed by their therapeutic framework on their feminist practice (Trevithick, Adams, Heenan). Some have also explored the usefulness of neutrality and how this might in fact be problematic for feminist practices (Marecek, Jones). Following on from that, I also want to question the intrinsic neutrality of the 'therapeutic space' and interrogate it as a possible site of the reproduction of women's oppression.

This chapter is concerned with the use of language as ideological activity in psychotherapy. It suggests that we turn our attention to the implications of the value systems we live in, contribute to and re/create when we wonder what is feminist in our practice. I argue that the employment of discourse analysis can be beneficial in investigating the ideological implications of the language we ordinarily use; but I also caution against the dangers of a postmodern turn in psychotherapy.

This chapter is divided into three parts. In the first part, I offer a brief introduction to what in social sciences is referred to as the 'turn to language'. This will touch on current debates concerning the nature of the subject and subjectivity and on the questioning of language as a neutral means of expression. Attention to language as social action which constructs reality also involves interrogation of the ideological functions of our therapeutic language.

In the second part, I explore this issue in depth through the analysis of an extract from an interview which is part of a research project I have been involved in. The particular extract I will be discussing has been selected for this chapter because it gives an account of how therapy has contributed to the interviewee's change in terms of self-esteem and her relationships. It focuses on the interviewee positioning herself as the 'responsible subject'. In reconnecting this account to wider social issues I will try to show some of the implications for our feminist practice of adopting an individualistic model.

Part three explores some alternatives put forward in line with a 'postmodern' turn in psychotherapy and looks at its possible benefits and intrinsic dangers. In contrast with the relativistic attitude put forward by some postmodern theories of psychotherapy, I conclude by arguing for an increased rather than reduced accountability as feminist psychotherapists. Accepting this might mean, however, having to take a closer look at what we do with our power as therapists and how we position ourselves in the therapeutic space we construct with our patients.

When talking about psychotherapy in this chapter, I will be referring to one-to-one psychodynamic psychotherapy, as this is the framework in which I practise.

PSYCHOTHERAPY AND IDEOLOGY

Psychoanalysis looks for explanations of people's actions inside the person, through an inquiry into their unconscious minds and their intrapsychic conflicts. The analyst's task is to attempt 'to grasp the real that underlies surface appearances' and to combat the patient's resistance to knowing it; resistance being, according to Freud, the main pathological factor in neurosis (Flax, 1990: 65–6). The patient is made aware of the unconscious motivations in their actions through their unwitting repetitions in the analytic process. It is in this context that the analyst's objectivity and neutrality, according to Freud, are crucial. If we accept that human relationships are based on an interplay of mutual projections of unconscious desires and conflicts, it is essential that the analyst functions as a 'blank screen' in order to mirror back the projections to the patient who, with the help of interpretation, will come to acknowledge them. Thus 'the unconscious compulsion to repeat is gradually replaced by a greater degree of conscious choice' (Flax, 1990: 69).

In total opposition to this view, the French philosopher Michel Foucault (1981) strongly objected to the existence of anything deep inside us that can be uncovered through recourse to experts (psychoanalysts, psychologists) whose knowledge provides privileged access to the person's self. He argued against any essentialist notion of 'human nature' and claimed instead that subjectivity in Western cultures is constructed through disciplinary and confessional practices. These practices are organized through discourses which can be described as patterns of meaning, accounts of actions and experience which describe the world in a particular way (Parker, 1997). For example a 'medical discourse' will lead us to speak about distressing experiences as if they were a reflection of an underlying disease (Parker, 1997: 285). It is through discourses, particularly those relating to human behaviour, that we come to learn what it is to be human, what is true and normal. In other words 'they "normalize" the "individual" who is constituted and named by these discourses' (Flax, 1990: 207).

Foucault argued that it is through discourse that external coercion becomes internal regulation through the person exercising surveillance upon themselves. This apparently voluntary self-discipline, however, is said to lead to self-knowledge. Psychoanalysis according to Foucault is a particularly powerful, ideologically driven, confessional practice which normalizes oppressive social norms, pathologizes difference and perpetuates the oppressive status quo (Foucault, 1981). Thus, studies of discourse look at a particular 'regime of truth' which constructs the way we talk and the way we experience our self and the world (Parker, 1997), and how certain discourses reproduce power relations (Foucault, 1977).

Language is a form of social action because it *constructs* rather than merely describes the self, people's experience, social and psychological phenomena (Wetherell and Potter, 1992; Potter, 1996). These constructions of the world, however, are not purely theoretical abstractions, but each carries different implications (Burr, 1995) and has crucial repercussions on the way we view and value ourselves and others (Burman and Parker, 1993). As people construct versions of reality in their daily interactions through language, discourse analysts have made it the subject of their inquiry. Discourse analysts believe that language is not a neutral, transparent medium between the social actor and the world, nor a blank window through which the researcher or the therapist regards the psyche of the subject, but an ideologically charged social activity (Potter and Wetherell, 1987) which 'plays its part in legitimizing or challenging, supporting or ironizing, endorsing or subverting what it describes' (Parker, 1997: 290).

Another fundamental issue in Foucauldian discourse analysis is the analysis of power and resistance which moves away from a conceptualization of power as located in definable sites of oppression to a study of how power and ideology permeate our social practices in many complex ways (Hall, 1988). Foucault did not conceptualize power as an institution nor as a structure, but as a 'multiplicity of force relations', simultaneously 'intentional' yet 'non-subjective' (Smart, 1985: 77). Power, according to Foucault, finds expression in forms of internal regulation, i.e. when forces from 'outside' work as self-discipline from 'within'. Power, therefore, is not just a negative prohibition, but can be recognized when a subject willingly says 'yes' to some mode of behaviour, or sees this mode as particularly expressive of their real identity (Wetherell and Potter, 1992: 84). As we will see in the analysis of the extract, this is what is conveyed by the interviewee when she describes how her former identification with being angry and destructive is now replaced with an identification with a truer self: the responsible subject. This is why, from the rejection of a single locus of power or resistance, Foucault's interest moved to investigating the techniques which legitimize power and how these work 'at the level of those continuous and uninterrupted processes which subject our bodies, govern our gestures, dictate our behaviours, etc.' (Foucault as quoted by Smart, 1985: 79).

Through this form of regulation, discourse produces subject-positions. To follow the production of these discourses, and the subject-positions created within them, is to understand the way power unfolds and oppression is perpetrated, as studying ideology is to study the ways in which meaning (signification) serves to sustain relations of domination (Potter and Wetherell, 1987).

Both discourse analysis and psychoanalysis offer the possibility of looking at factors which militate against change and at the dynamic interplay between resistance to power and resistance to change. However, while psychoanalysis looks at resistance to change as an intrapsychic conflict, discourse analysis looks at the meaning and values attached to a person's practices and the power and constraints offered by different subject-positions, which allow the person to position themselves in relation to others (Hollway, 1984).

Hence, discourse analysts pay attention in linguistic analysis, not only to the position of statements, but also to the function that statements perform beyond the simple communication of information (Wetherell and Potter, 1992). In this way, a person's speech is looked at as built up of accounts or repertoires which, constructed out of existing resources, provide the speaker with the possibility of taking various, sometimes contradictory, subject-positions (Hollway, 1989). Subject-positions can be described as 'places' in the discourse which carry certain rights to speak and specifications for what may be spoken (Parker, 1997). The subject-positions the speakers take within these accounts will determine their self at that given moment. Subjectivity, however, cannot be equated with 'individual', nor with 'self' or 'identity'. I am referring to this term as it has been postulated by Henriques et al. (1984):

> We use 'subjectivity' to refer to individuality and self-awareness – the condition of being a subject – but understand in this usage that subjects are dynamic and multiple, always positioned in relation to discourses and practices and produced by these – the condition of being 'subject'. (Henriques et al., 1984: 3)

People must assume these places for the discourse to work (Davies and Harré, 1990). It has been argued that one of the ways in which discourse analysis can be employed as a political tool is by making visible the otherwise hidden implications of subject-positions (Burman and Parker, 1993).

THE 'RESPONSIBLE SUBJECT': A WOMAN'S ACCOUNT OF THERAPY

My political motivation in deconstructing speech, in this case deconstructing the function of the 'responsible subject', is to identify the process through which oppression becomes internal regulation and self-discipline (Foucault, 1981); in this particular extract, the self-oppression involved in taking the position of 'the responsible subject'. The political aim of this exercise is therefore to 'remake the link' with the historically gendered and social resources that both the woman interviewed and her therapists are likely to have drawn upon to construct this subject position. I believe that this process, by suspending the common-sense status quo and the belief in an intrinsically neutral psychotherapist, can open the way to a more political self-reflection on the models we use and the conceptualization of 'new frameworks of interpretation' which might empower our patients and ourselves.

The version of discourse analysis I have used in my research is influenced by a mixture of different approaches. It focuses mainly on the function of language and its relation to ideology (Potter and Wetherell, 1987; Wetherell and Potter, 1992), but with some reservations. Although I agree that we all use the same existing resources to construct our talk (Potter and Wetherell, 1987; Marshall and Rabe, 1993), I think that we are all imprisoned by language (Marks, 1993), and that we favour some subject-positions over others because they have positive implication for our sense of self and self-esteem (Burman and Parker, 1993) – i.e. they contain higher narcissistic supplies (Sandler et al., 1963). They may provide a sense of being in harmony with the world as represented by 'common sense' (see Weedon, 1994, for an illustration of the presentation of ideological situations as 'common sense') or they may supply us with more power in relation to others (Hollway, 1989). These are obviously always relative and contextual, which accounts for contradictions in speech (Potter and Wetherell, 1987).

The extract is taken from an investigation into women's experiences of shame. The semi-structured interviews were divided into two parts: in the first section the participants were asked general questions about their lives and interests. In the second part they were asked to report their experiences of shame. As previous studies have suggested a strong link between shame and low self-esteem, the participants were invited to discuss their self-esteem through open questions like 'Is there anything that you particularly like or dislike about yourself?'

According to classical psychoanalysis, the notion of self-esteem implies a large measure of reference to internal criteria: we judge ourselves in relation to an internalized sense of 'who we are', as well as in relation to our community. We are aware of our self-judgements, however dependent these judgements may be upon the approval and opinion of others (Ablon, 1985). It has been widely discussed in the literature how low self-esteem is related to conflicts in the self-representation (Sandler et al., 1963; Pines, 1995; Lewis, 1971, 1987; Wumser, 1981; Silberstein et al., 1987), and, more specifically, how loss of self-esteem derives from a discord between wishful self-images and a self that appears to be failing, defective, inferior, weak and contemptible by comparison (Lewis, 1971).

Within a psychodynamic model of intrapsychic conflict, then, low self-esteem can be constructed as resulting from the interaction of a judgemental part of the self as the agent and another as the object. The psychodynamic model can now be abandoned, as what I am interested in here is not using these two constructs as reflections of an unconscious, internalized intrapsychic conflict (which of course is a very useful way of looking at it within a therapeutic psychodynamic analysis), but the construction of a hateful/hated self with all the other attendant negative connotations. These representations of oneself carry a very strong emotional component, because subject-positions are not just theoretical constructs, but have implications for one's sense of self and self-worth (Burman and Parker, 1993).

When asked how she felt about herself, the participant (whom I shall call Moira) said that, although she had always had quite a low self-esteem, recently she had started to like herself more. This is how she described what had happened to her:

> I suppose in a funny way I think that the more I have become aware of things that I dislike about me I have also become aware of things that I like about myself, and I think that has got a lot to do with therapy (.) I don't know it is a matter of being able to pinpoint what these things are and where they come from (.) ahm (.) I suppose I have always had the feeling that I did not like myself and therefore that people would not like me, that was not based on anything objective, it is a very subjective experience.

The above is a crucial statement which prepares the listener for her account of what has made her change her perception of herself. In other words, Moira is setting the scene. There are three elements which are important to highlight. In the first three lines Moira warns us that this transformation is no simple straightforward matter. To like herself more she has had to dislike herself more too. This is presented as a fair deal, 'you give some and get some' sort of thing. She does however acknowledge that something 'funny' is going on and that perhaps this shift has required some mental gymnastics. What is clear is that this has mainly taken place in therapy.

She then goes on to say that an important part of this process had involved reframing where these things come from. (I assume she is referring to the things she does not like about herself.) I take this to mean that she originally thought that the source of her self-dislike was one place and that through therapy she has 'discovered' that in fact it comes from elsewhere. To be noted here is that she frames this process of disowning her perception in a positive way in terms of 'it is a matter of *being able* to . . .' This rhetorical device, as we will see later in more direct terms, plays a crucial role in warranting something we assume must have been very difficult and painful. This allows her to value the action and to feel proud of herself for having done it.

Finally, she qualifies what this process consisted of: her experience is removed from the realm of objectivity and located in the subjective sphere. This implies two fundamental dynamics. Firstly, it implies that what she experienced no longer carries the power of 'objectivity', i.e., of something that can be proved and is unquestionably a fact. Second, the arena has shifted from being 'out there' for anybody to see, to 'inside of her'.

Having done this, Moira is now on her own with her therapist and her internal world. I am not questioning that this might well be a necessary process if, indeed, one goes into therapy to explore one's internal world. It is the totality of the shift that worries me, as I am not sure that the intrapsychic is sufficient as a context for feminist practice.

Some of the consequences of this move are brought to the fore later in the interview where Moira describes how she deals with a situation that makes her feel bad about herself. This is what she says:

```
 1  M: I suppose I can be very self-punitive in that situation, my first reaction
 2     would be to blame or devalue the other person, like put the person
 3     down, in a kind of attack of rage but I suppose the second stage would be
 4     to take the blame on myself, in the sense of kind of realize that it had
 5     something to do with me therefore I would be resposible for it, it is kind
 6     of taking responsibility for what you are feeling/
 7  B: You also said self-punitive/
 8  M: I think that would be the second stage/
 9  B: To punish yourself (.)
10  M: Yes, punish myself or perhaps take the blame for it/not necessarily
11     punish myself I suppose, perhaps that what I think is not necessarily the
12     truth, realizing things that I haven't realized while in the process of being
13     angry (.) in general I am quite self-punitive, I don't know if it makes me
14     feel better or worse actually [laughs] [. . .] it is more kind of mental or
15     emotional, it begins with devaluing somebody and ends with devaluating
16     yourself, like making you feel small, envious and bad, it is sounding quite
17     awful but I don't necessarily see it as being quite bad/
18  B: Why do you think you punish yourself or what do you punish yourself
19     for?
20  M: um (.) because I feel responsible for what happens to me and the way I
21     am, so I suppose in a way it is a good thing because if you blame yourself
22     you take responsibility for it therefore it is in your hands to change it (.) if
23     you blame other people for doing bad there is nothing you can do about
24     it, while taking the blame for it is taking responsibility for it and change
25     can come from that
26     [. . .] I think when you manage to put a name to something maybe
27     because it makes it more manageable, that is my main defence now, to be
28     able to analyse the situation and understand what I feel and then why I
29     feel that way and I suppose once you get there I suppose it becomes less
30     relevant then, it does not stop the pain necessarily but becomes more
31     manageable.
```

Moira starts her account with a choice: she could turn her anger against someone outside or against herself; through these two actions it is decided who is in the position of being blamed. However, from the beginning the two actions, although basically the same, are constructed as carrying completely opposite connotations. So that 'to blame or devalue the other person' is described within the context of 'a kind of attack of rage'; alternatively, 'if you blame yourself you take responsibility for it'. I am interested here in the warranting strategy adopted by Moira, through which she manages to justify doing something to herself which sounds quite awful (line 17), makes her feel small, envious and bad (line 16) and that she is not sure makes her feel better or worse (line 14). The first option (turning her anger outwards) is rejected by representing it derogatively as an 'attack of rage', while the alternative is legitimized as positive action of taking responsibility for her feelings. Therefore, the desirable course of action is that of self-blame, following the acceptance that the situation 'had something to do with me' (lines 4–5).

This, I think, is the crucial point and on this statement hinges the whole strategy of warranting. Moira has to position herself as the one who in some way provoked or caused what happened to her. In lines 20 to 24 she specifies this by saying that she feels responsible for what happens to her and the way she is and that any explanation is better than no explanation (lines 26–31), and this 'defence' helps her to manage her pain.

This extract is a good illustration of the process of constructing an explanation and how any one reading is not 'intrinsically true' but becomes true through rhetorical devices and the way it is constructed in speech. Hence, attacking the other person has implications of irrationality and would position Moira as out of control, incapable of thinking while dominated by anger, as expressed in lines 12–13. This position warrants the second action of turning the anger against herself as being reasonable and mature. The need for doing this is in the discomfort provoked by the event and the helplessness which is implied in the lines quoted preceding the extract and in the extract (lines 20–5). The strategy is not totally successful as it does not really deal with the discomfort. This is acknowledged in line 13 where she does qualify it as self-punishment. The last few lines eventually construct the position of the 'responsible subject' which gives self-blame positive connotations; this is construed as self-empowering in that it allows her to be in a position of being able to change things.

This account contains two important elements. First Moira looks in herself for a solution to a problem as if it were entirely intrapsychically constructed. This solution involves positioning herself as the one who should be blamed, either for her action or for her intrinsic personal qualities (lines 20–1). Secondly, Moira presents this strategy as a defence against situations where she would feel helpless, implying that there are no alternative ways of understanding what is happening. However, this is contradicted in the text which does provide an alternative position: legitimizing her anger and attacking the source of the discomfort. This alternative position of power is undermined and discredited as an 'attack of rage'.

What I want to do at this point is to reflect on the consequences of the reading suggested above, with the idea of exploring the political implications of what could otherwise be considered as an exclusively 'therapeutic' intervention. Moira's accounts of what has happened in therapy are constructed around the following elements:

1 The 'responsible subject' obviously resorts to modern ideas of the self as initiator of action and a place where people's identities reside (see Potter, 1996); i.e., it uses an epistemological framework which constructs the self as unitary, responsible and capable of change.
2 It contains elements of the Foucauldian view of therapy being embedded in a medical discourse of 'cure' or as confessional practice (Foucault, 1981).
3 Language is described as a means to access hidden parts of the self (which interestingly the therapist can access better than the patient).

In this way the subject is removed from the social arena and the link with her historical and political position is lost. It is precisely this link that I want to remake and suggest a mixture of sociological and psychological accounts to explore the ideological implications of the 'responsible subject'. These accounts might seem disparate, but they all have in common the attempt to explain the production of self-blame and acquiescence.

Marx used the concept of false consciousness in an attempt to understand the acquiescence of subordinate social classes to systems of stratification which are patently unjust. On similar lines, Scheff (1990) looks at the role played by the subordinated classes' internalization of the opinions and values of their oppressors in the perpetuation of their own oppression. If the members of the dominated class are ashamed of their own putative characteristics, and this shame is not acknowledged and dispelled, it might result in a permanent undervaluation of self and overvaluation of the ruling class.

At a psychological level, I find Silberstein et al. (1987) on shame and gender very interesting in this context. They suggest that society fosters women's self-denigration and that the shame is even greater when blame is imputed as well, for the self is derogated not only for its initial inadequacy, but also for its inability to overcome it. The punishment also reinforces a view of the self as bad and is an attempt to rectify the problem rather than to reassert it. In this context Scheff (1990) talks of 'feeling traps'. According to Scheff (1990), a chain reaction, which takes place between and within interactants, occurs when there is a real or imagined criticism, insult, defeat on one or both sides without the resulting emotions being acknowledged (Lewis, 1971, 1987; Scheff, 1990). At the core of this issue is the phenomenon of having emotional reactions to one's emotional reactions, which easily becomes a closed loop. These inner storms are very disruptive and can interfere with the person's capacity to deal with the world (Lewis, 1987; Scheff, 1987) and *to feel certain about one's understanding of reality* (emphasis added). These 'feeling traps' are characteristic of most systems of social deference or unequal status.

This dynamic is highly present in Moira's extract, particularly because, as I have pointed out, for the warranting to be effective she has to position herself as 'small, envious and bad' and that she is to be blamed for what happened to her. Further, I want to argue that taking this position implies being in a disempowering and vulnerable position and that this process does not pertain exclusively to issues of gender, but to inequality towards minorities in general.

The description of inner storms and spirals of self-attack resonate with what Shere Hite describes as the language of power used to undermine women's perception of reality and entitlement. She makes reference to a 'big, foggy area' of emotional inequality which manifests in private between a woman and a man. This psychological discrimination blankets everything and is built into language. So often women are labelled as 'neurotic' and 'insecure', especially when wanting to address an issue emotionally:

> These arguments usually happen in the middle of the night, there is nobody there but the man and the woman. The whole power of this society is behind the man using that kind of language and the worst forms of it are something like, 'You know, you are being irrational, when you get hold of yourself I'll talk to you.' Eventually the woman will feel as if she has a voice in her head repeating that she is a nag. (Hite quoted in Brunt, 1989)

I find these explanations useful and problematic at the same time: useful because they do look at the power of language to re/produce oppression and because they look at the multiple manifestations of inequality. In line with Hollway (1983, 1984, 1989), however, I find problematic how these reactions are deterministically attributed to women, rather than being looked at as 'gendered positions', i.e., as socially constructed positions made available to women. This would avoid positioning women as intrinsically passive victims, while to think in terms of positions would include women as agents in their own oppression and hence, in the possibility of their liberation. Therefore I would say that the fact that women repeat the self-derogatory remarks in their heads is not, as Hite claims, a mechanistic passive act, but shows how it is not only men who take the position of oppressors towards women (although they certainly do), but also women to other women and indeed to themselves. In contrast to a mechanistic view of oppression I would argue that by unquestioningly adopting oppressive discourses as 'common sense', women, from being defined as 'naggers', end up defining themselves as such. Focusing exclusively on the intrapsychic world, however, hides very effectively other social dimensions of patients' suffering as well as the power dynamics in the therapist/patient relationship.

Is the Postmodern Turn the Alternative?

What I have tried to illustrate so far is the existence of different readings and competing narratives in psychotherapy. This obviously has serious implications for clinical practice, as we unavoidably carry into the consulting room our everyday interpretative models and framework. What needs questioning is what we do with these frameworks when working clinically within a psychodynamic model, interpreting our interactions with our clients exclusively in intrapsychic terms. I am particularly concerned with the power granted to us by our status of neutral 'experts' with no investment in the process. Although this is obviously the case to a certain extent in any properly professional practice, at another level we all have investment in our world-views. It is within those world-views that who we are and what we do acquires meaning and gains other people's recognition. Through sharing and having our world-views validated we acquire a solid sense of self and self-esteem. It is therefore essential to question what social arrangements a particular view of the world is sustaining; in other words, what the ideological investments underpinning it are.

To question the intrinsic truth and neutrality of psychodynamic theoretical frameworks can be a way of producing scepticism and space for reflection; however, some of the alternatives are, as I will endeavour to argue, unfortunately equally dangerous.

Deep concern for the power imbalance in therapy has produced, in recent times, a very important shift in psychotherapy to narrative and discursive approaches (see, for example, White and Epston, 1989; McNamee and Gergen, 1991). One of the main issues motivating this shift concerns the way in which the therapeutic process can be a hegemonic and subjugating process (Gergen and Kaye, 1992). To start with, privileged knowledge is attributed to the therapist, and although therapist and patient might hold equally valid views of the patient's story, therapy is effectively a process of translating the patient's story into the therapist's framework (White, 1991). Thus therapy is pathological in itself as it weakens the patient's capacity to trust her judgement (Kaye, 1996). As an alternative to this, it has been argued that as the therapist's account is not intrinsically better than the patient's and all accounts are equally valid, therapy should take 'not knowing' as its starting point (Kaye, 1996). Others (Schafer, 1981, 1983; Spence, 1982) have claimed that as psychoanalytic interpretation is more a creation than a discovery, instead of searching for truth, the therapist should aim at internal coherence or maximal rhetorical force when formulating interpretations; i.e., the interpretation becomes an 'aesthetic experience'. The argument is that psychoanalysis can be 'curative' through making the patients aware of the analytic process itself, i.e., its relativistic or fictional nature. In this way the patient learns to accept the essentially created nature of all reality, thus 'liberating' the patient from the danger of taking too literally what is in fact only a narrative she happens to be living by.

These positions, in true postmodern fashion, seem to claim an intrinsically liberating potential in relativism; they offer a very seductive and yet potentially dangerous reading. In order to stress how insidious these readings are I will comment on these two points in turn.

I feel very suspicious of the invitation for the therapist to start from 'not knowing' (Goolishian in Kaye, 1996) which I find problematic on epistemological, political and ethical grounds (some of these criticisms overlap with more general critiques of the relationship between post-structuralism and political action: see Gill, 1995, for a full discussion).

My objections start with questioning Gergen and Kaye's (1992) argument that the therapeutic process must inevitably result in the slow but inevitable replacement of the client's story with that of the therapist. This position hinges on the idea of ownership of stories; as if accounts belonged to and resided inside of people, in this case the therapist and the patient. Instead I would argue that 'stories', 'discourses', 'repertoires' exist in the social world and that we use different and contradictory ones at different times. The point therefore is not 'who the story belongs to', but what the implications are of adopting one story at the expense of another. Thus the proposed solution of striving to operate in a vacuum of knowledge (a 'story' in itself) could be little more than a revamping of the neutral, unbiased therapist, the criticism of which is precisely the starting point of any discursive inquiry. I would tend to see this invitation to disown our knowledge as a rhetorical manoeuvre to favour the therapist rather than as potentially liberating for patients.

This leads to my second, political question: who would benefit from this supposed 'tabula rasa' therapist? I would argue that the ideological function of this position is to hide issues of power. Patients and therapists are not equally situated and resorting to this discourse of purity is, in my view, a device for avoiding our responsibilities as therapists by claiming that we can somehow lift ourselves out of history and material conditions. What should we do in the case of sexual abuse or violence against women, for example? Are we invited 'not to know'? This seems to go totally against any kind of feminist stance (see Walker and Jones in this book).

As far as the 'aesthetic experience' is concerned (Schafer, 1981, 1983) surely patients would not invest vast quantities of time and money if they believed (although at times they might) that they could gain equally from talking to the greengrocer or having a stroll in an art gallery. Ethically and professionally, therapists have responsibility towards those who, primarily out of suffering, seek help, not an 'aesthetic experience', from therapy. The state of vulnerability of the patient, I believe, should be a crucial concern. Sass (1992), for example, warns against the possible effects of postmodernist, relativistic approaches to psychotherapy when working with narcissistic, schizoid or borderline personalities whose fundamental problems are around feelings of emptiness, meaninglessness and incapacity to relate. Although it is unquestionably very positive to support the development of self-awareness and flexibility, we also need, he argues, to worry about the resulting confusion, lack of direction and paralysing self-doubt in what might present itself as an 'anything goes' attitude on the side of the therapist.

To me the fundamental choice is whether we think there is a complete absence of basic reality, replaced by a never-ending stream of equally valid constructions of reality, or whether we want to hang on to a basic belief in the existence and importance of a core self, a core reality, without neglecting the fact that the various readings and accounts of it are always culturally and historically constructed (Habermas, 1987a, 1987b). We therefore need to consider very carefully a differentiation between the positive *use* (see Swan in this book) of a theoretical framework and its dangerously reactionary elements, albeit presented as innovative and liberating for the patient.

Feminist critiques of relativism have been arguing for the need to re-invent a new vocabulary of value (Soper, 1991; Squires, 1993) with which we can make political interventions (Gill, 1995: 165). In line with these arguments I also claim that in the same way in which researchers are accountable for their interpretations (Henwood and Pidgeon, 1995), our task as feminist therapists is not to deny the knowledge we have of women's inequality, but instead to increase our responsibility by making the concern of these inequalities a more explicit part of our work.

In order to illustrate how I suggest this could be done, I will use another extract from an interview with a woman whom I will call Dawn.

> *Dawn*: I feel ashamed in certain situations of my background, like being in Oxford and being surrounded by people who are middle class, and being in a social situation and being asked what your father does and not accountant, not doctor, but painter and decorator and your mother is a cleaner and that annoys me because I shouldn't feel ashamed of my background.

In Dawn's quote, the subject, according to specific social norms, is positioned as comparatively inferior, inadequate, or at least different. The subject is exposed and made visible in her inferiority. What is interesting is that Dawn feels annoyed with herself for feeling ashamed. There is no doubt, in my eyes, that Dawn's shame is grounded in a social construct and yet the annoyance tells us that she feels she should not feel ashamed. This is understandable if Dawn takes her shame to signify a betrayal of loyalty to her background; however, within the context of Oxford University it is a reality that having a builder as father and a cleaner for a mother does position her in the minority. In this context her expectation to get rid of the shame is unrealistic and, as I have repeatedly come across in the interviews, there is the danger that Dawn constructs her shame as her personal failure. Alternatively, however, there is the position of pride also available, but not considered by Dawn; that she has found her way into a highly elitist institution, not out of social privilege but as the result of her own work and strength.

I think that the therapist has a potentially crucial role to play in this kind of situation, by making other subject-positions available to Dawn, by preventing her from turning her anger against herself, instead of, for example, directing it against the inequality of the education system and the privileges which come from belonging to a certain social class. I believe it is possible to interpret unconscious contents connected to her shame, as well as confirming that her perception of being part of a minority is not the fruit of her paranoia. This would go some way to break the isolation and self-blame that Dawn experienced and relieve the burden which so many women carry on their own. Validating patients' perceptions of inequality (particularly when it involves their therapists) is in no way antithetical to working with the unconscious and, I believe, a therapeutic intervention in itself.

In this sense, the use of a post-structuralist deconstruction is a necessary but not sufficient tool for feminist psychotherapy. As an instrument of analysis, deconstruction helps us to be aware of the existence of different narratives. This, however, does not relieve feminist therapists from having to choose which narrative to adopt.

In this chapter I have explored the positive potential that post-structuralist deconstruction can offer to feminist psychotherapies. I have looked at the differences and similarities between classical psychoanalysis and Foucauldian theory of discourse. I have then illustrated, through a discursive analysis of an extract, the constructed nature of therapy and the dangers, implicit in psychodynamic psychotherapy, of adopting an exclusively intrapsychic framework. I then moved on to look at the contributions and dangers of a postmodern turn in psychotherapy and conclude by urging for more accountability and the need to make a concern for inequalities a more explicit part of the work of feminist therapists.

In summary, the thrust of this paper is to define feminist psychotherapies in terms of reflecting on the political implications of our daily practice rather than in identifying in principle with a political movement. However, this might mean that we can no longer rely on being intrinsically feminist by virtue of an act of will or being unquestionably oppressed by virtue of our gender. We might need to entertain the uncomfortable thought that positioning ourselves on the same side as the patient might hide the prejudices and ideology we bring into our consulting rooms. To me, it is surprising that the therapeutic space has ever been held as a place that could escape from the same ideological dynamics which govern the rest of our lives. Our position is not intrinsically certain but is constantly negotiated as is that of our patients. In this sense we never act neutrally.

NOTE

I would like to thank Colleen and David for their insightful comments and help with earlier versions of this chapter.

REFERENCES

Ablon, S. L. (1985) 'Affect and self-esteem', in J. E. Mack and S. L. Ablon (eds), *The Development and Sustaining of Self-Esteem in Childhood*. New York: University International Press.

Brunt, R. (1989) 'Love on the rocks – interview with Shere Hite', *Marxism Today*, Dec: 14–19.

Burman, E. and Parker, I. (eds) (1993) *Discourse Analytic Research: Repertoires and Readings of Text in Action*. London: Routledge.

Burr, V. (1995) *An Introduction to Social Constructionism*. London: Routledge.

Davies, B. and Harré, R. (1990) 'Positioning: the discursive production of selves', *Journal for the Theory of Social Behaviour*, 19 (4): 43–63.

Flax, J. (1990) *Thinking Fragments: Psychoanalysis, Feminism and Postmodernism in the Contemporary West*. Berkeley and Los Angeles, CA: University of California Press.

Foucault, M. (1977) *Language, Counter-Memory, Practice: Selected Essays and Interviews*. London: Blackwell.

Foucault, M. (1981) *The History of Sexuality. Vol. 1: An Introduction*. Harmondsworth: Penguin.

Gergen, K. J. and Kaye, J. D. (1992) 'Beyond narrative in the negotiation of the therapeutic meaning', in S. McNamee and K. J. Gergen (eds), *Therapy as a Social Construction*. London: Sage.

Gill, R. (1995) 'Relativism, reflexivity and politics: interrogating discourse analysis from a feminist perspective', in S. Wilkinson and C. Kitzinger (eds), *Feminism and Discourse; Psychological Perspectives*. London: Sage.

Habermas, J. (1987a) *The Philosophical Discourse of Modernity* (trans. F. Lawrence). Cambridge: Polity Press.

Habermas, J. (1987b) 'An alternative way out of the philosophy of the subject: communicative versus subject-centred reason', in *The Philosophical Discourse of Modernity*.

Hall, S. (1988) 'The toad in the garden: Thatcherism among the theorists', in C. Nelson and L. Grossberg (eds), *Marxism and the Interpretation of Culture*. London: Macmillan.

Henriques, J., Hollway, W., Urwin, C., Venn, C. and Walkerdine, V. (1984) *Changing the Subject: Psychology, Social Regulation and Subjectivity*. London: Methuen & Co.

Henwood, K. and Pidgeon, N. (1995) 'Remaking the link: qualitative research and feminist standpoint theory', *Feminism and Psychology*, 5 (1).

Hollway, W. (1983) 'Heterosexual sex: power and desire for the other', in S. Cartledge and J. Ryan (eds), *Sex and Love*. London: The Women's Press.

Hollway, W. (1984) 'Gender difference and the production of subjectivity', in Henriques et al., *Changing the Subject; Psychology, Social Regulation and Subjectivity*. London: Methuen & Co.

Hollway, W. (1989) *Subjectivity and Method in Psychology: Gender, Meaning and Science*. London: Sage.

Kaye, J. D. (1996) 'Towards a discursive psychotherapy', *Changes*, 14: 3.

Lewis, H. B. (1971) *Shame and Guilt in Neurosis*. New York: International University Press.

Lewis, H. B. (ed.) (1987) *The Role of Shame in Symptom Formation*. Hillsdale, NJ and London: Lawrence Erlbaum Associates Publishers.

Marks, D. (1993) 'Case-conference analysis and action research', in E. Burman and I. Parker (eds), *Discourse Analytic Research*. London: Routledge.

Marshall, H. and Rabe, B. (1993) 'Political discourse: talking about nationalization and privatization', in E. Burman and I. Parker (eds), *Discourse Analytic Research*. London: Routledge.

McNamee, S. and Gergen, K. J. (eds) (1991) *Therapy as Social Construction*. London: Sage.

Nietzsche, F. (1973) *Beyond Good and Evil*, trans. R. J. Hollingdale. London: Penguin.

Parker, I. (1997) 'Discursive psychology', in D. Fox and I. Prilleltensky (eds), *Critical Psychology*. London: Sage.

Pines, M. (1995) 'The universality of shame: a psychoanalytic approach', *British Journal of Psychotherapy*, 11 (3): 346–58.

Potter, J. (1996) *Representing Reality: Discourse, Rhetoric and Social Construction*. London: Sage.

Potter, J. and Wetherell, M. (1987) *Discourse and Social Psychology*. London: Sage.

Sandler, J., Holder, A. and Meers, D. (1963) 'The ego ideal and the ideal self', *The Psychoanalytic Study of the Child*, Vol. XVIII.

Sass, L. A. (1992) 'The epic of disbelief: the postmodernist turn in contemporary psychoanalysis', in S. Kvale (ed.), *Psychology and Postmodernism*. London: Sage.

Schafer, R. (1981) *Narrative Actions in Psychoanalysis*. Worcester, MA: Clark University Press.

Schafer, R. (1983) *The Analytic Attitude*. New York: Basic Books.

Scheff, T. J. (1987) 'The shame–rage spiral: a case of an interminable quarrel', in H. B. Lewis (ed.), *The Role of Shame in Symptom Formation*. Hillsdale, NJ and London: Lawrence Erlbaum Associates Publishers.

Scheff, T. J. (1990) *Microsociology: Discourse, Emotion and Social Structure*. Chicago and London: University of Chicago Press.

Silberstein, L. R., Striegel-Moore, R. and Rodlin, J. (1987) 'Feeling fat: a woman's shame', in H. B. Lewis (ed.), *The Role of Shame in Symptom Formation*, Hillsdale, NJ and London: Lawrence Erlbaum Associates Publishers.

Smart, B. (1985) *Michael Foucault*. London: Tavistock Publications.

Soper, K. (1991) 'Postmodernism, subjectivity and the question of value', *New Left Review*, 186.

Spence, D. (1982) *Narrative Truth and Historical Truth*. New York: Norton.

Squires, J. (ed.) (1993) *Principled Positions: Postmodernism and the Rediscovery of Value*. London: Lawrence and Wishart.

Weedon, C. (1994) *Feminist Practice and Poststructuralist Theory*. Oxford: Blackwell.

Wetherell, M. and Potter, J. (1992) *Mapping the Language of Racism: Discourses and Legitimation of Exploitation*. London: Harvester Wheatsheaf.

White, M. (1991) 'Deconstruction and therapy', *Dulwich Centre Newsletter*, 3: 21–40.

White, M. and Epston, D. (1989) *Literate Means to Therapeutic Ends*. Adelaide: Dulwich Centre Press.

Wumser, L. (1981) *The Mask of Shame*. London: Johns Hopkins University Press.

13

Conclusion: Questions, Answers and Absences in Feminist Psychotherapies

M. Colleen Heenan and I. Bruna Seu

All therapies are informed by a political perspective. Many psychotherapists often make the mistake of offering up their clinical work as though it were value-free. In this sense they are unconscious of how a political view of the world shapes a psychological view of women and how this in turn will provide a particular viewpoint. As feminist psychotherapists we bring in our political and personal attitudes, biases and values to the work we do. We hear what our clients say with a particular ear, no more special in its particularity than other therapists, but with a stated bias that sees women as the oppressed sex within patriarchy. (Eichenbaum and Orbach, 1982: 69)

This book is about multiplicity. It has illustrated that contemporary feminist psychotherapy is not a unitary and coherent school of thought, nor does it manifest itself as an easily identifiable set of techniques or clinical applications. This has been shown precisely in the diverse and rich answers that the contributors have given, when asked to question their practices as feminist psychotherapists. The different chapters showed how feminist practitioners and researchers struggle with these difficult issues in their practice and scholarly work. The creative potential of being able to tolerate the contradictions and resist the temptation to 'throw away the baby with the bath water' is often reiterated. In this final chapter of the book, we will try to bring the multiple threads together into a summary of how the questions raised by the book were answered by its authors, as well as attending to those issues left remaining. In doing this, we illustrate how aspects of particular chapters answered two of the questions we posed to the contributors; that is, what is feminist therapy and how does your therapeutic theory inform your feminist practice? This is a strategic use of the contributors' work, for the purposes of our editorial needs, and not a value judgement on them.

WHAT IS FEMINIST PSYCHOTHERAPY?

When we approached the contributors to this book, our first selection criterion was that the contributors would identify themselves as feminists, working in, or researching about, clinical practice with women. This narrowed the field down to some obvious choices, such as well-established authors, or women's therapy centres. However, in contacting some less well-known writers, whose work we respected, we were immediately faced, as editors, with having to deal with one of the questions we wanted to pose to the contributors; that is, what kind of feminist are you? We had to define what we considered feminism to be, in order to negotiate whether or not this was a book which included, not just those women who wouldn't necessarily define themselves primarily as feminists, but also those who did consider themselves to be feminists, but who wanted to be able to write about their concerns and criticisms of feminist therapy.

In this context, we were very lucky to have had the chapter by Jeanne Marecek and Diane Kravetz, whose empirical research on the epistemological, political and therapeutic belief systems of feminist therapists raised a number of pertinent issues. First and foremost, they make clear the ways in which 'feminism' has tended to be adopted unquestioningly within this field, as a singular theory. Moreover, this singular feminist theory belies not just a belief in essential differences between men and women, but the belief that *women* have particular qualities which are better than men's. This has led to the conflation of feminist therapy with what they call *feminine* therapy, therapy which celebrates and encourages the development of 'women's capacities'. The authors made clear that, by taking the stance that feminism was somehow value-free, this exacerbated the ways in which feminist theory has tended not just to privilege gender, but also to depict itself as a universal concept, thereby functioning to exclude those feminists whose framework of reference was different.

Because of the tensions highlighted in the introduction, we asked the authors not just *which* feminism they subscribed to, but also whether or not gender should take priority over other issues of inequality and discrimination. The answer was no, although this answer in itself highlighted the complexities of the question. In her chapter, Aileen Alleyne argued for a more self-critical approach to a feminist stance claiming to be in aid of all women. She invited us to deconstruct the very notion of woman, a notion which universalizes *white* women's experience, thereby positing black women as different, as 'other'. Through exploring some of the historical background which contextualizes contemporary differences between black and white women's feminisms, Alleyne offered some critical insights into some of the unconscious processes which can result from being positioned as 'different'. At the same time, she does not ignore differences within the black community – in terms of culture and history, as well as gender. The uniqueness of her model, a culturally specific and socially contextual, psychodynamic 'Cycle of Events', is that it has implications, not just for *black* British feminist therapy, but also for white feminist therapists, and indeed, white feminist theorists.

Pam Trevithick also answered 'no', although her chapter addressed a very different issue, that of material oppression. Trevithick made clear that in thinking about the value and application of therapy to the needs of working-class and often severely impoverished women, it is necessary to address economic differences above and beyond gender differences. However, at the same time, the position of working-class women is also different from that of men, in that they are often worse off economically, owing to gender oppression. Moreover, many working-class women will face even harsher deprivation, in that supporting and maintaining their families will often mean having to place their needs second. However, Trevithick outlined the contribution made by feminist psychodynamic psychotherapy to developing and facilitating a therapeutic project for working-class women, one which addressed the very real, day-to-day material oppressions which all psychotherapy is usually accused of ignoring.

We also asked the authors how their feminism was expressed in their therapeutic practice. In answering this, Vanessa Swan argued that she regarded taking a feminist stance as a necessary condition. However, while this heightens awareness of contemporary Western society as a site of discrimination and oppression, thus making feminism a position of resistance and a starting point for interrogation of other inequalities, it is far from being sufficient. On the contrary, through her own self-reflective experience, she showed how sometimes that very *feminist* stance allows for avoiding an awareness of positions of privilege and oppression. It was her position as a *therapist* working with Aboriginal Australians, more so than her *feminist* stance, which forced her to confront her position of power and privilege as a white middle-class professional woman. These encounters enabled her to think more clearly about the ways in which racist beliefs were being masked by a therapeutic, as well as feminist, framework.

However, while taking a critical stance in relation to feminist theory, the authors have also reminded us that there is cause for celebration in acknowledging the enormous contributions that feminist thinking has brought to the field of psychotherapy. The value of these came to the fore when issues particularly salient to gender were addressed by feminist therapy. One such powerful statement came from Moira Walker, who pointed out, in her chapter, the fundamental contributions of feminism to both identifying the gender biases in current theories on sexual abuse, and taking a stance against violence towards women and children. Walker argued that through this, feminist thinking has not only constructed a space in which the voices of women can be formulated, validated and heard, but crucially, it has also provided a critique of the family and the social construction of gendered sexuality. In turn, by making use of feminist object relations theory, Walker demonstrated that it was possible for feminist psychodynamic therapists to sensitively address issues relating to sexual abuse, particularly in the context of mother-blaming and father-idealizing, without losing sight of the individual meanings of these events.

Even in those rare cases where there seemed to be some obvious compatibility between feminist principles and therapeutic model, as in Robin Sesan and Melanie Katzman's chapter on empowerment therapy with women who have eating problems, the authors indicated that contradictions and compromises were central to their practice. The subject of women's relationship to food, eating and body size has been a catalyst for developing the theory and practice of feminist therapies. At the same time, by accepting a diagnosis of eating 'disorder', of having to consider hospitalization as a 'therapeutic' option, a feminist therapist is faced with the very *material* substance of the client's body, and thus the very materiality of the world. Sesan and Katzman grapple with what the notion of 'empowerment' means to both client and therapist in these situations. For example, there is an inherent contradiction in empowering clients in the consulting room while they are disempowered by society. This highlights the conflict between a belief in empowering women to make different choices, and the fact that their range of choices remains unaltered. Moreover, they point out how at times the therapist may be required to help clients to adapt to a culture which is hurtful to them, suggesting that feminists using this framework continually need to reflect on its aims and ethics.

The preceding chapters have dealt in differing ways with one of the main issues identified in this book, the conflict between clinical work with individual clients and the 'external world'. In exploring the 'external world' of violence in heterosexual relationships, the issue of compromise was also brought up by Elsa Jones. She illustrated how the feminist therapist, working with couples where the woman is abused and attacked by her male partner, often faces the dilemma of having to hold back her condemnation of the man's action in order to keep him in a therapy which will ultimately benefit the woman. Here, the therapist invites both members of the couple to clarify their differing constructions of their gendered relationship, always having to deal with the reality that exploration may provoke further violence. At the same time, through a gendered and therapeutic deconstruction of the couple's stories, the therapist is able to facilitate both partners in shifting out of gender-stereotypical deadlocks. Making use of the contributions which feminist thinking has made to the systemic therapeutic framework, Jones demonstrates that it is possible to reconcile feminist and psychotherapeutic practices.

IN WHAT WAY DOES YOUR THERAPEUTIC THEORY INFORM YOUR FEMINIST PRACTICE?

While the preceding chapters have all addressed this issue in varying ways, aspects of the following chapters could be said to focus more specifically on this particular question. And again, in answering this, they address further complexities. For instance, Colleen Heenan's critique of feminist object relations theory and practice clarified some of the ways in which notions particular to psychoanalytic thought have been adopted by Chodorow, Benjamin, and Eichenbaum and Orbach, as tools which could enhance feminist understanding of the difficulties inherent in both individual and social change. The complex ways in which these authors deconstructed the gender biases within psychoanalytic theory contributed to making aspects of this framework available for the use of feminist theorists, and feminist therapists, with Eichenbaum and Orbach outlining the tenets of a feminist psychodynamic practice. However, despite their attempts to situate unconscious processes as gender-, sexually-, culturally- and historically-specific, the authors still adopted universalistic notions of woman which fail to address differences between women. This was illustrated in various ways, but perhaps most specifically in relation to their adoption of the notion of the Oedipus complex as universal. This has implications for clinical practice, particularly in dealing with sexuality.

Jocelyn Chaplin's description of the history and development of her 'rhythm model' of therapy made clear how a humanistic therapeutic framework could be beneficial to working with women. Indeed, Chaplin argued that it was more helpful than a psychoanalytic framework. However, in exploring the differences between these models, Chaplin also teased out some further areas for consideration. What became clear were the hidden dualisms between psychotherapies, dualisms which reflected the epistemological tenets of humanist thinking. The author suggested that this left women trapped in a dualistic, hierarchical system of thought antithetical to their creative potentials. This led her to reflect back on the assumptions underlying her rhythm model, to take on board the sorts of critiques set out in the introduction, and to explore the implications of these further. She concluded that humanistic therapy had the potential to embrace not only aspects of women's spiritual thinking, but also aspects of postmodern theory.

In her chapter on the use of the Jungian analytical psychology for feminist therapy, Joy Schaverien acknowledged that this therapeutic model has been regarded by feminists as embedded in patriarchal ideology. However, she argued that even the metaphor of the *coniunctio*, from Jungian psychology, despite its heterosexual bias, could be drawn on in an informed way in feminist therapeutic thinking and practice. Schaverien's clinical illustrations demonstrated that, by opening the boundaries of the unconscious, and allowing herself to be open to the eroticism which ensues from this, the feminist therapist, whatever the sexual orientation of herself or her client, allows herself and her thinking to be challenged. This opens up possibilities for the further development of both theory and practice.

In a chapter which critiqued the epistemological framework of psycho-analytic theory, Tessa Adams addressed the implications for feminist therapeutic theory when the very language which constructs theory means itself that women are left out of the symbolic order. She asked how feminist concerns, which challenge patriarchy, can be reconciled with a psychodynamic analysis, which, through the fundamental role attributed to language, re-establish male primacy. She invited psychotherapists to resist the need for a secure, unequivocal meaning in their practices, and to accept that creative intention stands apart from everyday systems of human communication. In this way, by allowing space for the creative feminine, therapists might enable their patients to reconnect with a productive hidden maternal discourse.

Conspicuous Absences

Having focused on the assumptions and exclusions present within both feminist and therapeutic theories leads to the fundamental question of who and where the 'other' is, in feminist therapies. This question links with a wider debate in feminism (see, for example, Wilkinson and Kitzinger, 1996). There are some obvious and yet invisible absences in this book which we have identified, although no doubt the reader will find more. The first of these became apparent when we saw that many of the initial drafts of the chapters talked of women, and women clients, without specifying their class, racial identity or sexual orientation, for instance. This tendency belies some of the ways in which working within psychotherapeutic theories involves a tendency towards universalism. Connected to these issues of ideology, what might have contributed to these absences is the belief that those authors who are therapists are above these differences, working with the suffering of 'human beings' regardless of their specificity. This ostensibly benign and humanitarian position, however, hides behind the notion of neutrality, denying material difference and preserving inequality and oppression.

This book also does not contain any reference to working specifically with, for instance, lesbians, or disabled women. These omissions certainly warrant attention and, again, raise further issues. We intended the book to address issues of inclusion and exclusion on a general level, within feminist therapies. This involved a commitment from each author to do just this, and each has, in different ways. Nevertheless, the only chapters which specifically address the issue of working with those women who do not 'represent the norm', Alleyne's chapter on black feminism and therapy, and Trevithick's chapter on working-class women and therapy, come from a black and a working-class contributor respectively. On the other hand, we were also concerned not to 'ghettoize' those authors who might well have written about specific women, as if only *they*, through virtue of 'being one of them', could, or should, take on this theorizing. Indeed, one additional factor in compiling the book was the pressures on those women who *are* prepared to theorize about particular groups of women, meaning that it has not been possible for some of those we would have liked to have included to make space in their schedules for meeting our deadlines.

What do we do with these problems of representation and exclusion? What do they say about our various feminist stances? First, they draw attention to issues of difference: feminist psychotherapists, like feminists in general, are not a unified group, nor are we exempt from reproducing the same power dynamics we so strongly criticize in patriarchy. Therefore, it could be suggested that the contributions in this book imply that, by and large, we are in danger of reproducing the same hierarchical structures by situating white, middle-class, heterosexual, able-bodied women as the norm. In this way issues of 'difference' are often left to those of us who are intrinsically positioned as 'the other'. This book does address some of the difficulties involved in attempting to step out of ideological frameworks in which we are totally immersed, of which we are often comfortably unaware. However, attention to language is not an intellectual activity divorced from consequence, as those who argue against 'political correctness' would suggest; it is crucial because 'language locks people into place as it encourages them to think about themselves in certain ways and to place them in particular relations of power' (Parker, 1997: 198).

There are other absences in the book which are of a different, albeit related, category. One noticeable absence is that of women's therapy centres, only present in Trevithick's mention of Womankind. Unfortunately, although two of the centres in Britain initially accepted our invitation to contribute, they subsequently withdrew. There are important reasons behind this. One is connected to material restrictions such as the lack of mainstream funding over the last ten years, which has increasingly forced these organizations into an ongoing battle for survival. Inevitably, this reduces the time, space and security needed for reflecting and developing projects. Further, some readers will be disappointed to find that we have not included work on body therapies, on cognitive-behavioural therapies, gestalt therapies, or other therapeutic models. Indeed, we also note the lack of detailed attention to therapeutic group-work. However, while some of these absences arose simply due to lack of space, one reason for this shortage has been our desire to include work from authors who were prepared to address the tensions we have described. Not every feminist therapist was prepared to take this on board.

REFLECTIONS ON THE PROCESS

Issues of difference and power have been an inevitable part of the process of writing and editing the book, too. It has been indeed a challenge as it has involved us, as editors, being positioned differently from the other contributors. Our power was reflected in our position of access to, and control over, the book as a whole. The convoluted negotiations involved in attempting to circulate copies of others' chapters to all the authors made this impossible. This means that the authors in this book will also be amongst its readers, having not seen a complete copy until its publication. This has had an impact on individuals writing in isolation, and perhaps particularly on those who were never able to – indeed may never – meet each other, prior to settling down to the task of writing. For some, a fantasy then ensued that it was *only* they who were struggling to convey their ideas.

Our authority as editors was also manifest in our ability not just to suggest but to strongly advise changes to individual chapters. Not surprisingly, at times this led to some emotionally charged negotiations. The difference in our positions was also to do with our multiple identities as practitioners, academics and researchers. It is very noticeable that some contributors also took on one of the three positions as their identity, often constructing the 'other' as a *critical* other. This led to us being regarded as either the sole representatives of critiques of ideas in chapters, or – by voicing the possible responses which the authors might receive from potential readers – as then denying them the right to their opinions. We think that this says something very important about the insularity of psychotherapy practice which is not exposed to either academic or political debate. This problem, however, cuts both ways as academic theorizing is often too far removed from the intricacies of practical applications.

Open Questions – Where Do We Go from Here?

In the final chapter of this book, Bruna Seu made clear the need for *accountability* in feminist therapy. Seu argued that, while postmodern theory makes clear that the notion of self is constructed through language, selves are also positioned through discourse. Thus, the feminist therapist, whether or not working within a postmodern framework, is always positioned as 'knowing'. Moreover, through her research on shame, Seu demonstrated that, while an analysis of gender oppression moves debate beyond individual explanations, it also explicates one of the salient tensions in feminist psychoanalytic therapy; that is, by adopting a therapeutic framework which focuses on individual change, the therapist positions the client as a *responsible* subject. The ideas raised in this chapter have implications across the range of therapeutic frameworks.

As editors, we hope that the differences in feminist therapies addressed in this book have fuelled the debates surrounding this topic in a creative manner. However, as well as recognizing the dangers of taking a relativistic position, for both feminist and therapeutic theory and practice, we are aware too that multiplicity may also undermine a sense of the strength which a unitary position has often provided for feminists.